Leyla Rouhi.

KNOWLEDGE AND ILLUMINATION
A Study of Suhrawardī's Ḥikmat al-Ishrāq

Number 97
KNOWLEDGE AND ILLUMINATION

by
Hossein Ziai

KNOWLEDGE AND ILLUMINATION

A Study of Suhrawardī's Ḥikmat al-Ishrāq

by

Hossein Ziai
University of California, Los Angeles

Scholars Press
Atlanta, Georgia

KNOWLEDGE AND ILLUMINATION

Library of Congress Cataloging-in-Publication Data

Ziai, Hossein.
Knowledge and illumination : a study of Suhrawardī's Ḥikmat al -ishrāq / by Hossein Ziai.
p. cm. -- (Brown Judaic studies : n. 97)
Includes bibliographical references.
ISBN 1-55540-142-2 (alk. paper)
1. Suhrawardī, Yahyá ibn Ḥabash, 1152- or 3-1191. Ḥikmat al -ishrāq. 2. Ishrāqīyah. I. Title. II. Series.
B753.S83H559 1990
181'.5--dc20 90-8073
CIP

Printed in the United States of America
on acid-free paper

For Dad-Ali and Mahasti

از صدای سخن عشق ندیدم خوشتر
یادگاری که در این گنبد دوّار بماند

Table of Contents

Acknowledgments xi

Introduction 1

Chapter One 7

The Philosophy of Illumination

1. How to Define the Philosophy of Illumination *7*
2. The Works of Suhrawardī on the Philosophy of Illumination *9*
    - 2.1 The Four major Works Defined *9*
    - 2.2 Position of the *Flashes of Light* *11*
    - 2.3 Character of the Four Works *14*
    - 2.4 The Period of Composition: Remarks on Suhrawardī's Life *15*
    - 2.5 Abu' l-Barakāt al-Baghdādī and the Philosophy of Illumination *19*
3. The Major Works Examined *20*
    - 3.1 The *Intimations* *20*
    - 3.2 The *Apposites* *23*
    - 3.3 The *Paths and Havens* *24*
    - 3.4 The *Philosophy of Illumination* *29*
        - 3.4.1 Suhrawardī's Reasons for Composing the *Philosophy of Illumination* *31*
        - 3.4.2 Methodology of the Philosophy of Illumination *34*
        - 3.4.3 Suhrawardī's View of the History of Philosophy *36*
4. Conclusion *38*

Chapter Two 41

The Position of Logic in the Philosophy of Illumination

1. Introduction *41*
2. Suhrawardī's View of Logic *42*
    - 2.1 Logic of the *Intimation.* *42*
    - 2.2 Logic of the *Paths and Havens* *45*

2.3 Logic of the *Philosophy of Illumination* 48
3. Synopsis of the Structure of Illuminationist Logic 50
3.1 Structure of Logic in the *Intimations* 51
3.2 Structure of Logic in the *Paths and Havens* 56
3.3 Structure of Logic in the *Philosophy of Illumination* 58
4. Assessment 78

Chapter Three...**77**
The Illuminationist Theory of Definition: Formal Method and Knowledge

1. Terminology of Definition 77
1.1 Basic Illuminationist Divisions of Logic 78
1.2 Typology of Definition 81
2. Definition and the Methodology of Philosophy 83
2.1 The Methodology of Definition and its Position in Metaphysics 85
2.2 Two Approaches to Definition: Platonic and Aristotelian 86
2.3 Plato's Method of Definition Examined 88
2.4 Aristotle's Method of Definition Examined 92
3. Suhrawardī's Theory of Definition: First Part of the Cycle 97
3.1 The *Intimations* 99
3.2 The *Paths and Havens* 104
4. An Illuminationist Theory of Definition 114
4.1 A Formulation of the Illuminationist Theory of Definition 122

Chapter Four...**129**
Knowledge, Illumination and Cosmology

1. Is Knowledge Possible? Suhrawardī's Assessment of the Peripatetic View 129
1.1 The Ontological Basis for the Lack of Certitude in Peripatetic Epistemology 130
2. Conception and Assent: A First Epistemological Division 136
2.1 Suhrawardī's Objections to the Peripatetics 136
2.2 The Illuminationist Division of Knowledge 139
3. Knowledge by Means of Illumination 143

3.1 Suhrawardī's Critique of the Peripatetic View of Knowledge as Union with the Active Intellect *143*
3.2 Suhrawardī's Dream-Vision of Aristotle *145*
3.3 Illuminationist View of Self-Knowledge *147*
3.4 Self-Consciousness and Illumination *150*
3.5 Illuminationist Epistemology: The Process of Intuition and Vision-Illumination. *155*
3.5.1 Intuition. *155*
3.5.2 Vision-Illumination. *155*
4. Illumination and Emanation *162*
5. Being and Light *166*
5.1 Being and Its Primary Determinants *166*
5.2 Being and Cosmology *168*

Appendixes..**173**

Appendix A: Translation of Suhrawardī's "Introduction" to the *Philosophy of Illumination* *173*

Appendix B: Translation of "Part One: The Seventh Rule [On Definition and its Conditions]" of the *Philosophy of Illumination* *179*

Appendix C: An Analysis of Abu'l-Barakāt al-Baghdādī's *Evidential: Logic,* I, 13 *183*

Glossary of Terms..**185**

Arabic English *185*
English Arabic *193*

Bibliography...**203**

Index..**211**

Index of Greek Terms *223*

Acknowledgements

I wish to thank Muhsin S. Mahdi for his generous and painstaking guidance, and I am indebted to Wheeler McIntosh Thackston, Jr. for his invaluable suggestions. For their kind assistance I would also like to acknowledge the Middle East Division of Widener Library at Harvard University and extend my gratitude to Dr. David Partington. I would like to offer my thanks to Ms. Chrisine Desjarlis-Leuth and to Ms. Corrie V. Marsh of Brown University Library who obtained for me the microfilm of a manuscript I had been trying in vain to obtain for many years. I am grateful to my former students, Messers Chase Robinson and Anselm Snodgrass, who read parts of the manuscript and offered useful comments. I wish to thank Oberlin College for the support I received during the short but most rewarding year I spent there. During the final stages of the completion of this book I received support from the Academic Senate at U.C.L.A. for which I am most grateful. I wish especially to thank Mr. Dunning Wilson of the University Research Library who obtained for me microfilms of manuscripts without the use of which Chapters Two and Three would have reminined incomplete. Finally, I would like to take this opportunity to thank Jacob Neusner for his warm encouragement and for offering to publish this work in Brown University's Judaic Studies Series.

Introduction

میان عاشق و معشوق هیچ حایل نیست
تو خود حجاب خودی حافظ از میان برخیز
(حافظ، از دیوان)

The philosophical thought of Shihāb al-Dīn Suhrawardī has not been systematically studied. This book is an attempt to fill this lacuna. It is hoped that it will serve as a preliminary to a comprehensive investigation of the ideas of a man who has had monumental influence on philosophical thought in Islam in general, and on Iranian speculative mysticism in particular. At a time when the *Zeitgeist* of Islamic history had become more a manifestation of the lack of spirituality than the process of recovering it, Suhrawardī's legacy provided an alternative method of inquiry into the nature of things. From its initial formulation in the late twelfth century, the philosophy of illumination was adopted by those thinkers who questioned synchretic Peripateticism as genuine Islamic philosophy. It marks the beginning of a well-formulated religious and mystical philosophy in Islam. It transcends Peripatetic philosophy by according a fundamental epistemological position to revelation, personal inspiration, and mystical vision. Its allegorical and symbolic language is evidenced in a wide range of Persian and Arabic mystical works in prose and poetry.

The impact of Suhrawardī's new methodology, his reconstruction of philosophy more along the lines of Platonism, is a monumental one. This impact can, for example, be readily seen on a hitherto little studied work by the 13th century Jewish philosopher and logician Sa'd b. Manṣūr Ibn Kammūna, himself among the great commentators on Suhrawardī's logical works, whose philosophical composition was given the title *al-Jadīd fi'l-Ḥikma* (*The New Philosophy*, a *Novum Organum* as it were).

Suhrawardī's thought constitutes neither a theology, nor a theosophy, nor *sagesse orientale*, as the volume of scholarship to date may suggest. Instead it represents systematic mystical philosophy. To ignore completely the logical and epistemological component of his works, guarantees an incomplete and therefore unsatisfying analysis. Suhrawardī's thought is characterised by a lack of dogmatism, with a dynamic disposition that permits for change as the subject changes. Although it embraces wisdom, σοφία, in the strict sense, it is ultimately a philosophy that aims at examining things as well as the responses they evoke in the human being; and it endeavors to express coherently and systematically the results of this examination.

The study of the origins and development of religious and mystical philosophy in Islam, as well as of non-Aristotelian logic and epistemology, is beyond the scope of the present work. The twelfth- century philosopher Hibat Allāh Abu'l-Barakāt al-Baghdādī's *Evidential,* a major anti-Aristotelian philosophic encyclopaedia, will be examined, however, because of its special impact on Suhrawardī in his illuminationist reconstruction of philosophy.[1] Both Baghdādī and Suhrawardī claim that their constructivist methodology is founded upon the primary intuition of a knowing subject whose immediate grasp of the totality of existence, of time and space, of the whole as a self-constituted inherently manifest and knowable object, determines what-is being and what-is knowledge. The influence of illuminationist concepts and methodology on philosophy will be exemplified through an examination of a number of major commentaries on Suhrawardī. These include, in the thirteenth century, the commentaries of Shams al-Dīn Muḥammad al-Shahrazūrī,[2] himself an illuminationist philosopher, and of Sa'd b. Manṣūr Ibn Kammūna;[3] in the fourteenth century, that of Quṭb

[1] See below, Chapter One, §2.5.

[2] Shahrazūrī's *Sharḥ Ḥikmat al-Ishrāq [Commentary on the Philosophy of Illumination]* has not been published. I have prepared a preliminary type-script critical edition: however, prior to its publication I shall refer to the folios of the Istanbul, Saray Ahmad III, MS # 3230.

[3] Moshe Perlman's text edition and translation of Ibn Kammūna's polemics *Tanqīḥ al-Abḥāth li'l-Milal al-Thalāth* are the only studies on Ibn Kammūna. See Moshe Perlman, *Sa'd b. Manṣūr Ibn Kammūna's Examination of the Inquiries into the Three*

al-Dīn al-Shīrāzī;[1] in the sixteenth century, that of Jalāl al-Dīn al-Dawwānī;[2] in the seventeenth century, that of Muḥammad Sharīf Niẓam al-Dīn al-Harawī,[3] and of the famous philosopher of the School of Isfahan Ṣadr al-Dīn al-Shīrāzī, better known as Mullā Ṣadrā.[4] While the impact of Suhrawardī's thinking in the west, specifically on the development of Jewish mysticism in the fourteenth century, is beginning to receive some attention,[5] it will not be examinied in this work.

Faiths: A Thirteenth-Century Essay in Comparative Religion (Berkeley and Los Angeles: University of California Press, 1967—the text and 1971—the translation). Ibn Kammūna is an important figure in the history of post-Avicennan philosophy. The section on logic of his *Sharḥ al-Talwīḥāt [Commentary on Suhrawardī's Intimations]* has been printed on the margins of Suhrawardī's, *Manṭiq al-Talwīhāt [Logic of the Intimations]*, ed. Ali Akbar Fayyāz (Tehran: Tehran University Press, 1955), but the editor does not mention Ibn Kammūna by name and refers to him only as "The Commentator" *(al-Shāriḥ)*. I make use of both the printed marginalia as well as the Berlin manuscript of *al-Talwīhāt* (Berlin # 5062). Ibn Kammūna is also an important logician of the post Avicennan period. His *al-Ḥikma al-Jadīda fi'l-Manṭiq [Neue Abhandlungen über die Logik]*—which is probably the section on logic of his *al-Jadīd fi'l-Ḥikma*— and his commentary on Avicenna's *Directives and Remarks* entitled *Sharḥ al-Uṣūl wa'l-Jumal min Muhimmāt al-'Ilm wa'l-'Amal [Kommentar zu den Grundlehren und dem Gesamtinhalt aus dem Gewichtigsten für Theori und Praxis]* deserve a special study; see Leo Hirschfeld's short monograph, *Sa'd b. Manṣūr Ibn Kammūna* (Berlin, 1893), pp. 11-13.

[1]Shīrāzī, *Sharḥ Ḥikmat al-Ishrāq [Commentary on the Philosophy of Illumination]*, lithograph edition by Ibrāhīm Ṭabāṭabā'ī (Tehran, 1313 A.H.).

[2]Dawwānī, *Sharḥ Hayākil al-Nūr [Commentary on the Temples of Light]*, Tehran, Majlis Library, MS #1412.

[3] Harawī, *Anwāriyya [Abodes of Light]*, ed., with introduction and notes, Hossein Ziai (Tehran:Amir Kabir, 1980). This is the only Persian commentary of Suhrawardī's work known to have survived. Harawī, perhaps a Chishtī ṣūfī, in his commentary on Suhrawardī's work also compares epistemological and cosmological principles of illuminationist philosophy with the Advaita system of Indian mystical philosophy.

[4]Mullā Ṣadrā's *Ta'līqāt [the Addenda to Ḥikmat al-Ishrāq]* is printed on the margins of Shīrāzī's *Sharḥ Ḥikmat al-Ishrāq.*

[5]Christian Jambet in his "Introduction" to *Shihāboddīn Yaḥya Sohravardī, Le Livre de la Sagesse Orientale, traduction et notes par Henry Corbin* (Paris: Veridier, 1986) states "Peut-être verrons-nous un signe de la grandeur universelle de Sohravardī en ce que nous apprend M. Paul Fenton, dans le livre quil fait paraître au moment précis où cette traduction voit enfin le jour. Rabbi David Maïmonide, chef de la communauté juive

The initial phase of the present work was fraught with difficulties, some of which seemed insurmountable. The frame of reference against which Suhrawardī's thought was to be examined and presented had to be carefully chosen to avoid a historical approach, which is not our primary concern, and the quasi-philosophical. The terminology to be used in presenting Suhrawardī's thought posed the type of difficulties that are inherent in every attempt at finding exact equivalents for technical terminology from one conceptual, linguistic, and historical context to another. In this case, the choice of terminology was additionally burdened by the limitations of an older Orientalist philological tradition, while every attempt had to be made to also avoid the analytic implications of modern philosophical terminology. I tried to be clear, yet not pedantic, nor yet overly literary. My terminology, though in places tenuous and even perhaps enigmatic, reflects an attempt to convey the thought of a twelfth-century thinker in terms that are intelligible in the context of present-day philosophical thinking and expression.

This study begins by showing that Suhrawardī's philosophy of illumination is not contained solely in his *Philosophy of Illumination.* Rather, there are four major works constituting a cycle in which this philosophy is taught and developed. I then try to show that the philosophy of illumination begins with an attack on the Peripatetic notion of definition, which Suhrawardī modifies and expands into a more comprehensive theory of knowledge that emphasizes self-knowledge and self-consciousness as the grounds of all knowledge. This view of knowledge then serves as the foundation for a cosmology in which real essences or the true being of things are set forth in a continuous sequence of self-conscious and self-subsistent monads, depicted as "lights," which together constitute the whole cosmos. The God of this cosmos is the Light of Lights, from whose self-radiating being emanates a light that covers all of existence, and where light

---

d'Égypte au XIVe siècle, écrit un «Guide du détachement» Ce livre, écrit P. Fenton, «est tout entier imbibé par la terminologie illuministe de l'école sohravardienne» Que ce descendent direct du grand Maïmonide ait choisi la structure même du système du mystique iranien, et voici que l'image que nous devons former des spiritualités et de leur histoire échappe aux lieux communs des orthodoxies." p. 74. See also, Ibid., p. 75, n. 85 where notice of Paul Fenton's forthcoming book, *Deux traités de mystique juive,* is given. See also, Paul Fenton, *Treatise of the Pool* (London: Octogan Press, 1983).

is no longer, is the world of privation, of non-being, and of the darkness wherein resides evil. According to illuminationist epistemology, knowledge is obtained when both the subject and the object are present and manifest, i.e., when there is no obstacle between them. Then and only then is the knowing subject able to grasp the essence of the object.

Chapter One

The Philosophy of Illumination

1. How to Define the Philosophy of Illumination.

Since the early part of this century, Orientalists and historians of philosophy have notised that Suhrawardī is an important figure in the formation of post-Avicennan philosophical thought. Eminent scholars such as Carra de Vaux[1] and Max Hörten[2] wrote short essays on Suhrawardī. In the late twenties, Louis Massignon gave a classification of Suhrawardī's works.[3] In the mid-thirties, Otto Spies edited and translated a few of his philosophical allegories;[4] and Helmut Ritter discussed aspects of his life and distinguished him from three Muslim mystics with the same name.[5] Starting in the mid-forties, Henry Corbin's text-editions of many of Suhrawardī's philosophical writings kindled a special interest in the thought of the man who has been traditionally known as the Master of the philosophy of illumination *(Shaykh al-Ishrāq).*[6] In more recent years, Seyyed Hossein Nasr has

[1] See Carra de Vaux, "La philosophie illuminative d'après Suhrawerdi Meqtoul," *Journal Asiatique,* xix, vol. 19 (1902), pp. 63-64.

[2] See Max Hörten, *Die Philosophie der Erleutung nach Suhrawardī* (Halle, 1912).

[3] See Louis Massignon, *Receuil de textes inédits* (Paris: Paul Gauthner, 1929), pp. 111-113.

[4] See Otto Spies, *Three Treatises on Mysticism by Shihabuddin Suhrawardī Maqtul* (Stuttgart: Kohlhammer, 1935).

[5] See Helmut Ritter, "Philologika IX: Die vier Suhrawardī," *Der Islam,* vol., 24 (1937), pp. 270-286; and vol. 25 (1938), pp. 35-86.

[6] See H. Corbin, *Suhrawardī d'Alep, fondateur do la doctrine illuminative* (Paris, 1939); idem, *Les Motifs zoroastriens dans la philosophie de Sohravardī* (Tehran, 1946); idem, *L'Homme de Lumière dans le soufisme iranien* (Paris: Sisteron, 1971). See especially Corbin's *Prolégomènes* to each of his following critical editions of Suhrawardī's works: *Opera Metaphysica et Mystica I* (Istambul: Maarif Matbaasi, 1945); *Opera Metaphysica et Mystica II* (Tehran: Institut Franco-Iranien, 1954); *Opera*

devoted a number of studies to the spiritual and religious dimension in Suhrawardī's teachings.[1] There has been no serious attempt made, however, to study the logical and epistemological foundations of the philosophy of illumination from a philosophical point of view, and to date a few pages in Muhammad Iqbāl's doctoral thesis, *The Development of Metaphysics in Persia,* remain the best general account of Suhrawardī's philosophical thought.[2]

Recent scholars, notably Corbin and Nasr, have stressed the significance of Suhrawardī as a reviver of ancient Iranian thought. These authors have pointed repeatedly to what they consider to be the profoundly mystical quality of Suhrawardī's thought without, however, undertaking a systematic study of the foundations of the philosophy of illumination. Such general characterizations, though useful, do not provide us with a comprehensive view of the philosophy of illumination.

In order to assess in some detail Suhrawardī's role in the development of post-Avicennan philosophical thought, one has first to delineate the

---

Metaphysica et Mystica III (Tehran: Institut Franco-Iranien, 1970). See also Corbin's translations of Suhrawardī's works: *Archange empourpré, Quinze traités et récits mystiques traduits du persan et de l'arabe,* présentés et annotés par Henry Corbin (Paris: Fayard, 1976); and *Le Livre de la Sagesse Orientale, Kitāb Ḥikmat al-Ishrāq,* traduction et notes par Henry Corbin, établies et introduit par Christian Jambet (Paris: Verdier, 1986).

[1] See S.H. Nasr, *Three Muslim Sages* (Cambridge: Harvard University Press, 1964), Chapter II; idem, "Suhrawardī," in *A History of Muslim Philosophy,* ed. M.M. Sharif (Wiesbaden: Otto Harrassowitz, 1963), vol. I, pp. 372-398. Nasr, in his pioneering work has pointed out the religious significance of Suhrawardī's life and teachings, as well as the religious dimension in his cosmology. See, in this regard, idem, *An Introduction to Islamic Cosmological Doctrines* (London, 1978), Chapter XII.

[2] See Muhammad Iqbāl, *The Development of Metaphysics in Persia* (London, 1908), pp. 121-150. In his analysis of *Ḥikmat al-Ishrāq,* Iqbāl relies almost totally on Muḥammad-Sharīf al-Harawī's Persian commentary available to him during his student days in Berlin at the Königlichen Bibliothek (part of the *Bibliotheca Orientalis Sprengeriana,* Spr. 766). My critical edition of Harawī's commentary, based on the same unique manuscript available to Iqbāl, has now been published: see *Anwāriyya: An 11th century A.H. Persian translation and commentary on Suhrawardī's Ḥikmat al-Ishrāq,* edited with introduction and notes by Hossein Ziai (Tehran: Amir Kabir, 1980, second edition 1984).

character of his thought. Suhrawardī's role as the synthesizer of Greek and Iranian "wisdoms" together with Islamic religious and mystical principles and intentions, cannot be determined before we have looked into his handling of the problems of logic, physics, mathematics, and metaphysics, which together constitute his philosophy of illumination. To simply say that Suhrawardī was a mystic who was given to the glorification and revival of ancient Iranian philosophy and wisdom, and to portray him as a "perennial," "wise," and "profound" sage, does not determine the exact nature of his thought—not even whether Suhrawardī was a mystic, a theologian, a systematic philosopher, or the ideologue of some form of medieval Iranian nationalism.

To say anything significant regarding Suhrawardī's thought, we have to determine first the precise nature of the logical and epistemological foundation of the philosophy of illumination. Only on the basis of such a systematic analysis can we find out whether Suhrawardī was a mystic or a philosopher, or whether, and what part of, his systematic philosophy is a defense, clarification, or systemization of mystical experiences as a method of discovering reality. In order to undertake such a systematic approach, we must first determine the works of Suhrawardī that deal with what is specifically named the philosophy of illumination *(ḥikmat al-ishrāq)* by him.

2. The Works of Suhrawardī on the Philosophy of Illumination

2.1 The Four Major Works

We shall begin by examining the four major Arabic philosophical works of Suhrawardī: the *Intimations (al-Talwīḥāt)*, the *Apposites (al-Muqāwamāt)*, the *Paths and Havens (al-Mashāri' wa'l-Muṭāraḥāt)*,[1]

[1] Only the sections on metaphysics of the three works the *Intimations*, the *Apposites*, the *Paths and Havens* (each referred to by Suhrawardī as "The Third Science On Metaphysics" *[al-'Ilm al-Thālith fi'l-Ilāhiyyāt]* have been edited and published in *Opera Metaphysica et Mystica I*, ed. H. Corbin (Istanbul: Maarif Matbaasi, 1945), (hereafter cited as *Opera I*).

and the *Philosophy of Illumination (Ḥikmat al-Ishrāq),*[1] in order to show that, based on Suhrawardī's own explicit statements, these works constitute an integral corpus in which he presented in writing the genesis and development of the philosophy of illumination, from its analytical, discursive beginnings to its experiential, allegorically and symbolically depicted illuminationist end. To answer satisfactorily the question, "What is the philosophy of illumination?" we cannot limit ourselves to the study of any one of these four works, but rather we are obliged to examine all of them as a coherent whole. Only such a study will enable us to delineate a comprehensive account of the philosophy of illumination.[2]

The following is the most explicit statement by Suhrawardī on the interrelation of these works: "This book *(the Paths and Havens)* should be read before the *Philosophy of Illumination* and after the short examination called the *Intimations.*"[3] Since the *Apposites* is stated to be an "addendum to the *Intimations,*"[4] it follows that the proposed cycle of reading and teaching the philosophy of illumination is as follows: 1- the *Intimations,* 2- the *Apposites,* 3- the *Paths and Havens,* and 4- the *Philosophy of Illumination.* It is evident, then, that these works should be read together and in a particular sequence, and that only as such do they constitute the philosophy of illumination. Now, in light of certain facts we shall presently examine, it is equally evident that the major works were written, taught, and revised within a span of no more than ten years. This indicates that the idea of the philosophy of illumination, either partially or perhaps even fully, was present in Suhrawardī's mind while composing each of these works. In fact, I aim to show that the impetus behind the composition of each of these

[1] Published in *Opera Metaphysica et Mystica II,* ed. H. Corbin (Tehran: Institut Franco-Iranien, 1952), (hereafter cited as *Opera II).*

[2] The question as to the intention of the author in any examination of medieval philosophical texts is a crucial one. This is so specifically because of the implicit elliptical style of all such texts.

[3] Suhrawardī, *Opera I,* p. 194.

[4] Suhrawardī, *Opera I,* p. 124. Since the structure of this "addendum" to the *Intimations* corresponds to the structure of the *Intimations,* we shall only examine the structure of the *Intimations,* save in the case of specific points, to which we shall refer in the notes.

works was nothing other than the systematic presentation of the philosophy of illumination. This means that when Suhrawardī states that the *Intimations,* for example, is written according to the "Peripatetic method,"[1] it is not an independent work written solely as an exercise in Peripatetic philosophy, nor does it represent a Peripatetic "period" in Suhrawardī's life and writings. Rather, it points to the fact that certain parts or dimensions of the philosophy of illumination are accepted Peripatetic teachings, mostly Avicennan doctrines as found in his two most famous works, the *Healing (al-Shifā')* and in the *Directives and Remarks (al-Ishārāt wa al-Tanbīhāt).* To compose a philosophy in a corpus that covers logic, physics, and metaphysics (and the philosophy of illumination is a complete system of philosophy in this sense) meant that, to a great extent, Suhrawardī had to work within the methodological and conceptual framework of some established scientific and philosophic tradition, which in this case is explicitly said to be the Peripatetic tradition, most notably the Avicennan (to whom Suhrawardī refers on a number of occasions in his texts), and not that of Alfarabi nor Alkindi (neither of whom are ever mentioned).

The philosophy of illumination does emphasize certain intuitive elements over and beyond discursive thought, but it is not a system that is in complete opposition to, or totally different from, Peripatetic philosophy. In fact, Peripatetic philosophy, as studied and understood by Suhrawardī, is both the point of departure and an inseparable component of certain aspects of illuminationist methodology. Only in comparison with Peripatetic philosophy can one realize how the philosophy of illumination aims at expanding man's view of things; then, and in those terms, can its success in achieving that aim be assessed.

2.2 Position of the *Flashes of Light* and Other Works

For several reasons we are excluding Suhrawardī's work, the *Flashes of Light (al-Lamaḥāt)* from our study. To begin with, Suhrawardī mentions the *Flashes of Light* only once in the four works mentioned earlier, while there are a number of cross-references among the latter. Also,

[1] *'Alā ṭarīq al-mashshā 'īn.* Suhrawardī, *Opera II,* p. 10.

nowhere does he indicate that the *Flashes of Light* is part of the corpus that should be read by the student of the philosophy of illumination. The one instance where Suhrawardī does mention the *Flashes of Light* is in his "Introduction" to the *Philosophy of Illumination,* where he indicates that among his works this one occupies a position "below" the *Intimations,* itself the first of the group of works that make up the philosophy of illumination.[1] In his "Introduction" to the *Flashes of Light* Suhrawardī refers to it as a work of "utmost brevity, including only the most important elements of the three sciences [logic, physics, and metaphysics]."[2] The "most important elements" turn out to be only an outline or a short syllabus of the major topics of Peripatetic philosophy, as presented, for instance, in Avicenna's major philosophical work, the *Healing*. The *Flashes of Light* is a simple, non-argumentative presentation of the central Peripatetic philosophical principles and rules of logic, physics, and metaphysics.[3] In all the four major works, in contrast, Suhrawardī takes issue in varying degrees with certain carefully selected Peripatetic principles and rules, which are either refuted, or revised, or finally reformulated within a new illuminationist framework, and expressed using a modified technical language in harmony with a cohesive account of the philosophy of illumination. The *Flashes of Light* includes no such characteristics.[4]

Among Suhrawardī's other works, the following, for the reasons stated below, will not be part of our present study of illuminationist philosophy, but will be examined in a forthcoming work on the use of allegory in the philosophy of illumination.

[1] Ibid., pp. 10-11

[2] Suhrawardī, *Kitāb al-Lamaḥāt* [*the Flashes of Light*], ed. Emile Maalouf (Beirut: Dar An-Nahar, 1969), p. 57 (hereafter cited as *Flashes of Light).*

[3] E. Maalouf in his "Preface" to the edition of the *Flashes of Light* (p. vii), states that the work is to be considered as an "epitome of an epitome of Peripatetic theory."

[4] Suhrawardī himself stipulates his intention for composing the work to be an exposition of the most important topics of Peripatetic philosophy (*Flashes of Light*, p. 57). As it is customary in all of his works, Suhrawardī rarely refers to Peripatetic views by using the name *al-Mashshā'ūn,* this being the only instance in the *Flashes of Light.*

1. *Partawnāma [Sun Rays]*[1] is a work in Persian, and is among Suhrawardī's independent compositions. It should be considered a Persian epitome of illuminationist philosophy. I have chosen not to include this work in the present study because an analysis of it presupposes an understanding of what illuminationist philosophy is, itself our aim here. It should be mentioned that in this work Suhrawardī discusses in detail the position of the fundamental self-conscious knowing subject in epistemology. His concept "I-ness" *(manī)* is expanded to include "thou-ness" *(tu'ī)* and "he/she/it-ness" *(ū' ī)*.[2] These generalized terms signify self-consciousness in the knowing and evident *(ẓāhir)* subject.

2. *Hayākil al-Nūr [Temples of Light]* of which there exists both an Arabic[3] as well as a Persian version.[4] This work too falls within the category of epitomes of illuminationist philosophy. In this work Suhrawardī uses Qur'ānic exegesis *(ta'wīl)* to a much greater extent than in other of his major didactic works. Since I plan to examine the question of exegesis in Suhrawardī's methodology, making use of Jalāl al-Dīn al-Dawwānī's *Sharḥ Hayākil al-Nūr [Commentary on the Temples of Light]*, on a separate occasion, I shall not deal with this work now.

3. Persian and Arabic allegorical tales.[5] These eleven tales represent the final "poetic" expression of the results of the experience of illumination *(ishrāq)*. Suhrawardī's works *Kalimat al-Taṣawwuf [Maxim on Sufism]*, and *al-Alwāḥ al-'Imādī ['Imādī Tablets]*,[6] though not allegorical in the

[1] Published in Suhrawardī, *Opera Metaphysica et Mystica III*, ed. H. Corbin, and S.H. Nasr (Tehran: Institut Franco-Iranien, 1970), (hereafter cited as *Opera III)*, pp. 12-34.

[2] Suhrawardī has here generalized the concept *huwiyya* (ipseity, τὸ ὄν) by taking the Persian term *ū'ī* and applying it to the second and first persons as well. Thus *manī* for "I-ness," *tu'ī* for (thou-ness), and *ū'ī* for "he/she/it-ness."

[3] Suhrawardī, *Hayākil al-Nūr*, ed. Abu Rayyan (Cairo, 1960).

[4] The Persian version is published in *Opera III*, pp. 54-67.

[5] See, *The Mystical and Visionary Treatises of Suhrawardi*, translated by W. M. Thackston, Jr. (London: Octagon Press, 1982). Thackston's artful translations are to be considered among the best English renditions of Arabic and Persian mystical works .

[6] The two treatises are published in *Si Risāla az Shaykh-i Ishrāq [Three Treatises by the Master of Illumination]*, ed. by Najaf-Ali Habibi (Tehran, 1977), pp. 1-121. I

strict sense, should be included in the category of "poetic" and allegorical compositions and not among the "theoretical" systematic works on the philosophy of illumination.

2.3 Character of the Four Works.

Our grouping here of the four works is in conformity with Corbin's scheme of the "grands traités dogmatiques."[1] However, we wish to go beyond what Corbin has suggested, and propose that the four works, when considered together, form an integral unit which constitutes the attempt made by Suhrawardī to present systematically a new formulation of philosophy. This new formulation employs a special technical language, accentuates the creative act of intuition, and posits as a primary axiom that the soul's knowledge of itself is the foundation and starting point of knowledge. Suhrawardī's intention of establishing an intuitionist foundation for the reconstruction of Peripatetic philosophy is the intention of each of the four books mentioned.

The four books are related one to another and form a whole which includes a cycle starting with discursive philosophy *(ḥikma baḥthiyya)*[2] and ending with intuitive philosophy (*ḥikma dhawqiyya*).[3] This basic view of philosophy, which attempts to combine the discursive with the intuitive, is present in each of the works taken separately as well, i.e., every one of the works combines discursive principles, rules, methods, and technical terms with intuitive ones, but the first work in the cycle, *Intimations,*

---

have also made reference to *Kalimat al-Taṣawwuf,* MS, Tehran, Majlis Library, *Majmū'a,* 3071.

[1] *Opera I,* p. xvi

[2] For Suhrawardī, "discursive philosophy" is a philosophical attitude, methodology, and technical language, associated mostly with certain (but not all) Avicennan Peripatetic works. His use of terms such as *baḥth, al-ḥikma al-baḥthiyya, ṭarīq al-mashshā'īn,* and *madhhab al-mashshā'īn,* all refer to this philosophy, with certain principles of which he does not agree. What is significant for Suhrawardī, however, is not the refutation of *baḥth* but the incorporation of a reformulated *baḥth* in reconstructed philosophy of illumination.

[3] For Suhrawardī, "intuitive philosophy" is both a method and a starting point for the reconstruction of philosophy, as well as an objective (that which is acquired by the "practitioner") of *ḥikmat al-ishrāq* taken as a complete system. Terms used such as *dhawq, al-ḥikma al-dhawqiyya, al-'ilm al-ḥuḍūrī, al-'ilm al-shuhūdī,* though they all refer to "intuitive philosophy," differ in specific detail, as will be made clear.

stresses the discursive, while the final work in the cycle, *Philosophy of Illumination*, emphasizes the intuitive. This combination is absent from all but the four major works of Suhrawardī with the exception of the *Sun Rays*, the *'Imādī Tablets*, and the *Temples of Light*.[1]

2.4 Period of Composition of the Major Works: Remarks on Suhrawardī's Life.

Let us now examine relevant historical facts in Suhrawardī's life, not to provide the reader with a biography, but to establish the time span during which Suhrawardī may have composed his major works and the places where he may have been involved with teaching the philosophy of illumination.

We know only a few dates and specific details of events in Suhrawardī's life. We know that he was born in the village of Suhraward in northeastern Iran in the year 549/1155, and was executed in Aleppo in the year 587/1191, which means that he lived for thirty-eight lunar years or thirty-six solar years.[2] We are informed that Suhrawardī entered Aleppo in

[1] Dawwāni stipulates the work to be allegorical *(marmūza)*, containing the secrets of illuminationist wisdom, the kind that is bestowed upon the chosen in God's proximity *(al-qirāba al-ilāhiyya)*, fols. 2r-3v; 82v-84r.

[2] Shahrazūrī, *Nuzhat al-Arwāḥ* (MS. Istanbul, Yeni Cami, 908), fol. 233v. Shahrazūrī's work on the history of philosophy is the only extensive source in its treatment of Suhrawardī's biography. Sahrazūrī may have had oral sources for this material, for we have not been able to locate any possible written sources for the biography as treated in *Nuzhat al-Arwāḥ*. However, there does exist some additional information on Suhrawardī', which though not extensive, adds to our understanding of his life. We shall indicate these as we proceed in our present study. A recentlly printed version of Shahrazūrī's work is also available See Shahrazūrī, *Nuzhat al-Arwāḥ wa Rawḍat al-Afrāḥ fī Tārīkh al-Ḥukamā' wa'l-Falāsifa*, ed. Seyed Khurshid Ahmed (Hayderabad: Osmania Oriental Publications Bureau, 1976). Also a 16th century Persian translation of the work by Maqṣūd 'Ali Tabrīzī has been recently published. See Shahrazūrī, *Nuzhat al-Arwāḥ wa Rawḍat al-Afrāḥ (Tārīkh al-Ḥukamā')*, ed.with an introduction on histories of Islamic philosophy, by M.T. Danesh-Pajouh and M. S. Mawlā'ī (Tehran, 1986)

the year 579/1183.[1] Suhrawardī himself states that he completed the *Philosophy of Illumination* in the year 582/1186.[2] Shams al-Dīn Muḥammad Shahrazūrī states in his *Nuzhat al-Arwāḥ* that Suhrawardī was approximately thirty years old at the time of the completion, or near completion, of the *Paths and Havens* (i.e., that this book was completed around the year 579/1183).[3]

We may safely assume that Suhrawardī had completed all of his studies prior to his departure for Aleppo and may have completed most of his writings prior to that date as well. We know the names of a number of his teachers, but have no exact information as to when or what specific texts or types of works he studied with them. As far as we know, Suhrawardī's first teacher was Majd al-Dīn al-Jīlī, who taught him philosophy and theology in Marāgha. Suhrawardī's next teacher was Fakhr al-Dīn al-Mārdīnī (d. 594/1198), who taught him philosophy in Isfahan or in Mārdīn,[4] and was probably his most important teacher. We know that al-Mārdīnī was in the area of Aleppo in the year of Suhrawardī's execution, which he is reported to have predicted,[5] but we do not know whether there was any contact between the teacher and his student in Syria, nor that he played a role, positive or negative, in the intrigue that led to Suhrawardī's trial and execution.[6] It is important to note that al-Mārdīnī had been a contemporary of the famous anti-Aristotelian Abu'l Barakāt al-Baghdādī (d. after 560/1164) and a student of Baghdādī's namesake and rival in Baghdad;[7] and this as well as other reasons (with which we deal in section 2.5 of this chapter) might explain why al-Baghdādī is one of the very few "contemporary" philosophers to whom Suhrawardī refers by name. Al-

[1] This fact has not been noticed by Corbin nor other scholars. It is given by Ibn Abī Uṣaybi'a, *Ṭabaqāt al-Aṭibbā'*, ed. A Müller (Köningsberg; Pr., 1884) I, 168; and by Yāqūt, *Irshād al-Arīb*, ed. D.S. Margoliouth, VI, 269.

[2] Suhrawardī, *Opera II*, p. 258.

[3] Shahrazūrī, *Nuzhat al-Arwāḥ*, fol. 231r.

[4] Yāqūt, *Irshād*, VII, 269.

[5] Ibn Abī Uṣaybi'a, *Ṭabaqāt*, I, 299-301.

[6] It seems that Mārdīnī, who had spent a few years (587-589) in Damascus, went to Aleppo and was received by al-Malik al-Ẓāhir. Ibid., pp. 289-290.

Baghdādī, like Suhrawardī following him, claims that his major work, the *Evidential (al-Mu'tabar)* had been composed on the basis of "personal reflection."[1] Both philosophers admit that the certainties of intuition are as valid as those of reason and sense perception and claim that only the latter type of certainty is accepted by the Peripatetics. Finally, we know the name of another teacher of Suhrawardī, Ẓahīr al-Fārsī, with whom he studied the *Observations (al-Baṣā'ir)* of the famous logician 'Umar ibn Sahlān al-Sāwī (fl. 540/1145), who is also among the few philosophers whose name is mentioned by Suhrawardī, especially in connection with certain intricate problems of logic.[2] Suhrawardī was a young philosopher who left his native land and went to Syria in a period of political turmoil and intrigue, then entered Aleppo in the year 579/1183, where he taught and was involved with the prince Malik Ẓāhir Shāh, the son of the Ayyūbid Ṣalāḥ al-Dīn. We further know the date of the composition of two of his major works. On the basis of this scanty information we want to attempt to ascertain the approximate span of time during which Suhrawardī wrote his major works.

We may never know exactly when Suhrawardī finished his studies or when he commenced with teaching and writing, but the following assumptions seem reasonable to make. Suhrawardī probably finished his studies with al-Jīlī in his early twenties, and his studies with al-Mārdīnī in his middle twenties. Let us assume that, after the completion of his studies, a period of three to five years could have elapsed prior to the time when a group of students or disciples, to whom he refers as his "brethren" or "companions," attached themselves to him. For them, at their insistent

---

[7] al-Qifṭī, *Tārīkh al-Ḥukamā'* (11th century Persian translation), ed. Bahman Dārā'ī (Tehran: Tehran University Press, 1347 A.H.), p. 345.

[1] Abu'l-Barakāt al-Baghdādī, *Kitāb al-Mu'tabar* (Haydarabad, 1357 A.H.), I, 7. For a discussion of the position of "personal reflection" and intuition in Abu'l-Barakāt's views on the epistemological position of personal and intuitive knowledge in philosophy, see S. Pines, *Nouvelles études sur Awḥad al-Zamān Abu'l-Barakāt al-Baghdādī* (Paris: Librarie Durlaches, 1958), pp. 8, 17. See also, below section 2.5.

[2] Suhrawardī, *Opera I*, pp. 146, 278, 352. It is interesting to note that Sāwī wrote a Persian commentary on Avicenna's *Risālat al-Ṭayr (GAL* I, 456.44), an allegorical treatise which was re-composed in Persian by Suhrawardī (translated in *The Mystical and Visionary Treatises of Suhrawardī*, tr. Thackston, pp. 21-25). Sāwī is among the forerunners of illuminationist thinkers in Islam.

request, he composed most of his works. This would mean also that Suhrawardī may have been engaged for some time in teaching his doctrines orally prior to setting them down in writing. It is improbable that Suhrawardī's major works could have been written before his late twenties. Suhrawardī had a maximum of ten years to compose all his major works and possibly the majority of the other ones including the allegorical tales. Now ten years is not long enough for a thinker to have two distinct periods of fully developed thought, one Peripatetic and the other illuminationist, as some scholars have suggested.[1] I find it difficult to believe in this hypothesis; and the fact that Suhrawardī wrote a few synopses of Peripatetic doctrines (whose dates of composition are not certain) does not seem to support it.

In any case, the four major works of Suhrawardī here examined make references to each other; and, judging by the extent of the cross-references, they must have been either composed more or less concurrently, or at least each was constantly revised, when taught, with a view to the others.[2] Perhaps the year 582/1186, the stated year of the completion of the *Philosophy of Illumination,* is the year when a version had been made available, but this was surely revised up to the end of Suhrawardī's life as the book was taught. Also, in 579/1183, the year when Suhrawardī had entered Aleppo and had finished the *Paths and Havens,* he may have had

[1] Recent scholars have too readily accepted Suhrawardī's works such as the *Intimations,* the *Apposites,* and the *Paths and Havens* as Peripatetic works not essentially related to the philosophy of illumination composed in a period in which Suhrawardī had not yet developed illuminationist principles, rules, and methods. See Louis Massignon, *Recueil de textes inédits* (Paris: Paul Geuthner, 1929), pp. 111-113; Carl Brockelman, *GAL* I, pp. 437-438, *GAL* SI, pp. 481-483; Henry Corbin, "Prolégomènes," *Opera II;* Sayyid Hossein Nasr, "Shihāb al-Dīn Suhrawardī Maqtūl," *A History of Muslim Philosophy,* ed. M.M. Sharif (Weisbaden: Otto Harrassowitz, 1963), p. 374; as well as others who have followed the same incomplete classification of Suhrawardī's works as these authors.

[2] E.g., Suhrawardī, *Opera I,* pp. 59, 121, 128, 131, 146, 183, 185, 192, 194, 195, 278, 340, 361, 371, 401, 484, 506. Suhrawardī considers all of the major texts to be related.

with him "drafts" (or versions) of all the four major works, which he discussed during the many gatherings arranged by Malik Ẓāhir Shāh.[1]

2.5 Abu'l Barakāt al-Baghdādī and the Philosophy of Illumination.

Abu'l Barakāt al-Baghdādī is among the very few philosophers Suhrawardī ever mentions by name while discussing specific philosophical problems, and in many instances he is identified in manuscripts of Suhrawardī's works in marginal annotations in reference to the subject being discussed in the text. Also, Suhrawardī clearly stipulates on several occcasions Baghdādī's Platonist position—a prefared position by himself—and in regards key philosophical issues Baghdādī's methodology reverberates in Suhrawardī's own reformulations of the principles of philosophy. Concerning the most significant queston of the foundation of philosophy both Suhrawardī, and Baghdādī before him, take an intuitionist position by allowing for primary intuition to play a principle role in philosophical construction. The structure of Baghdādī's philosophical work, the *Evidential,* is also reflected in Suhrawardī's philosophical works. It seems, thus evident to me that Baghdādī should be regarded as an important immediate source for many of Suhrawardī's non-Peripatetic approaches to problems of philosophy. Avicenna's methodology of philosophy, his use of technical terminology and his philosophical intention were the standard in view of which later systematic Arabic and Persian philosophy was studied and further elucidated. Baghdādī and Suhrawardī both make serious attempts at reformulating many Avicennan philosophical principles, something no other philosopher does in such systematic manner. It is in this repect that Suhrawardī's reading of Baghdādī's philosophical work, the *Evidential,* is to be examined, as it helps explain the construction of the philosophy of illumination.

In what follows, I will refer to Baghdādī's the *Evidential* while analyzing Suhrawardī's philosophy of illumination in order to show the relation between the two methodologies and to point to their common anti-Avicennan themes. I do not aim to make an exhaustive comparison. The

[1] Yāqūt, *Irshād,* VII, 269.

philosophy of illumination, however, is finally distinguished from Baghdādī's philosophical work in its use of the metaphore "light," in its ontological position, in its illuminationist theory of emanation, in its epistemological theory of knowledge by presence and in its being well defined as fundamentally non-Peripatetic systematic philosophy so designated as a separate *illuminationist* system. This is clear when the *Evidential* is examined with a view to Suhrawardī's philosophical works.

3. The Major Works Examined.

3.1 The *Intimations*.

In his "Introduction" to the "third science" (*al-'ilm al-thālith,* i.e. metaphysics) of the *Intimations,* Suhrawardī states:

> [In this book] I have not paid attention to the well-known doctrine of the Peripatetics, but rather I am reviewing and revising them as far as I can and mention only the core of the theorems (*qawā'id*) of the First Teacher.[1]

Further, in his "Introduction" to the *Philosophy of Illumination,* he states that the *Intimations* is a work composed according to "the Peripatetic method,"(*'alā ṭarīq al-mashshā'īn*)[2] while at the end of the *Intimations,* he stipulates:

> I have provided in this book what enables one to dispense with [Peripatetic methods], plus amazing and unique matters. It includes carefully laid down rules of science. In it there are no discrepancies nor scattered thought. I advise you not to follow me blindly, nor any one else. For the true measure of things is demon-

[1] Suhrawardī, *Opera I,* p. 2.

[2] Suhrawardī, *Opera II,* p. 10. There are several instances in all of Suhrawardī's four major works where he discusses the relevance of the "Peripatetic method" (*ṭarīq al-mashshā'īn*) for the student of the philosophy of illumination. These we shall examine in detail in later chapters. Most scholars have failed to see that illuminationist methodology does not negate Peripatetic methodology, but rather it incorporates it as a tool in the reconstruction of metaphysics. We may readily ascertain, at this preliminary juncture, the significance of Peripatetic methodology from the statement made by Suhrawardī himself at the end of the *Philosophy of Illumination:* "Do not bestow the philosophy of illumination except upon those who are worthy of it and have become fully competent in the Peripatetic method." (*Opera II,* p. 258)

stration . . . Turn to "experiential sciences"[1] in order that you may become one of the philosophers.[2]

We may infer from these statements that the *Intimations* is a work in which Suhrawardī, using the "Peripatetic method," analyzes central discursive philosophical problems and presents certain conclusions, or truths of a symbolic nature—these being, as he says, the "secrets"—and presents a view of philosophy that points to "experiential knowledge" as the highest kind of knowledge that serves also as the ground for epistemology. Experiential knowledge, as primary intuition of time-space, needs to be explained, or discussed—hence *baḥth,* or discursive philosophy is necessary—and Peripatetic methodology *must* be employed in the process of explaining what this intuition is. This is an important feature also of Suhrawardī's view of the history of philosophy, especially of the history of philosophy in Islam. This view, also discussed in detail in the *Paths and Havens* and in the *Philosophy of Illumination,* is presented in the *Intimations* through Suhrawardī's recollection of a dream-vision of Aristotle, who tells him in the dream that among the Islamic "wise" men *(ḥukamā')*, only the mystics like Abū Yazīd al-Bastāmī and al-Ḥallāj have achieved union with the Active Intellect; they are the only true wise men because they have surpassed discursive philosophy through their personal experience.[3] In an earlier passage Suhrawardī informs us that certain types of knowledge, of the same rank as that obtained as the result of union with the Active Intellect, had been obtained by philosophers such as Aristotle and Plato, and others among the ancients, as well as by mystics in Islam,[4] and

[1] *al-'ilm al-tajarrudī al-ittiṣālī al-shuhūdī.* Cf. R. Arnaldez, *EI* 2, s.v. "Ishrāq."

[2] Suhrawardī, *Opera I,* pp.120, 121.

[3] Ibid., pp. 70-74.

[4] Essentially this is the view of Suhrawardī's "sources," not in the strict historical sense, but in the sense of spiritual lineage. This view considers the existence of two branches in the spiritual genealogies, one Western comprising Empedocles, Pythagoras, Plato, and in Islam (still Western) Dhū al-Nūn al-Miṣrī, and Sahl ibn 'Abd Allāh al-Tustarī; and the other Eastern branch comprising Gayomarth, Farīdūn, Kay-Khusraw, and in Islam (still Eastern) Abū Yazīd Bastāmī, Manṣūr Ḥallāj, and Kharraqānī. Both branches start with Hermes "the father of philosophers" *(wālid al-hukamā'),* and end with Suhrawardī. See R. Arnaldez, *EI* 2, s.v. "Ishrāḳiyyūn" It should be noted that each illuminationist philosopher is bestowed with a special "mark," or quality, reminiscent of

such "truths" *(ḥaqā'iq)* thus obtained are said to be results of a special intuitive, experiential mode of knowledge.[1] Concerning this very important epistemological principle, Suhrawardī refers the reader to his *Paths and Havens,* where he deals extensively with the problem of the soul's knowledge of things in relation to self-knowledge and other related epistemological problems. Suhrawardī's position regarding what philosophy is, as well as his views on the the epistemological significance of the creative acts of intuition, the question of personal experience, and the "secrets" (*rumūz*), as explained in the *Intimations,* are definite marks of his philosophy of illumination. In many places in the *Intimations,* especially in the section on the dream-vision of Aristotle, illuminationist principles are discussed at length by Suhrawardī, albeit while employing a non-illuminationist technical language, and this is a clear indication of his intention in this book: to lay the foundation of the philosophy of illumination by presenting the "core" of Aristotle's philosophical doctrine. This shows that the work cannot be regarded as an isolated Peripatetic composition independent of, and unrelated to, the philosophy of illumination.

Suhrawardī, in his "Introduction" to the *Philosophy of Illumination,* clearly stipulates that "discursive philosophy" *(ḥikma baḥthiyya)* is a necessary component of "intuitive philosophy" *(ḥikma dhawqiyya).*[2] He further states that only a perfect combination of the two methodologies will lead to true wisdom *(ḥikma)*—the aim of illuminationist philosophy—and if we here make the identification between "discursive philosophy" and the "core" of Aristotle's doctrine, we realize why the *Intimations*, as a philosophical composition, is to be considered the first step in the illuminationist reconstruction of philosophy. The *Intimations* is primarily the "discursive" part of the methodology of the philosophy of illumination. Suhrawardī

---

the δαιμόνιον of Socrates, and equated with the Persian *khvarnah*, referred to by Suhrawardī as *kiyān kharra,* or *farra-yi īzadī..*

[1] *Opera I,* p. 58.

[2] Suhrawardī, *Opera II,* p. 12. Cf. Quṭb al-Dīn al-Shīrāzī, *Sharḥ Ḥikmat al-Ishrāq [Commentary on the Philosophy of Illumination]* (Tehran, 1313 A.H.), pp. 3,4 (hereafter cited as *Sharḥ II).* Suhrawardī's own introduction to the work is very significant: we have thus provided the reader with a complete translation. See below, Appendix A.

outlines that part of Peripatetic methodology he needs to employ in his own work. This, however, is only one component of the *Intimations*, the most obvious one, and the one which has led scholars and commentators to think of the work as merely an epitome of "standard" Peripatetic doctrine. The less obvious component of the *Intimations*—to be examined more carefully later on—can be determined by observing that the work is not simply an exposé of the "core" of Aristotle's doctrine. It is more than that. Consider the following passage in the *Paths and Havens:*

> A person who needs to may find what is necessary to know prior to the [study of] the *Philosophy of Illumination* in the book *Intimations* where I have stated the points on which I differ from the master of discursive philosophy, Aristotle.[1]

Suhrawardī's discussion of the "core" of Aristotle's doctrine is in accordance with what he has reformulated that doctrine to be, and not a simple epitome of it. The main intention of the *Intimations* is to accept a reformulated Peripatetic methodology as a necessary component of illuminationist method, and to teach this to the students of illuminationist philosophy.

3.2 The *Apposites*

What I have said so far concerning the *Intimations* is in many ways also pertinent to the *Appposites*, simply because this work is said to be an addendum to the *Intimations* by the author and not substantially different, certainly not in its main intention nor structure. However, the *Apposites* is one step further towards a more specific and comprehensive explication of illuminationist doctrine, and employs more non-standard technical terminology than the *Intimations*. There are several references to the *Intimations* in the *Apposites*, mostly indicating that the same subject is treated there as well.[2] On one occasion Suhrawardī states that the *Apposites* is in conformity with the "method of the *Intimations*,"[3] so that the

[1] Suhrawardī, *Opera I*, p. 484.

[2] Ibid., pp. 128, 146, 183, 188.

[3] *Ṭarīq al-talwīḥāt*. Ibid., p. 188. The "secrets," or "metaphores" (*al-rumūz*) of the *Intimations* are here said to be understood only in connection with the discussion in the *Apposites*.

Apposites, too, is to be considered a further "discursive" component of illuminationist methodology. At the end of the *Apposites* Suhrawardī indicates its relation to his other works when he anticipates the *Philosophy of Illumination,* points to the *Paths and Havens* as the work wherein details of his illuminationist philosophy are to be found, and further informs the reader that the *Apposites* is a work in which a deeper level of the subject matter of the *Intimations* is discussed.[1] It is indeed my view that the *Apposites* is a more argumentative and a more advanced work than the *Intimations*.

3.3 The *Paths and Havens*

The *Paths and Havens* is Suhrawardī's most well-known work after the *Philosophy of Illumination.* If we set aside the more elegant stlye of the latter, we must make it clear that the *Paths and Havens* is *the* most important illuminationist work, containing, as we are informed by Suhrawardī himself, the "detailed analysis" of his doctrine. It is a work that is considerably more lengthy than the *Philosophy of Illumination.*[2] In this work Suhrawardī works out the details of illuminationist principles, rules and methodologies which he discusses only briefly in the *Philosophy of Illumination.* The commentators of the *Philosophy of Illumination* refer to the *Paths and Havens* more than to any other of Suhrawardī's works. While the *Philosophy of Illumination* may be designated a more poetic statement concerning the unitive experience of illumination, the *Paths and Havens* is a well-structured philosophical analysis of it.

The most explicit statement about the nature of the *Paths and Havens* is given by Suhrawardī himself in his "Introduction" to the work:

> This book contains the three sciences [logic, physics, metaphysics]. I have composed it on the suggestion of you my brethren. In it I have dealt with subjects and theorems that are not to be found in other works [on philosophy].

[1] Suhrawardī, *Opera I,* p. 192.

[2] The published part of the *Paths and Havens* (in Corbin, *Opera I*), which consists of only *al-Qism al-Thālith: fi'l-'Ilm al-Ilāhī* [*The Third Part: on Metaphysics*], comprises less than one-third of the total and yet is considerably larger than the whole of the *Philosophy of Illumination.*

> [These theorems] are truly beneficial, and have been obtained and refined through my own personal experiences.[1] However, I have not greatly departed from the path of the Peripatetics, even though I have given in this work certain points which hint at noble principles [of philosophy] in addition to what the Peripatetics have dealt with. An unbiased person who has carefully deliberated upon the Peripatetic works will find this work to be complete where the others are deficient. Whoever does not become proficient in the discursive sciences will not be able to understand our book called the *Philosophy of Illumination*. The *Paths and Havens* should be read before examining the *Philosophy of Illumination* and after examining the short work called *Intimations*. Here we do not comply with the [prescribed] structure [of Peripatetic works], nor do we adhere, in some instances, to the [established] subject of the science [under examination], but rather our intention in this work is discursive philosophy, even though this should involve [the discussion of] rules belonging to various other sciences. So when the student of discursive philosophy learns this method well, let him commence with illuminating ascetic practices by the command of the one who is proficient in illumination (*al-qayyim 'ala'l-ishrāq*),[2] in order that some of the basic principles of illumination manifest themselves to him. After [such a beginning] he will be in a position to understand the principles of things (*al-ashyā'*). As for the three forms *(al-ṣuwar al-thalātha)* mentioned in the *Philosophy of Illumination,* they are: (the Corbin edition gives three cryptograms).[3] The starting point of philosophy is in abandoning the world, its midpoint is [marked by] the vision of the Divine Lights (*al-anwār al-ilāhiyya*), and its end has no limit. I have called this book the *Paths and Havens.*[4]

We note from this "Introduction" that the *Paths and Havens* is not a work solely composed in accordance to the Peripatetic methodology. Like the *Philosophy of Illumination,* this work, too, is based on Suhrawardī's

[1] *Mukharraja mushaḥḥadha min taṣarrufātī.* Cf. al-Baghdādī, *al-Mu'tabar* [*the Evidential*], I, 2-4.

[2] There are a number of references to the person called *al-qayyim 'ala'l-ishrāq* in Suhrawardī's works. In the *Philosophy of Illumination* this person is called *qayyim al-kitāb* (*Opera II,* p. 258). Shahrazūrī refers to the person as *al-qayyim bi-'ilm al-kitāb fī 'ahdinā* (*Opera II,* p. 260). The function of such a person, not unlike that of the ṣūfī *murshid,* must have been to "protect" the secrets of the philosophy of illumination and discuss them only with the initiates for whom he would serve as guide and mentor. Quṭb al-Dīn al-Shīrāzī refers to this person as "the person who is conscious of the secrets *(asrār)* of the philosophy of illumination." (*Sharḥ II,* p. 561.)

[3] The cryptograms are not deciphered. See *Opera I,* p. 124, notes to line #12.

"personal reflection." It is not just a work in which the deficiencies of the Peripatetic doctrines are reported, but also a work that leads the reader to a deep discussion as to what the philosophy of illumination is. As stated by Suhrawardī himself the work also differs in its structure from standard Peripatetic works.

The *Paths and Havens* includes a number of references to the *Philosophy of Illumination,* and to the latter's "amazing," "symbolic," metaphorical and illuminationist characteristics.[1] In many instances in the *Paths and Havens* Suhrawardī refers to his *Philosophy of Illumination* as the work in which the "key" to the "secrets" of his teachings is to be found.[2] There are indications, too, that while composing the *Paths and Havens,* Suhrawardī had placed certain restrictions upon himself. All of this quite obviously indicates that a complete version of the two works had been available concurrently:

> As for what I believe regarding this problem, it is mentioned in my book called *Philosophy of Illumination.* I cannot mention it explicitly here [in the *Paths and Havens*] because my aim in this book is to [discuss] discursive analysis in such a way as not to stray too far from the approach of the Peripatetics.[3]

There are a number of characteristics of the *Paths and Havens* which indicate its importance as an indispensable work in the study of the philosophy of illumination. Firstly, as noted, there are a number of references to the *Philosophy of Illumination.* Secondly, this major work includes rigorous and detailed study of Suhrawardī's own philosophical system not to be found, in such detail, in the *Philosophy of Illumination.* One such important instance is where Suhrawardī discusses the concept of symbolic language and composition as the only means of writing about experiential knowledge, and where he discusses the semantics of the "language of illumination" *(lisān al-ishrāq).*[4] Suhrawardī places great emphasis on the proper use of language in philosophy, but nowhere in the *Philosophy of Illumination* does he treat the subject "language of illumination" as he does

---

[4] Suhrawardī, *Opera I,* pp. 194-195.

[1] E.g. Ibid., pp. 361, 401.

[2] Ibid., p. 505.

[3] Ibid., p. 483.

in the *Paths and Havens*. The reader is expected to know the latter work, where the details of the position of language in the reconstruction of metaphysics are fully examined.

Illuminationist philosophy employs a special language, a special set of technical terminology, and emphasizes the use of a symbolic mode of expression based, to a large extent and in principle, on the imagery of light and darkness. The symbolism of light is used when specifying being and the determinants of being, form and matter, God, primary and secondary intelligibles, intellect, soul, individual ipseity, and degrees of intensity of mystical experience. In short, the use of symbols is an integral feature of the illuminationist construction of philosophy, and this symbolic mode of expression is also a prominent feature of the *Paths and Havens*. In this work the symbolic mode is always presented within a framework of Peripatetic philosophy and its technical terminology so as to, it seems, instruct the reader concerning the new language employed. Now, it is clear that discursive Peripatetic philosophy uses a language which had been used by Alfarabi and Avicenna and more or less standardized by the time of Suhrawardī. But, in view of Suhrawardī's use of the "language of illumination," the question should be raised: How much of Suhrawardī's novel philosophical system is a symbolic expression and a specific use of language? Such a question leads us to examine the illuminationist system in relation to the Peripatetic in order to discern how the two are related and to ultimately indicate essential differences between the two. Once the two "languages" are identified, as the commentators on the philosophy of illumination have indicated, we may realize that: 1- there is an hitherto unnoticed connection between the two systems; 2- the "language of illumination" is a necessary mode for the construction and expression of the philosophy of illumination; and 3- any discussion of the concept of "illumination" itself, which asserts experience to be the foundation of epistemology, requires a language of its own in order to express "experience" in a way that what that experience is will not be lost in the analysis of it.

As we shall see, this is a basic illuminationist principle, i.e., that to know something is to obtain an "experience" of it, tantamount to a primary

---

[4] Ibid., p. 494.

intuition of the determinants of the thing. Experiential knowledge of a thing is analyzed only subsequent to the intuitive total and immediate grasp of what it is. Is there something, we may ask at this point, in a subject's "experience," which necessitates that what is obtained by the subject be expressed through a specifically constructed symbolic language? The answer to this question will be examined from multiple points of view, but it is clear, even at this preliminary juncture, that Suhrawardī's "language of illumination" is an attempt by him to use a specific language through which the experience of "illumination" is to be depicted. It is equally clear that the interpretation of the symbolism of illumination and its implications are the central aspects of the controversy as to what is illuminationist philosophy. It must be kept in mind that the symbolism of illuminationist construction of philosophy is developed in detail by Suhrawardī in the *Paths and Havens*, and thus this work is indispensable in our attempt to understand the philosophy of illumination.

There must have been a very significant "oral" side to Suhrawardī's teachings, a teaching that would have dealt more freely, without the constraints of the written word, with the symbolic language of the philosophy of illumination. The "oral" teachings would have been confined to a circle of initiates and close companions around Suhrawardī.[1] Our inference is substantiated by Suhrawardī's own reference to a person who is "proficient in illumination," analogous to the ṣūfī master, or guide, together with his numerous statements to the effect that illuminationist philosophy cannot be discussed with everyone, and surely not with those outside the circle of initiates. An oral teaching of illuminationist philosophy, addressed to a group of companions, would have been the means to penetrate the symbol, unfolding its intended meaning. Discussion of illuminationist experience itself, according to Suhrawardī, cannot be confined to a purely discursive analytic and ordinary mode of expression. Symbols (signs and secrets) have to be used. The symbol (including metaphor and allegory) is of such a character that it will elicit a response in the soul and in the mind of

[1] This we infer from the numerous references in all of Suhrawardī's works to "my brethren" *(ikhwānī)*, "our companions" *(aṣḥābunā)*, etc. E.g. Suhrawardī, *Opera II*, pp. 10, 257-260.

the subject, expressive of the experience which remains, however, personal and can only be communicated fully within the closed circle of initiates. In the *Paths and Havens* we find an explicit statements to this effect:

> The great and noble mystery covered by the symbolic [and metaphorical] expression of our book the *Philosophy of Illumination*, we can only address to our companions the illuminationists *(aṣḥābunā al-ishrāqiyyūn)* [1]

The "illuminationist companions," to whom Suhrawardī also refers as "brethren," who make up the circle of the "brethren of abstraction" *(ikhwān al-tajrīd)*,[2] would have had access to a level of understanding of the philosophy of illumination not contained in books. Such an illuminationist level would have been the level at which Suhrawardī would have conducted his discourses while alive, and, presumably, continued by the person "proficient in illumination" after his death. It is only at this point that we realize that such works of Suhrawardī as the *Intimations* and the *Apposites* (to which there are a number of references in the *Paths and Havens*), composed having the "Peripatetic method" in mind, are also meant to show the weakness of that method, as we are indeed so informed in the *Paths and Havens*.[3] The message is then clear: The "Peripatetic" method and ordinary language fail to convey the essence of "experience" which is the foundation of illuminationist epistemology.

3.4 The *Philosophy of Illumination*

Suhrawardī's best known work is the *Philosophy of Illumination*. This is the last of the four major works here examined. It is a work in which illuminationist principles of philosophy are systematically, though at times quite briefly, presented in a polished and perfected manner. It is a work that is said by Suhrawardī to contain his own intuitive grasp of the foundation of philosophy as well as a work that systematically formulates results obtained

[1] Suhrawardī, *Opera I*, p. 334.

[2] *Ikhwān al-tajrīd* constitute a group that includes Suhrawardī and his immediate disciples, but transcends them to include earlier philosophers and mystics as well. It is a spiritual brotherhood not confined to time and space. See Suhrawardī, *Opera I*, pp. 74, 95, 103, 506.

[3] Suhrawardī, *Opera I*, p. 334.

from Suhrawardī's own mystical experiences and incorporates them in the reconstruction of philosophy. This work contains the final formulation of Suhrawardīs novel system succinctly and in a predominantly symbolic mode, the details of which had been worked out in the previous three works mentioned. Yet this work, too, includes both discursive as well as illuminationist methodologies, rules and principles of philosophy. The harmonious and perfect blend of discursive philosophy *(al-ḥikma al-baḥthiyya)* and intuive philosophy *(al-ḥikma al-dhawqiyya)* is both the intent and the distinguishing mark of the philosophy of illumination.

Suhrawardī refers by name only to his *Intimations* and his *Flashes of Light* in the *Philosophy of Illumination.*[1] Quṭb al-Dīn al-Shīrāzī, in his *Commentary on the Philosophy of Illumination,* states that this indicates that Suhrawardī had started but not completed both of these other works prior to the composition of the *Philosophy of Illumination.*[2] As we noted above, Suhrawardī must have written, or revised, all of his major works concurrently. Suhrawardī does not mention the *Paths and Havens* in the *Philosophy of Illumination* specifically, but its significance had been known and well established.[3] Quṭb al-Dīn al-Shīrāzī, however, believes that, in his statement, "I have composed the *Intimations,* and below it the *Flashes of Light,* and others following the Peripatetic method,"[4] Suhrawardī means by the "others" the *Paths and Havens* and the *Apposites.*[5] In view of what I have said above, I do not agree with this view. By mentioning the *Intimations,* Suhrawardī is, in effect, already referring to the *Apposites,* since we know the latter to be an addendum to the former. Also, as we have shown, the *Paths and Havens* is not a work expressly composed according only to the "Peripatetic method" In light of Suhrawardī's own repeated statements delineating the importance of the *Paths and Havens* for a true understanding of illuminationist philosophy, we cannot simply place the work in the same category as the *Flashes of Light,* and thus dismiss it as irrelevant for the study of illuminationist

[1] Suhrawardī, *Opera II,* p. 11.

[2] Shīrāzī, *Sharḥ II,* p. 15.

[3] Suhrawardī, *Opera I,* pp. 361, 401, 484, 488.

[4] Suhrawardī, *Opera II,* p. 11.

philosophy. By *not* mentioning the *Paths and Havens* in this passage of his "Introduction" to the *Philosophy of Illumination,* Suhrawardī may even be indicating what would have been obvious to his companions that the work is *not* to be counted among the works composed as a simple didactic epitome of Peripatetic philosophy. A work such as the *Doctrines of the Philosophers (Risāla fī I'tiqād al-Ḥukamā')* fits much better Suhrawardī's statement about "others" in that passage, because the work can more appropriately be designated a short epitome of Peripatetic doctrine, and is quite clearly within the Peripatetic mode of expression.

As we examine the *Philosophy of Illumination* itself it will become clear that the work is the culmination of Suhrawardī's philosophical goal: a systematic reconstruction of philosophy. This he had commenced with in the *Intimations,* refined further in the *Apposites,* and fully formulated in the *Paths and Havens.* The *Philosophy of Illumination* is only understood fully when taken as part of the cycle of illuminationist reconstruction of philosophy as carefully composed by Suhrawardī in his major four books, albeit the most important work in the cycle. The work is best characterized by Suhrawardī himself in his own "Introduction" to it, which we shall now examine.

The "Introduction" to the *Philosophy of Illumination* deals with three subjects that underlie the illuminationist reconstruction of philosophy; it also defines the intentions of the author himself. The first subject deals with Suhrawardī's reasons for composing the work and with the group of people for whom it is intended. The second addresses the question of methodology. The third deals with the history of philosophy as well as the place of the philosophy of illumination and the position of the "wise" philosopher in this history. Let us examine the three subjects in question.

3.4.1 Suhrawardī's Reasons for Composing the *Philosophy of Illumination*

As with most of Suhrawardī's other works, the *Philosophy of Illumination* is said to have been actually written as a result of persistent

---

[5] Shīrāzī, *Sharḥ II*, p. 15.

requests by Suhrawardī's companions and pupils. We noted above that the implication of such statements is that the subject matter of Suhrawardī's works may have been taught orally to a close circle of initiates prior to their being set down in writing. This in turn suggests that, in the context of the oral discourses given by Suhrawardī, the disciples had the opportunity to engage in a discussion of the central doctrines of the philosophy of illumination and of the inner intentions of the symbolism employed in the written works. Symbolic depiction of illuminationist doctrine is an integral component of Suhrawardī's method, as he himself indicates on several occasions, notably in §4 of the "Introduction" to the *Philosophy of Illumination.* We have also to bear in mind the "difficulties," according to Suhrawardī, of committing foundations of the philosophy of illumination to writing. Such "difficulties" may be due to inherent complications encountered in writing about the qualitative element of experience to which, in an oral mode of expression, the "presence" *(ḥuḍūr)* of the teacher who has had the experience himself, bears direct testimony. However, there are enough indications in the writings which, when examined carefully, may enable us to penetrate the intended meaning of the symbols. This will then lead us to construct the view of what Suhrawardī's philosophy of illumination is. The intended meanings of the metaphorical language are, here and there, examined at first instance by Suhrawardī himself, and further by the commentators.

There is an unusual statement made by Suhrawardī at the very beginning of his "Introduction" to the *Philosophy of Illumination,* and nowhere else in the works of Suhrawardī is such a statement repeated. The statement can be interpreted in two different ways, with divergent implications. The statement is:

> Were it not for an incumbent obligation, a message that has appeared, and a command given from a place disobedience of which will lead to going astray from the path, I would not have felt obliged to step forward and openly reveal the philosophy of illumination.[1]

The first interpretation of this statement, which is the one given by the commentator Quṭb al-Dīn al-Shīrāzī, is that the "source" of the command

[1] Suhrawardī, *Opera II*, p. 10.

given is the Divine.[1] The second way in which this statement may be interpreted, is to regard the source of the command given to be an earthly one, perhaps issued by a prince or a king. It is not unlikely that there was, in fact, a political motive for the composition of the work. We know that in the year 579/1183 Suhrawardī had gone to Aleppo, where the *Philosophy of Illumination* was composed in the year 582/1186, and that there had been an amicable relationship between the Ayyubid Malik Ẓāhir Shāh and Suhrawardī. It is therefore possible that the command to write the *Philosophy of Illumination* had been given to Suhrawardī by Malik Ẓāhir Shāh, presumably after he had heard Suhrawardī lecture on the philosophy of illumination. We know that Suhrawardī was killed at the instigation of some of the 'Ulamā' around the young Malik, who had convinced his father, the great Sultan Saladin that Suhrawardī was corrupting the *Sharī'a*.[2] There may, however, have been more specific political reasons for the intrigue. Could there have been a connection between the open composition and publication of the *Philosophy of Illumination,* to which, it seems, Suhrawardī reluctantly had succumbed, and the political intrigue that led to his trial and death? If so, what? It is neither unlikely nor without precedent that a philosopher would have had the desire to influence a ruler with whom he had a close relationship. After all, the 11th and 12th centuries had witnessed many political intrigues instigated by esotericists, mystics and others philosophically inclined and politically motivated. It is likely that the *Philosophy of Illumination* may have been viewed as the "constitution" for a new "city" to be ruled by the philosophically educated Malik Ẓāhir Shāh with the aid of the philosopher Suhrawardī, who would serve as the spiritual power behind the throne. Through him the king would have access to unrestricted "wisdom" based on the illuminationist experience and knowledge of the wise philosopher in his court. Such a design, as I said, is not without precedent. This may indicate a viable reason for the courtly intrigue that ultimately caused Suhrawardī's execution. Such a reason

[1] Shīrāzī, *Sharḥ II,* p. 13. See also Shahrazūrī, *Sharḥ,* fol. 19r.

[2] Ibn Shaddād in his biography of Saladin refers to Suhrawardī as the "youth Suhrawardī" and also as the "ṣūfī." He states that the king was warned of the philosopher's corrupting influence on the Divine Law. See Ibn Shaddād, *al-Nawādir al-Sulṭāniyya,* pp. 10, 59.

would involve reactions to the plan spearheaded by Suhrawardī, of establishing a new order in (at least) Aleppo, and would be a welcome one in view of the fact that none of the historians of philosophy have been able to furnish a viable reason for Suhrawardī's death sentence, save the vague explanation that the jurists of Aleppo had considered Suhrawardī's teachings heretical.[1]

3.4.2 Methodology of the *Philosophy of Illumination*

The terse statements made by Suhrawardī in his "Introduction" to the *Philosophy of Illumination* are suggestive of the general theory of the philosophy of illumination, especially of the position of intuition and experience in the foundation of epistemology. Among all of Suhrawardī's works, the "Introductions" of only two of them, the *Paths and Havens* and the *Philosophy of Illumination,* include specific statements concerning the methodology of the philosophy of illumination. In the "Introduction" to the *Paths and Havens,* Suhrawardī indicates that the book contains an exposition of the results of his personal experiences and intuitions, and further stipulates his view of how knowledge is to be obtained.

These principles are formed as the result of a process consisting of several stages. The first stage is marked by an activity on the part of the philosopher: he has to "abandon the world." The second stage is marked by certain experiences: the philosopher attains visions of a "Divine Light" *(al-nūr al-ilāhī).* The third stage is marked by the acquisition of unlimited and unbound knowledge, which is the illuminationist knowledge *(al-'ilm al-ishrāqī).* Suhrawardī's account of the same methodological question in his "Introduction" to the *Philosophy of Illumination* is more elaborate and more detailed but is essentially the same as the account given in the *Paths and Havens.* The philosophy of illumination consists of three stages which concern the question of knowledge—how to prepare for the experience of it, receiving it through illumination, and constructing a systematic view of it, as in the previous work—plus an additional stage, consisting of the process of setting down the results of the experience of illumination and of

[1] Shahrazūrī relates that the jurists accused Suhrawardī of claiming to be a prophet. Shahrazūrī, *Nuzhat al-Arwāḥ,* fol. 232v.

the inquiry concerning it, in written form. As we examine the stages mentioned in more detail we further observe that the first stage is an activity through which the philosopher prepares himself for illuminationist knowledge, a certain way of life which he must follow to arrive at the readiness to accept "experience." The second stage is the stage of illumination. The third stage is the stage of construction. The last stage is depicting, symbolically whenever necessary, in written form, the structure that has been constructed during the third stage. Let us now examine these stages.

The very beginning of the first stage is marked by such activities as going on a forty-day retreat, abstaining from eating meat, and preparing for inspiration and revelation.[1] Such activities fall under the general category of ascetic and mystical practices, though not in strict conformity with the prescribed states and stations of the mystic path, or ṣūfī *ṭarīqa,* as known in the mystical works available to Suhrawardī. Through these activities, the philosopher with intuitive powers, in whom, as we are told by Suhrawardī, resides a portion of the "light of God" *(al-bāriq al-ilāhī),* is able, through "personal revelation" and "vision" *(mushāhada wa mukāshafa),* to accept the reality of his own existence and admit the truth of his own intuition. The first stage therefore consists of 1- an activity; 2- a condition (met by everyone, since we are told that every person has intuition and in everyone there is a certain portion of the light of God); and 3- personal revelation.

The first stage leads to the second, and the Divine Light enters the being of the human. This light then takes the form of a series of "apocalyptic lights" *(al-anwār al-sāniḥa),* and through them the knowledge that serves as the foundation of real sciences *(al-'ulūm al-ḥaqīqiyya)* is obtained.

The third stage is the stage of constructing a true science *('ilm ṣaḥīḥ).* It is during this stage that the philosopher makes use of discursive analysis. The experience is put to the test, and the system of proof used is the Aristotelian demonstration *(burhān)* of the *Posterior Analytics.*[2] The same certitude obtained by the movement from sense-data (observation and concept formation) to demonstration based on reason, which is the basis of

[1] Suhrawardī, *Opera II,* p. 248.

[2] *al-'Ulūm al-ḥaqiqiyya lā yusta'mal fīhā illā al-burhān.* Cf. Suhrawardī, *Opera II,* pp. 40-46.

discursive scientific knowledge, is said to obtain when visionary data upon which the philosophy of illumination rests are "demonstrated." This is done through a discursive analysis aimed at demonstrating the experience and constructing a system in which the experience itself can be situated and its validity readily deduced, even when the experience has ended.

The last stage is writing down the philosophy of illumination. This stage, and the above mentioned third stage, are the only components of the philosophy of illumination to which *we* have access. The practitioner, the disciple of the illuminationist way, would have recourse to the first two stages through experience. The disciples would have joined Suhrawardī in his retreats and would have experienced the "presence" of the experience for themselves, either individually or as part of a group. Suhrawardī may have (we so presume based on indications in the texts) discussed his visions with the disciples;[1] his personal way, his "presence," would have served as the testimony for such visions, and the physical manifestations, the observed phenomenon, associated with the visionary experience, described in the *Philosophy of Illumination*,[2] would have been witnessed by the ones present. What *we* have access to are the texts which are said to be symbolic portrayals of the phenomenon of the visionary experience, and we have to decide what they symbolize.

3.4.3 Suhrawardī's View of the History of Philosophy

Much has been written in recent years concerning Suhrawardī's view of the history of Philosophy, and the emphasis is usually on his role as the reviver of a special type of Iranian "wisdom" designated with the epithet

[1] Suhrawardī has composed several allegorical mystical and visionary tales. Each one is addressed to his pupils and to his companions. There has recently appeared an English translation of the tales, most of which are in Persian (unlike his more theoretical works, which are mostly in Arabic), by W.M. Thackston, Jr., *Mystical and Visionary Treatises of Suhrawardī* (London: Octagon Press, 1984).

[2] There are fifteen visionary stages described by Suhrawardī, and each stage is described in terms of a "light" associated with the experience starting with a "flashing light" *(nūr bāriq)* for the "beginners" *(ahl al-bidāya)*, and increasing in intensity as the initiate makes progress in terms of the visionary experience. The last stage is described as a light so powerful that will tear apart the body at the joints. See *Opera II*, pp. 253- 254.

pahlavī, or *fahlavānī*, and *kiyānī*. One important aspect of his view on philosophy is his attitude towards Aristotle and discursive philosophy. In his "Introduction" to the *Philosophy of Illumination*, Suhrawardī explicitly states that the perfect philosopher is he who combines intuitive ability with discursive methodology. Suhrawardī believes that his own philosophy of illumination is such a perfect combination.

Plato is the admitted master of intuitive philosophy, and he is said to be part of a long tradition that comprises a Græco-Egyptian branch and an Iranian branch, both of which are traced back to Hermes, "the father of philosophers." Aristotle is the admitted master of discursive philosophy. Suhrawardī, through his philosophy of illumination, considers himself the perfect harmonizer of the two types of philosophy. In his view, the role of the philosopher in history is that of the "wise" man who has combined intuitive knowledge with discursive methodology, to whom he refers as the Divine philosopher *(al-ḥakīm al-muta'llih)* in possession of a special "wisdom" This wise man should be considered the leader *(imām)* of society, be the leadership an actual, temporal one or an esoteric, spiritual one.Wisdom, in this sense, is what distinguishes virtuous political governance from that which is unjust and corrupt. Thus Aristotle's doctrine, and Peripatetic philosophy in general, must not be regarded as a system of philosophy distinctly separate from the philosophy of illumination, nor should it be viewed as some type of philosophy with which Suhrawardī was preoccupied in his youth, or only in some of his books. The combination of discursive philosophy *(ḥikma baḥthiyya)* and intuitive philosophy *(ḥikma dhawqiyya)*, the combination of which is said to be Divine philosophy *(ḥikma muta'alliha)*, is what distinguishes the philosophy of illumination from both theosophy and quasi-philosophical mysticism.[1]

[1] Several categories of wise men are enumerated. This is done by taking proficiency in Divine philosophy *(tawaghghul fī al-ta'alluh)* and proficiency in discursive philosophy *(tawaghghul fī al-baḥth)* as qualities that are combined in one man (or not) to a perfect or a less perfect degree (the actual categories are ten in number). See Harawī, *Anwāriyya*, pp. 12-14.

4. Conclusion

Suhrawardī has written four major philosophical works. In each of these works he deals with philosophical problems in a complete manner, yet each work leads to the other, and there are explicit statements by Suhrawardī himself that the four works are related and that they should be read in a specified order. Each work has its own particular emphasis on terminology, and yet there are definite indications that Suhrawardī has an overview of all four works when he is writing each one of them, and other indications that a single set of terminology, which is complementary to the conceptual framework of the works, is being developed. We have shown that, based on Suhrawardī's own explicit statements, the four works are related and form and integral whole.

The intricate nature of the relationship among the four works necessitates an analysis of the process of thought commencing with the *Intimations* and culminating in the *Philosophy of Illumination*. We have so far examined the relationship among the works on the basis of specific remarks made by Suhrawardī himself. Our next task is to examine the contents of the works. This task is not an easy one. We face the problem that the "process" is not a smooth one. It is not a process which can be seen to start, with a simple exposé of Aristotle's, doctrine in the *Intimations,* followed by emphasizing some problems not adequately treated by Aristotle or ignored by him, and finally ending up with a new, different, complete, and coherent theory presented in the *Philosophy of Illumination*. In fact the process is a tortuously winding one, at times circular, and quite often presupposes that some basic results presented in the *Philosophy of Illumination* are conclusions of an "earlier" work in the cycle, or that they are understandable only in terms of the development of the mode of thought from the *Intimations* through the *Paths and Havens*. What compounds the difficulty is Suhrawardī's style and terminology, which is sometimes particular to a specific work and at other times runs through all four works. Such an apparent change in style is due in part to Suhrawardī's experimenting with philosophical style and analysis. He examines an idea in an earlier work of the cycle within an established Peripatetic conceptual, methodological, and metaphysical framework, using a "standard" set of technical terminology, but with noted changes, and subsequently examines an idea, even the same idea, in an illuminationist manner, trying to capture the essence of experience, the "I" of human existence, in words and symbols. Such is the case in the *Intimations,* which has been supposed to be a purely Aristotelian work. For even in this work there is no one clear method of approaching the problems. Often without warning, a new idea is thrown in and examined from the vantage point of illuminationist doctrine.

All of this means that quite often we have to read back and forth among the four books in order to comprehend the unity of thought that underlies all of them. We have to have the final results of Suhrawardī's analysis as presented in the *Philosophy of Illumination* available before us in order to fully comprehend an "earlier" work, which in turn has to be carefully examined if we are to make sense of the end construction. This requires us to examine the major philosophical works from two points of view. We have to examine each work separately in order to ascertain its unity of thought and the manner in which philosophical problems are treated therein, and subsequently we have to examine the major works as a whole, considering them to be a virtual unit in order to recover Suhrawardī's own unified thinking. After such a two-fold examination, we shall be in a position to present a coherent account of the philosophy of illumination.

Chapter Two

Logic in the Philosophy of Illumination

1. Introduction

Our aim in this chapter is to examine Suhrawardī's treatment of logic and the way in which logic relates to the philosophy of illumination. In doing this we shall delineate the special areas and problems of logic thought by Suhrawardī to be especially pertinent in his reformulation of the principles and rules of philosophy. We shall first examine Suhrawardī's explicit accounts of the nature and scope of logic in the *Intimations,*[1] the *Paths and Havens,*[2] and the *Philosophy of Illumination.* Secondly, we shall provide the reader with a synopsis of Suhrawardī's logic and compare it with Peripatetic logic.[3] It is hoped that by so comparing the overall structure of Suhrawardī's logic, the reader will gain an understanding of both the depth and breadth of his logical works. Since the most systematic account of the logic of Peripatetic syncretism available to Suhrawardī was the logic of Avicenna's major philosophical work the *Healing (al-Shifā'),* to which he refers on numerous occasions, this work will serve, for the most part, as

[1] Suhrawardī, *Manṭiq al-Talwīḥāt [The Logic of the Intimations],* ed. A.A. Fayyāz (Tehran: Tehran University Press, 1334 /1955) (hereafter cited as *Intimations:Logic).*

[2] The logic and physics of Suhrawardī's *Paths and Havens* have not been published. I have used the following MS of the work, dated 707 A.H.: *al-Mashāri' wa'l-Muṭāraḥāt,* MS Leiden Or. 365 (hereafter cited as *Paths and Havens:Logic).*

[3] Special emphasis will be placed on the logic of Peripatetic syncretism, i.e., the logic of the Peripatetic school after Theophrastus, and on that of the Stoic-Megaric schools. For a discussion of the logic of Peripatetic syncretism see I.M. Bochenski, *Ancient Formal Logic* (Amsterdam: North-Holland, 1951), pp. 9-13; William and Martha Kneale, *The Development of Logic* (Oxfrod: Oxford University Press, Clarendon Press, 1968), pp. 101-117; and for a discussion of the transmission of Stoic-Megaric logic to the world of Islam, see Fehmi Jadaane, *L'influence du stoicisme sur la pensée musulmane* (Beirut: Dar El-Machreq, 1968), pp. 43-98.

the basis for our comparison. These are problems of logic that have been re-examined and reformulated by Suhrawardī within a well-defined illuminationist logical and epistemological scheme. The reader who finds this chapter too technical or dry may safely turn to the overall assessment of Suhrawardī's logic at the end of this chapter, and then proceed to the next, where the epistemological position of definition in illuminationist philosophy is discussed in detail.

2. Suhrawardī's View of Logic

2.1 Treatment of Logic in the *Intimations*

In the opening section of the *Intimations,* entitled "The First Intimation: On the Aim of Logic,"[1] Suhrawardī presents a view of logic which is similar to that presented by Avicenna in the *Healing:Isagoge,* I, 4. In the first paragraph of this section Suhrawardī commences his study of logic with the well-known division of knowledge into conception *(taṣawwur)* and assent *(taṣdīq),* and states that: 1- conception is the obtaining of the form of the thing *(ṣūrat al-shay')* in the mind; and 2- assent is the positive, or negative, judgement *(ḥukm)* regarding the conception.[2] Each one of these two types of knowledge is in turn divided into that which is innate *(fiṭrī)*

[1] *Intimations:Logic,* pp. 1-3.

[2] Such a view of conception and assent conforms to the views held by Baghdādī and Sāwī. See Baghdādi, *al-Mu'tabar [the Evidential],* I, 34-37; Sāwī, *Tabṣira,* ed. M.T. Danesh Pajooh in *Tabṣira va Du Risāla-yi Dīgar Dar Manṭiq* (Tehran: Tehran University Press, 1958), p. 4. The same account is given by Suhrawardī in his *Flashes of Light* (pp. 58-59). The theory of conception and assent has an important position in medieval Arabic and Persian philosophy. There are different views as to its Greek origins: Harry A. Wolfson regards the origin of "conception" to be either the Aristotelian νόησις or the the Stoic φαντασία λογική and regards the origin of "assent" to be either the Aristotelian λόγος ἀποφαντικός (de Int. $17^{a}8$) or the Stoic ἀξίωμα (Harry A.Wolfson, *Studies in the History of Philosophy and Religion,* ed. Isadore Twersky and George H. Williams [Cambridge: Harvard University Press, 1973], pp. 478-490.). Sohail Afnan and A.-M. Goichon regard "assent" to be a direct translation of νόησις. Afnan further compares "conception" with the Stoic περὶ φαντασίας (S. Afnan, *A Philosophical Lexicon in Persian and Arabic,* pp. 143, 154-155; A.-M. Goichon, *Lexique de la langue philosophic d'Ibn Sina: Supplement,* p. 15). See also, Jadaane, *L'influence du Stoicisme,* pp. 106-113.

and that which is acquired *(ghayr fiṭrī)*. This means that there are four epistemological divisions: innate conception, acquired conception, innate assent, and acquired assent. These divisions conform to those given by Avicenna in the *Healing:Isagoge,* I, 3, but Suhrawardī emphasizes the distinction between innate and acquired knowledge, and uses the term *fiṭrī* for innate.[1] These divisions are important to bear in mind, as we later deal with the significance given to innate knowledge by Suhrawardī in the way in which he incorporates the division in illuminationist epistemology in his systematic response to the questions "How is science constructed?" and "What is the first step in the process of obtaining knowledge?"

After having considered the distinction between innate and acquired knowledge, Suhrawardī discusses the process through which acquired knowledge is obtained in the mind, and he designates this process "cogitation," or "thought" *(fikr)*. The distinction between knowledge obtained through the process designated "thought," and knowledge obtained by some other means *(amr ākhar)*, is one of the most important methodological questions in illuminationist philosophy, as evidenced in Suhrawardī's statement:

> I did not at first obtain this [the philosophy of illumination] by *thought* (*fikr*), but through something else.[2]

[1] There may be a comparison to be made here with Baghdādī, who makes the same distinction between innate and acquired knowledge, incorporating it into his epistemology of "evidential" knowledge *(al-Mu'tabar,* I, 8, 40-46), however, the term used by Baghdādī for the innate, is *al-gharīzi*. The same term is used by al-Sāwī (*Tabṣira,* p. 31).

[2] *Lam yuḥṣal [ya'nī ḥikmat al-'ishrāq] lī awwalan bi'l-fikr, bal kāna ḥuṣūluhu bi-'amrin ākhar* (Suhrawardī, *Opera II,* p. 10). This is one of the most explicit methodological statements made by Suhrawardī, and commentators take note of it. Shams al-Dīn Muḥammad al-Shahrazūrī considers "something else" *('amr ākhar)* to be vision *(mushāhada)* and personal revelation *(mukāshafa) (Sharḥ Ḥikmat al-Ishrāq,* fol. 11v.); Quṭb al-Dīn al-Shīrāzī considers the same to be personal revelation and the special intuition (*dhawq* or taste) of the illuminationist Divine philosophers *(Sharḥ II,* p. 16); and Muḥammad Sharīf Niẓām al-Dīn al-Harawī considers it to be "inspiration" *(ilhām)*, personal revelation, and intuition *(Anwāriyya,* p. 6.). In a similar manner Baghdādī's major philosophical composition, *al-Mu'tabar,* is said by Pines to be "the book of what has been established by personal reflection." See Shlomo Pines, "Studies in Abu'l Barakāt al-Baghdādī's Poetics and Metaphysics," in *Scripta Hierosolymitana,* Volume

Thought, or cogitation, as a process, defined in this section of the *Intimations*, applies only to the activity of the mind when abstracting knowledge on the basis of given data, from conception to assent. This type of knowledge has to be proven, while innate knowledge is given an *a priori* status (considered part of the mind prior to any act of abstraction, or process of thought, and without temporal extension), is considered independent of sense-data or of other given data, and is self-proven, i.e. what it is, is its proof. When the process "thought" is used in order to obtain something not known prior to the process, then something else known prior to the knowledge obtained must be employed to determine its validity. To determine the validity of inference is to guard society against chaos *(harj);* so we are told by Suhrawardī. What guards the process of thought against error, is a "tool" *(āla =ὄργανον)* that is applied to judgements made by the mind. In Peripatetic logical writings, such as the *Healing*, this tool is called the "science of logic" *(al-'ilm al-manṭiq)*. Suhrawardī, too, accepts the importance of this tool in his illuminationist reconstruction of philosophy. But what is specific to the illuminationist view of the position of logic is that it is considered subordinate to the soul's own potential ability to be inspired by the Divine spirit, which results in a "confirmation"*(al-ayd) in* the being of the individual, which is what *truly* guards man against false judgements and inferences. This wisdom is obtained, in principle, through illumination *(ishrāq)*, and guarded, in part, by employing logic. In this view, then, the intuitive, the inspired, and the revelatory are things known prior to the logical investigation, and serve as the foundation for any subsequent elaboration on knowledge, and serve further as the first steps in constructing true science *(al-'ilm al-ṣaḥīḥ)*.

Suhrawardī ends his introductory remarks to the logic of the *Intimations* by stipulating that the tool itself, used in the methodology of science *(ṭarīq al-'ulūm)*, is composed of expository proposition *(al-qawl al-shāriḥ)* and proof *(al-ḥujja)*.[1] By "expository proposition" he means anything that connects conception of a thing to the idea *(mithāl)* of that

---

VI, *Studies in Philosophy*, edited by S.H. Bergman (Jerusalem: Magness Press, The Hebrew University, 1960), pp. 120-198. (Pines' statement just quoted appears on p. 123.)

[1] Suhrawardī, *Intimations:Logic*, p. 3.

thing in the mind. This is the process that serves to explain the thing, be the end result a definition *(al-ḥadd)* of the thing, or some other statement, or proposition, that serves to explain the thing. By "proof," Suhrawardī means anything that connects the assent *(taṣdīq)* given by the mind as to what the thing is to the constructed proof of that thing, be it based on demonstration *(burhān)* or another kind of "proof," such as vision or intuition. For Suhrawardī the most significant logical apparati are proofs and expository propositions. As we shall see later, this division covers logic *per se.*[1]

Compared to Avicenna's (the *Healing:Isagoge*, I, 2-4), Suhrawardī's view of logic, 1- emphasizes the division of knowledge into innate and acquired, with logic considered a tool applicable only to the latter; 2- stipulates that intuition, personal revelation, and inspiration are prior in essence to proofs constructed by formal methods; and 3- divides logic into expository propositions and proofs. This division reflects Suhrawardī's "new" structure of logic, and is different from the structure of the traditional Avicennan *Organon.*

2.2 Logic of the *Paths and Havens*

In the first two sections of the first chapter of the logic of the *Paths and Havens*, entitled "The First Path: on the *Isagoge*,"[2] Suhrawardī presents the reader with a general view of logic which, upon first examination, does not appear different from the view presented in the *Intimations*. However, as we examine the work more carefully we realize that Suhrawardī here presupposes that the reader is familiar with logic (something he had not done in the *Intimations*) ; and further, he argues against the Peripatetics on very basic principles of logic, offering illuminationist alternatives even to a number of purely formal problems. He also discusses in detail the question whether logic is part of philosophy, part of knowledge simply, or an independent discipline in itself. The analyses of problems of logic in these two sections are more advanced than their counterparts in the *Intimations*. Unlike the logic of the *Intimations*, where Suhrawardī was introducing the

[1] Sāwī makes the same two-fold distinction and uses similar terminology *(Tabṣira*, pp. 4-5).

[2] *Paths and Havens:Logic*, fol. 1r.

subject, in the logic of the *Paths and Havens* he assumes familiarity with it, and delves into the problem:

> You have so far learned from books that everything which is sought is either a conception or an assent, and that expository propositions connect the two. [You have learned] that proof is a logical deduction *(naẓar manṭiqī)* based on the two [or more] connectives [i.e., the expository propositions]; as well as the singular terms which comprise the expository propositions; and the figures of syllogism.[1]

Suhrawardī continues and states that logic is speculation based on matter *(mādda)* and form *(ṣūra)* of the two things connected, and goes one step further than he had done in the *Intimations* by rejecting the Peripatetic definitions of the logical notions both of conception and assent:

> Know that the statement of the person [Avicenna] who says that "conception occurs when the mind obtains the form of the things indicated by singular utterances" is wrong.[2]

By so taking issue with the Peripatetics on a fundamental division within logic, Suhrawardī is setting the tone for his major logical work, the *Paths and Havens,* which is to take issue with the Peripatetics on basic logical problems. The reasons given at this juncture by Suhrawardī for refusing to accept the Peripatetic position regarding conception are based on a view of semantics that does not admit the possibility of a one-to-one correspondence between the meaning *(al-ma'nā)* of the thing, the thing itself, and the utterance *(al-lafẓ)* that signifies it, be the utterance singular *(basīṭ)* or composite *(murakkab)*.[3]

Next, Suhrawardī argues against the Peripatetic view of assent:

> It is not correct to define assent as a judgement in regard to two things, judging that one is the other or not, because this type of assent is applicable only to the predicative proposition *(al-qaḍiyya al-ḥamliyya)* and not to the conditionals *(al-sharṭiyyāt)*.[4]

After having set the tone for the Logic of the *Paths and Havens,* Suhrawardī embarks on a discussion of whether logic is "part" of the

[1] Ibid., fol. 2v.

[2] Ibid., Cf., Avicenna, the *Healing: Isagoge* I, 3.

[3] *Paths and Havens:Logic,* fols.2r-3v.

[4] Ibid., fol. 2r.

sciences or a preparatory step for the study of science. He first distinguishes between the notions "knowledge as a whole" *(majmū' al-'ulūm)* and "knowledge simply" *(al-'ilm al-muṭlaq),* and argues that logic should be considered part of the whole of knowledge, a tool to be used in thinking, but not part of knowledge simply. Suhrawardī's arguments are further concentrated on the discussion as to whether logic can be regarded part of philosophy or not. At the outset he states that the differences of opinion regarding this issue are due to different implications of the technical terms used. The important issue for Suhrawardī, however, is that logic should *not* be considered as part of philosophy because it does not deal with things that are really out there *(fī' l-a'yān).* Logic, in this sense, is not applicable to things outside the mind, i.e. the subject matter of logic is considered to be non-real entities.[1] Suhrawardī's arguments here are reminiscent of his stand against the inclusion of mathematics in philosophy, since in his view mathematics, too, deals with non-real *(mawhūm)* subjects. This philosophical position is an important component of illuminationist philosophy.[2] But, while Suhrawardī does dispense with a separate discussion of mathematics in his philosophy, he cannot forego logic because of its significance as a tool guarding against error. However, though Suhrawardī has no separate "book" on mathematics, he does make extensive use of formal mathematical rules when they serve his constructivist intentions.

Suhrawardī ends his introductory remarks on logic by reiterating his view as to its definition. He states that logic is a speculative art *(ṣinā'a naẓariyya)* which deals with conception, assent, the figures of syllogism, and the secondary intelligibles; that it is an axiomatic art *(ṣinā'a qānūniyya)* which guards the human mind against error in thinking.The manner in which he treats logic is to provide the reader with a set of formal rules. Suhrawardī is a pragmatic user of logic and not a theoretical logician.

[1] Later Persian philosophers call this "logical being" *(wujūd-i manṭiqī).* See Mehdi Haeri Yazdi, *Hiram-i Hastī, [the Pyramid of Being]* (Tehran, 1980), pp. 21ff; Jalāl al-Dīn Ashtiyānī, *Hastī [Being]* (Mashhad, 1379 A.H.), pp. 4ff.

[2] The realist position of the philosophy of illumination is the subject of much controversy in later commentaries on the *Philosophy of Illumination.* Cf. Shīrāzī, *Sharḥ II,* pp. 35:8-36:9. See Ṣadr al-Dīn al-Shīrāzī, "Mullā Ṣadrā," *Ta'līqāt [Addenda],* Ibid., margin.

Though he demonstrates a remarkable in-depth understanding of intricate details of the problems of formal logic, his intention in using logic as a tool in philosophy does not coincide with that of the formal logician. The Peripatetics, he argues, fall into error by placing too much emphasis on formal details, and they are doubly at fault, he further argues, because when they finally arrive at important philosophical issues, these they do not deal with in sufficient detail.[1]

2.3 The Position of Logic in The *Philosophy of Illumination*

Unlike his sections on logic in the *Intimations* and in the *Paths and Havens,* Suhrawardī does not begin the *Philosophy of Illumination* by providing the reader with an introduction to logic (as is normally done in Peripatetic works), nor does he deal with logic in a standard manner. However, his treatment of logic in this work is rather special and novel. His intentions here are to provide his readers with what he deems to be a sufficient number of rules of logic for understanding illuminationist philosophy. He has no intention of playing the role of logic instructor here. Treatment of logic in the *Philosophy of Illumination* is very short, therefore, and is codified into a set of rules *(ḍawābiṭ)* given in the First Part *(al-Qism al-Awwal)* of the book, entitled "On Rules of Thought."[2] The codified nature of the logic of the *Philosophy of Illumination* is indicated by Suhrawardī himself:

> Concerning the well-known tool that safeguards thinking against error, we have presented here only a short epitome by way of laying down a set of rules that are few in number, but highly beneficial for the seeker of illumination. Whoever

[1] *Paths and Havens:Logic,* fol. 102v.

[2] Suhrawardī, *Opera II,* pp. 14 -105. It seems that Suhrawardī's use of the term "rule" *(ḍābiṭ)* is an extension of the term "canon" *(qānūn),* as usually applied to logic. See Sāwī, *Tabṣira,* pp. 129-131; and Avicenna, *al-Ishārāt wa al-Tanbīhāt [Directives and Remarks],* ed. Maḥmūd Shahābī (Tehran: University of Tehran Press, 1339/1960) p. 1. Suhrawardī's "On Rules of Thought," which comprises the First Part of the *Philosophy of Illumination,* includes rules that cover not just formal logic but sophistical refutations, psychology, and physics as well. This "extended" view of rules governing proper thinking is among the special features of the "new" methodology and structure of the philosophy of illumination.

needs detailed analysis of this science, which is a tool, should consult the comprehensive works on this subject.[1]

Suhrawardī is not satisfied with merely telling his readers his view that the treatment of logic should be short and beneficial to philosophy, but again attacks the Peripatetics for delving too deeply into logic:

> There is no need for the deep penetration of the Peripatetics into logic; one can dispense with their lengthy discussion by learning what I have done.[2]

Even within the areas of logic that Suhrawardī does actually deal with, there are topics deemed irrelevant and without any pertinence to the philosophy of illumination. It is as though Suhrawardī is hesitant to dispense with formal logic altogether, and wants to make certain by dealing with intricate problems of formal logic, that his readers are aware of his mastery of the subject:

> We mention conversion of syllogism *(al-'aks)*, negation *(al-tanāquḍ)*, etc. only to indicate what they are, for we do not need them in what follows.[3]

It is true that Suhrawardī has a pragmatic view of logic and is interested only in providing his readers with a set of rules, as short as possible, governing its use. In spite of all he himself says to this effect, however, there are certain areas of logic where Suhrawardī does take issue, painstakingly and in detail, with the Peripatetics; where he attempts to prove them wrong and to reformulate his own alternate view. To begin with, Suhrawardī gives emphasis to problems pertaining to the *Sophistical Refutations (al-Mughālaṭāt)*, and states his reasons:

> We have given only a short epitome of logic in this book of ours [the *Philosophy of illumination]*, relying on other works composed in this art which is logic. Most of what we have dealt with has been concerned with the *Sophistical Refutations* so as to warn the student, because he is more apt to find errors than truth in the proofs of various people.[4]

The special topics of logic in which Suhrawardī takes specific issue with the Peripatetics are given characteristic titles, such as "Illuminationist Theorem" *(qā'ida ishrāqiyya)*, "Illuminationist Wisdom" *(ḥikma*

[1] Suhrawardī, *Opera II*, p. 13.

[2] Ibid., p. 31.

[3] Ibid., p. 33.

ishrāqiyya), and "Illuminationist Clarification" *(daqīqa ishrāqiyya)*. They are: the problem of definition, reduction of all propositions into one special form of iterated modal proposition, theory of supposition, negation and quantification in negation, and the reduction of the second and third figures of syllogism to the first. These topics cover the most important problems of logic, as developed by Suhrawardī in his illuminationist philosophy. They are based on principles other than the standard Aristotelian of the period, and merit careful examination not just from the perspective of the study of the philosophy of illumination, but from the more broad vista of the history of logic as well. The most important topic among them is definition. Not only does Suhrawardī attempt to devise a different formal rule governing definition than that used by the Peripatetics, but his treatment of definition is a fundamental component of his illuminationist theory of knowledge as well. Suhrawardī's critique of the Peripatetic formal rules of definition and their use in science is the most substantial difference between his logic and theirs, and indicates an essentially different view of the logical and epistemological foundations of philosophy. We shall deal extensively with the problem of definition in the following chapters. The other topics mentioned above are more concerned with modifications of formal rules of logic and bear less of a direct methodological significance to the illuminationist reconstruction of philosophy.

3. Synopsis of the Structure of Suhrawardī's Logic

At the very outset of our examination of Suhrawardī's logic we observed that the structure of his logic is different from the structure of the Peripatetic logic set down in the traditional nine books of the *Organon*. Our aim here is to indicate this difference. It is hoped that, as we progress in our examination, we shall be able to ascertain Suhrawardī's reasons for reordering an existing structure, and indicate the significant characteristics of the "new" structure as well.

The nine books that constitute the *Organon* appear in the following order in Avicenna's *Healing: Isagoge (al-Madkhal); Categories (al-Maqūlāt);*

[4] Ibid., pp. 56, 57.

On Interpretation (Fi' l-'Ibāra); Prior Analytics (al-Qiyās); Posterior Analytics (al-Burhān); Topics (al-Jadal); Sophistical Refutations (al-Mughālaṭāt); Rhetoric (al-Khiṭāba); and *Poetics (al-Shi'r).* The most obvious difference between this arrangement in the *Organon* and the structure of the logical works of Suhrawardī is the absence of the book of *Categories* in the latter. Perhaps one reason for this is that Suhrawardī regards the categories as part of the subject matter of physics and metaphysics, and this is said to correspond to the Stoic theory of categories.[1] There are also no separate books on *Topics, Rhetoric,* nor *Poetics,* however Suhrawardī does examine their subject matter, albeit very briefly, and as a short appendix to his discussion of logical problems that pertain to the subject matter of *Prior Analytics.*

The second general characteristic of Suhrawardī's logical works is the apparent difference among their respective structures in the number of chapters, divisions, and "books." However, there is an underlying intention in the use of logic in each of the works, and there are a number of logical problems consistently dealt with in all the major works. The differences among them are in terms of emphasis and scope. The explicit, well-defined, and well-formulated dispute with specific problems in Peripatetic logic are presented in the *Philosophy of Illumination,* while the details are only fully worked out in the *Paths and Havens.* Let us now examine the structure of each of the works.

3.1 Structure of Logic in The *Intimations*

The logic of the *Intimations* is divided into six chapters, each called "Observation" *(Marṣad).* The first chapter is entitled "On the *Isagoge*" and consists of ten sections, each called "Intimation" *(Talwīḥ).* This chapter closely corresponds to Avicenna's *Healing: Isagoge.*[2]

[1] See Bochenski, *Ancient Formal Logic,* p. 87.

[2] *Intimations:Logic,* pp. 1-13. This chapter also includes a discussion on the "intention of logic" *(gharaḍ al-manṭiq).*

The second chapter is entitled "On Expository Propositions" and is the shortest chapter of the work; it consists of only three sections.[1] In this chapter, Suhrawardī deals with definition *(ḥadd)*, description *(rasm)*, and the rules that govern them. These subjects were usually considered part of the subject matter of *Posterior Analytics* (e.g., *Healing: On Demonstration*, IV, especially 2-7), and of the *Topics* (e.g., *Healing: Topics*, V). The place in which Suhrawardī treats these problems, therefore, does not correspond to the traditional structure of the Peripatetic *Organon*. The reasons for reordering the traditional structure are quite significant, and are in accordance with what Suhrawardī stipulated concerning the overall division of logic into expository propositions, which covers definition and description, and proofs. This covers more than the subject matter of the *Posterior Analytics*. Definition and description, therefore, fall within Suhrawardī's semantic theory and are not included in his theory of proof.[2] The most important precedent for including the discussion of definition and description in semantics and not in material logic is to be found in 'Umar ibn Sahlān al-Sāwī's *Beacon (al-Tabṣira)*, and also in Abu'l Barakāt al-Baghdādī's *Evidential*. This "new" attitude to the subject matter of logic, and to its structure, is faithfully followed by Suhrawardī in all of his works on logic, and is characteristic of illuminationist logic.

The third chapter is entitled "On Enunciative Composition" *(fī' l-tarkīb al-khabarī)*, and consist of four sections and one rule *(ḍābiṭ)*.[3] This chapter is a selective, short epitome of *On Interpretation* (e.g., *Healing: On Interpretation*, I, especially 6-10). One of the most important aspects of this chapter is Suhrawardī's use of both Arabic and Persian when discussing generalized logical rules.[4]

[1] Ibid., pp. 14-16. See also, Ibn Kammūna, *Sharḥ al-Talwiḥāt [Commentary on the Intimations]*, Ibid., pp. 15, n. 11; 16, n.3.

[2] Suhrawardī's theory of proof, designated *hujja*, covers topics taken from logic and epistemology, as well as from psychology. The "total" *relation* between the thing known (object) and the knower (subject) is what determines the proof of what is inferred.

[3] *Intimations:Logic*, pp. 17-27.

[4] E.g., Ibid., pp. 25-26. See also, Ibn Kammūna, *Sharḥ al-Talwiḥāt*, Ibid., p. 26, n. 2, n.3.

The fourth chapter is entitled "On Modality in Propositions" *(fī jihāt al-qaḍāyā)*, and consists of five sections. The subject matter of this chapter consists of selected problems of *On Interpretation* (sections 3-5 correspond to the *Healing: On Interpretation*, II) as well as of *Prior Analytics* (sections 1-2 correspond to the *Healing: Prior Analytics*, I, 4), and as such the chapter marks a departure from the traditional structure of the *Organon*. Suhrawardī places special emphasis on modal propositions (sec. 1-7), and he treats problems related to propositions such as contradiction *(al-tanāquḍ*, sec. 4) and conversion of proposition *(al-'aks*, sec. 5) in the same chapter.

The fifth chapter is entitled "On the Composition of Proofs" *(fī tarkīb al-ḥujaj)*, and consists of three parts, each called "ascendant" *(maṭla')*.[1] The first part consists of ten sections and is a selective, short epitome of *Prior Analytics*. The distinction is, however, in Suhrawardī's treatment of special topics relating to premises and methods such as induction *(al-istiqrā')*,[2] analogy *(al-tamthīl)*, enthymeme *(qiyās al-ḍamīr)*,[3] and division *(al-qisma)*, which are treated in parts two and three. In the second section Suhrawardī mentions also a special type of inference he calls "insight" *(firāsa)*.[4] By so dividing the traditional *Prior Analytics* into three parts, Suhrawardī distinguishes formal rules governing syllogism (Part One, cf. *Healing: Prior Analytics*, I, 1-19); inductive methods, which are used in obtaining the matter *(mādda)* of syllogisms (Part Two, cf. *Healing:*

[1] *Intimations:Logic*, pp. 46-73. See Ibn Kammūna, *Sharḥ al-Talwīḥāt*, Ibid., p. 47, n. 2-4.

[2] *Intimations:Logic*, pp. 66-67. See Ibn Kammūna, *Sharḥ al-Talwīḥāt*, Ibid., p. 66, n. 1-3.

[3] Enthymeme is defined as a syllogism whose Major Term has been omitted, such as "man is animal, *thus* it is a body" *Intimations:Logic*, p. 68.

[4] This inference, as a special kind of insight into things, is related to the subject's own natural disposition *(khulq)*,*(Intimations:Logic*, p. 69). It is possible that both *firāsa* and *ḥads*, are variations of the Aristotelian ἀγχίνοια, which may be translated as "quick wit," (e.g., *Eth. Nic.* 1142b6; *An.Post.* 89b10), and also has the sense of "prudence" and "insight." The important thing is that such concepts as insight, prudence, etc., all pertain to a special kind of inference where the subject may strike upon the conclusion without going through the steps of the inference. This kind of inference is made at once upon conception of the minor term.

Prior Analytics, IX, 20-22); and material logic, which he calls "the propositions which are the matter for syllogisms" (Part Three, cf. the *Healing: Prior Analytics,* IX, 4; *Posterior Analytics,* II, 3,9), one from another in a novel manner. This new division is apparently Suhrawardī's own; it also enables him to discuss very briefly dialectic, rhetoric, and poetry as special parts of material logic.

In *Intimations:Logic,* V, 3, i.e., the material logic component of *Prior Analytics,* Suhrawardī distinguishes seven classes of premises which serve as matter for syllogisms.[1] The first class consists of six premises: the primary *(al-awwaliyyāt);* the observed *(al-mushāhadāt);* the empirical *(al-mujarrabāt)*; the intuitive *(al-ḥadsiyyāt);* the repetitive *(al-mutawātirāt);* and the premises implicit in the conception of things. These premises are the only ones to be be accepted, so we are told by Suhrawardī, because they alone lead to certainty *(al-yaqīn)* in the construction of real sciences *(al-'ulūm al-ḥaqiqiyya).* The second class of premises are called the accepted *(al-mashhūrāt);* the third, the fancied *(al-wahmiyyāt);* the fourth, the received *(al-ma'khūdhāt),* which include the generally acceptable *(al-maqbūlāt)* and the given *(al-taqrīrāt);* the fifth, the supposedly true (the alleged) *(al-maẓnūnāt);* the sixth, the premises that only appear true *(al-mushshabbahāt).*[2] After having discussed the premises in detail, Suhrawardī goes on to define dialectic, rhetoric, and poetry as types of arguments that use forms of syllogism but special kinds of premises, which serve as their matter. The "matter" of dialectical arguments is said to consist of the given and/or of the accepted premises; and the "matter" of poetic arguments is said to consist of imagined premises.[3]

The sixth chapter is entitled "On Demonstration, its Conditions, its Relation to Definition, Sophistical Refutations, and Rules," and consists of six sections.[4] The first four sections constitute a selective, short epitome of the *Posterior Analytics,* with only the following topics treated: the

[1] *Intimations:Logic,* pp. 69-73

[2] See Ibn Kammūna, *Sharḥ al-Talwīḥāt,* Ibid., p. 72, n.1-2.

[3] See Ibn Kammūna, Ibid., p. 73, n.1-3.

[4] *Intimations:Logic,* pp. 76-93.

questions *(al-maṭālib,* sec. 1, cf. *Healing: Posterior Analytics,* I, 5);[1] the "why" and the assertoric demonstrations *(burhān lima wa 'anna,* sec. 2; cf. *Healing: Posterior Analytics,* I, 7; III, 3);[2] the divisions and conditions of the sciences (sec. 3; cf. *Healing: Posterior Analytics,* II, 6-9);[3] and the relation between demonstration and definition (sec. 4; cf. *Healing: Posterior Analytics,* IV, 2-7).[4] The fifth section deals with sophistical errors in syllogism, both material and formal, and consists of a simple enumeration of some of the problems of *Sophistical Refutations* (cf. *Healing: Sophistical Refutations,* I, 2; II, 3-6).[5] The sixth section, entitled "On Miscellaneous Rules," is not part of the traditional structure of the *Posterior Analytics*, nor part of the *Sophistical Refutations,* but is an appendix to the logic of the *Intimations* in which Suhrawardī deals with nine Rules relating to special problems of logic. In this part, a non-Peripatetic approach is evident and an important distinction is made by Suhrawardī between what he calls "Heavenly Rules" *(al-ḍawābiṭ al-'arshiyya)* and "Rules of the Tablet" *(al-ḍawābiṭ al-lawḥiyya).* In his commentary on the *Intimations,* Ibn Kammūna states that perhaps the "Heavenly Rules" refer to what Suhrawardī has obtained through his personal speculation, while the "Rules of the Tablet" refer to what Suhrawardī has learned from books.[6] The distinction is an important one, and it is used in the physics and metaphysics of the *Intimations* as well. In general, the "Heavenly Rules" deal with topics of special importance to the philosophy of illumination, and in this part of the logic of the *Intimations,* Suhrawardī's "Rules" comprise topics where he disagrees with the Peripatetics. These are as follows: Rule 1: on the general meaning (or,

[1] Ibid., p. 76. A distinction is made between "simple if" *(hal al-basīṭ),* and "compound if" *(hal al-murakkab).*

[2] Ibid., p. 75. See Ibn Kammūna, *Sharḥ al-Talwīḥāt,* Ibid., p. 74, n. 1.

[3] *Intimations:Logic,* pp. 75-80.

[4] Ibid., pp. 80-83.

[5] Ibid., pp. 83-87. See Ibn Kammūna, *Sharḥ al-Talwīḥāt,* Ibid., pp. 83, n.1-5; 85, n. 1, n. 3.; 86, n.1; 87, n. 1-4.

[6] Ibid., p. 88, n. 1: *hātān al-lafẓatān, a'nī al-'arshī wa al-lawḥī, qad ista'malahumā fī 'iddat mawāḍi' min hādhā al-kitāb wa lam yubayyin murādahu minhumā, wa li'alla murāduhu bi'l-'arshī al-baḥth al-ladhī ḥaṣalahu bi-naẓarihi, wa bi-al-lawḥī mā 'akhadhahu min al-kutub.*

universal); Rule 2: the universal has a being only in the mind; Rule 3: on the modalities;[1] Rule 4: on the relation of two equal parts of a thing in terms of quantity, to the thing itself; Rule 5: on the impossibility of two things becoming one except through connection *(ittiṣāl)* and admixture *(imtizāj);* Rule 6: on the relation of one thing to many things *(al-lāūlawiyya)*;[2] Rule 7: on presuppositions; Rule 8: on [explaining] that a thing not in place is non-being *('adamī)* ; Rule 9: on causal relations between two things.[3]

3.2 Structure of Logic in The *Paths and Havens*

The logic of the *Paths and Havens* represents Suhrawardī's most extensive treatment of logic. Its structure is slightly different from the structure of the logic of the *Intimations,* and the material is presented and analyzed in more detail and in a more advanced manner. There are nine chapters (as compared to six in the logic of the *Intimations),* each of which is called a Path *(mashra')* .

The first chapter is entitled "On the *Isagoge*" and consists of sixteen sections *(fuṣūl).* This chapter roughly corresponds to the *Healing:Isagoge,* and structurally corresponds exactly to the first chapter of the logic of the *Intimations.* However, greater emphasis is placed on the discussion of quiddity *(al-māhiyya),* which is treated in three sections (6, 7, 14) as compared to two sections in the *Healing: Isagoge,* I, 5, 7.

The second chapter is entitled "On Expository Propositions," and consists of twelve sections. This chapter corresponds to the second chapter of the logic of the *Intimations,* but with the following sections added: section 3, on the use of technical terms in logic; section 4, where Suhrawardī argues against Avicenna's use of the terms "concept" *(al-*

[1]In this Rule Suhrawardī states that the modals necessary *(wājib),* possible *(mumkin),* impossible *(mumtani'),* and probable *(muḥtamal)*—note the addition of probable—are all *necessary* if made part of the predicate *(maḥmūl).* This notion of an iterated modality is developed fully in the logic of the *Philosophy of Illumination,* where Suhrawardī considers a single proposition, the always necessary *(al-ḍarūriyya al-battāta),* as a form to which all propositions can be reduced.

[2] See Ibn Kammūna, *Sharḥ al-Talwīḥāt, Intimations:Logic,* p. 91, n. 3.

[3] Ibid., pp.88-93.

mafhūm) and "the named" *(al-musammā);* section 7, a critique of the Peripatetic definition of man as rational animal; section 10, in which Suhrawardī deals with the definition of soul; and section 11, devoted to a discussion of the logical use made of definition by analogy *(ta'rīf bi al-tamthīl)*.

Chapter three is entitled "On Enunciative Composition," and consists of nine sections. This chapter corresponds to chapter three of the logic of the *Intimations*. However, in the first section, Suhrawardī discusses the distinction between real being *(wujūd 'aynī)* and ideal, or mental, being *(wujūd dhihnī)* in detail. He had not dealt with these subjects in the logic of the *Intimations,* and they have no counterpart in Avicenna's *Healing*. This is an example of a section in logic that signifies the illuminationist method of discussing certain ontological problems within their logical context.

Chapter four is entitled "On the Modal Propositions," and consists of six sections. This chapter corresponds exactly to chapter four of the logic of the *Intimations*.

The next three chapters (five, six, and seven) correspond to chapter five of the logic of the *Intimations*. The subjects of its three parts are treated in more detail and each is given a separate chapter. We note that the fifth chapter, entitled "On the Second Composition of Proof," consists of twenty sections, and corresponds to the former work's first part; the sixth chapter, entitled "On the Classes of Things We Need: Things Dialectical, etc.," consists of six sections, and corresponds to the second part; and the seventh chapter, entitled "On the Classes of Propositions," corresponds to the third part.

Chapter eight is entitled "On demonstration," and consists of sixteen sections. This chapter is slightly different from the first four sections of the sixth chapter of the logic of the *Intimations,* and is closer in structure to the *Posterior Analytics*.

Chapter nine is entitled "On Sophistical Refutations," a short chapter that corresponds exactly to the fifth section of chapter six of the logic of the *Intimations*.

Finally, there is nothing in the logic of the *Paths and Havens* that corresponds to the sixth section of chapter six of the logic of the *Intimations*.

3.3 Structure and Scope of Logic in the *Philosophy of Illumination*

There are major structural differences between the logic of the *Philosophy of Illumination* and the sections of logic in the *Intimations* and the *Paths and Havens*. In the latter two works, logic comprises the first part, or "book," of a total of three books that constitute each work. Logic is treated in Part One of the *Philosophy of Illumination,* where selected problems of both physics and metaphysics are also discussed. Part One *(al-Qism al-Awwal)* of the *Philosophy of Illumination* is entitled "On the Rules of Thought,"[1] and Part Two *(al-Qism al-Thānī)* is entitled "On Divine Lights, the Light of Lights, and the Principles and Ranks of Being."[2] In Part One, the said Rules of Thought cover logic, and physics as well as metaphysics. Part Two is where we find a well-defined reconstruction of epistemology and ontology in illuminationist terms. However, in spite of major structural differences between the *Philosophy of Illumination* and the other two major works, the contents are similar and only differ in terms of emphasis and terminology.

From Suhrawardī's own statements, we have learned that the logic of the *Intimations* and of the *Paths and Havens* are posterior in rank, though prior chronologically, to the *Philosophy of Illumination.* We also know that the highly concise and formulaic style of the treatment of logic in the *Philosophy of Illumination* itself indicates that Suhrawardī assumes the reader to be familiar with his other major works. Recent scholars, notably H. Corbin and S.H. Nasr, have ignored the study of logic in the *Philosophy of Illumination* completely. We shall see in our following examination of the First Part, that a thorough examination of illuminationist

[1] *Fī ḍawābiṭ al-fikr*. Suhrawardī, *Opera II,* pp. 14-105.

[2] *Fī al-anwār al-ilāhī wa nūr al-anwār wa mabādī' al-wujūd wa tartībihā*. Ibid., pp. 106-257.

logic is in fact indispensable in any attempt to understand Suhrawardī's philosophical intention.

Part One of the *Philosophy of Illumination* is divided into three chapters, each of which is called a "treatise" *(maqāla)*. The third chapter is further divided into three sections. The first two chapters plus the first two sections of the third chapter are devoted to logic; together they constitute roughly half of Part One of the book.

Chapter one is entitled "On Known Things and Making Things Known," and consists of seven sections, each of which is called a Rule *(ḍābiṭ)*.[1] Suhrawardī's use of the term "Rule" for his section headings expresses his intention to provide the reader with a set of succinct and useful rules, or formulas, pertaining to important topics of logic, without much discussion as to their logical significance or analysis as to how they are formulated. He simply states a logical principle, or problem, and assumes the reader to be familiar with the details, as presented mostly in his own logic of the *Paths and Havens*.[2] It is reasonable to assume that each of the Rules which appear in Part One of the *Philosophy of Illumination* is carefully chosen for its use in the illuminationist reconstruction of philosophy.

The first rule of chapter one deals with semantic problems in relation to the signification *(al-dalāla)* of the meaning *(al-ma'nā)* of the thing *(al-shay')* by the utterance *(al-lafẓ)*.[3] Three types of signification are named: 1-

[1] Ibid., pp. 14- 21.

[2] The other instance where the term, rule, is used by Suhrawardī is in chapter six of the logic of the *Intimations* (which, as we noted, serves as an appendix) where nine rules are given governing problems of logic, as well as logical discussions of problems usually discussed in physics.

[3] While the explicit semantic scheme of Aristotle is rather a simple one—"written words are symbols of spoken words, which are symbols of mental experiences, and mental experiences are again symbols of things," writes Bochenski *(Ancient Formal Logic*, p. 29)—the Stoics developed semantics into a complex system through their theory of λεκτόν and related subjects. Stoic semantics perhaps serves as the origin of the highly developed semantics and semiotics of Arabic and Persian logic. For a detailed analysis of the Stoic theory of λεκτόν see Benson Mates, *Stoic Logic* (Berkeley and Los Angeles: University of California Press, 1961), pp. 11-27; W. and M. Kneale, *The Development of Logic*, pp. 138-158; and Bochenski, *Ancient Formal Logic*, pp. 82-86.

signification of intention (*dalālat al-qaṣd*), where a one-to-one correspondence exists between the utterance and the meaning; 2-implicit signification (*dalālat al-ḥīṭa*), where a partial correspondence exists between the utterance and the meaning; and 3- concomitant signification (*dalālat al-taṭafful*), where the utterance signifies one or many, but not all, of the concomitants (*lawāzim*) of the thing. This Rule is the counterpart of Chapter I, 2 of the logic of the *Intimations* and of Chapter I, 3 of the logic of the *Paths and Havens*. In the *Philosophy of Illumination,* however, different terms are used than in the *Intimations* and in the *Paths and Havens,* where the three more standard terms—signification of correspondence (*dalālat al-muṭābaqa*), signification of implication (*dalālat al-taḍammun*), and signification of concomitance (*dalālat al-iltizām*) are used.[1]

In the second rule of the first chapter Suhrawardī deals in a special way with the relationship between conception and assent. The terms "conception" and "assent" are not used by him, but the commentator Quṭb al-Dīn al-Shīrāzī refers to them.[2] In the first section of Chapter one of the *Intimations,* Suhrawardī, considers conception to be the "obtaining of the form of the thing (*ṣūrat al-shay'*) in the mind," a Peripatetic idea which he refutes in the first section of chapter one of the logic of the *Paths and Havens*. Here (*Philosophy of Illumination:Part One,* I, 2) Suhrawardī

The following comparison may prove useful in understanding Suhrawardī's semantic scheme. The denotation, i.e. the external object (τὸ ἐκτὸς ὑποκείμενον or τὸ τυγχάνον) should be compared with the thing (*al-shay'*); the sign (φωνή or σημαῖνον) should be compared with the utterance (*al-lafẓ*); and the significate (τὸ λεκτόν) should be compared with the meaning (*al-ma'nā*). Ibrahim Madkour, in his "Introduction" to his critical edition of Avicenna's *Healing: Isagoge* (p. 62) considers the Stoic theory of λεκτόν to be the origin of the Islamic science of signification (*'ilm dalālat al-alfāẓ*).

[1] Suhrawardī, *Opera II*, pp. 14-15. Cf. Shīrāzī, *Sharḥ II*, p. 36:13; Baghdādī, *al-Mu'tabar*, I, 8; Suhrawardī, *Flashes of Light*, p. 59, where different significations are dealt with in detail. See also Shahrazūrī, *Sharḥ*, fol. 14r.

[2] Shīrāzī, *Sharḥ II*, 38:13. The designation "illuminationist knowledge" (*al-'ilm al-ishrāqī*) is applied by the commentator to a kind of knowledge where the distinction between conception and assent does not apply. Knowledge of God and of the primary intelligibles, are examples of this kind of knowledge, where the mere "presence"(*ḥuḍūr*) of the object implies knowledge of it by a knowing subject.

presents, without much analysis, a different view, which should be considered a fundamental component of illuminationist principles concerning the foundations of knowledge. Suhrawardī states that cognition, or perception *(idrāk)*, of an absent thing *(al-shay' al-ghā'ib)* takes place when an idea *(mithāl)* of its reality *(ḥaqīqa)* is obtained, and he implies further that when the idea is obtained, an impression, or affection *(athar)*, appears in the being of the one who perceives which determines the state of knowledge obtained by him.[1] The few lines of this section have a great implication for our understanding of the illuminationist theory of knowledge. The distinction made by Suhrawardī between an absent thing (*al-shay' al-ghā'ib)* and a non-absent thing, i.e., a corporeal thing which is part of the sense-data, is an important one in illuminationist philosophy. Suhrawardī is in agreement with the Peripatetic formula that conception is the obtaining of the form of a thing in the mind—as long as the thing is corporeal and sensible. He is not satisfied with the Peripatetic formula when the thing to be perceived is not corporeal and not part of the sense-data. In such a case the illuminationist position is stated to be that knowledge is based on a relation *(iḍāfa)*, obtained in the mind, between the idea of the "reality" *(ḥaqīqa)* of the thing and the thing itself. This means that, for Suhrawardī, form and idea of sensible things are the same, but not so in the case of the non-sensible, where the idea of the thing is that which is related to the perception of it and hence is the epistemologically prior. In the rest of this section (Second Rule), Suhrawardī discusses the semantic problems connected to his previous account of the relation between knowledge, perception, and the "idea" *(mithāl)* of non-sensible things. In a novel manner he states that the meaning *(al-ma'nā)* that appears to the person is either a universal meaning *(al-ma'nā al-'āmm)*, and the utterance that

[1] Quṭb al-Dīn al-Shīrāzī regards the problem of conception and assent to be a "new science" which deals with the presence of the perceived thing *(al-mudrak)* in the perceiver *(al-mudrik) (Sharḥ II*, pp. 38:13-39:2). Shīrāzī goes on to stress the significance of this epistemological question for illuminationist philosophy and points to the distinction between formal knowledge *(al-'ilm al-ṣūrī)* and illuminationist knowledge by presence *(al-'ilm al-ishrāqī al-ḥuḍūrī)*. It should be noted that the question is debated at length by Mulla Ṣadrā in his *Ta'līqāt (Sharḥ II*, pp. 39-42 margin) who disagrees completely with the illuminationist epistemological position.

signifies it, a class name *(al-lafẓ al-'āmm);* or a particular meaning *(al-ma' nā al-shākhiṣ),* and the utterance that signifies it a particular or proper name *(al-lafẓ al-shākhiṣ).*[1] The subject matter of this Rule corresponds to the problem dealt with in the *Intimations:Logic,* I, 1, 3, 4, and the *Paths and Havens:Logic,* I, 1, 4, 5, 7. It should be noted that the terms used in this section of the *Philosophy of Illumination* are, however, different from the corresponding terms in the two other works.

In the Third Rule, Suhrawardī deals with the reality *(al-ḥaqīqa)* of a thing. This reality, which is equated with the standard Peripatetic term for quiddity *(al-māhiyya)* by Shīrāzī,[2] is said to be either simple *(basīṭ)* or non-simple *(ghayr basīṭ),* i.e. composite. A thing, then, has a reality associated with it, what-it-is or its quiddity, which may signify a meaning that corresponds either to the whole of the thing as-it-is, or only to part of it.[3] The "reality," or what the thing is as-it-is (*res* of the thing), may have "separate" accidents *(al-'awāriḍ al-mufāraqa)* or "concomitant" accidents *(al-'awāriḍ al-lāzima)* associated with it.[4] This section only partially corresponds to the *Paths and Havens:Logic,* I, 16.[5]

In the Fourth Rule Suhrawardī deals further with the what-of-the-thing he has called reality.[6] Both the separate accidents and the concomitant accidents are said to be posterior to the "reality" of the thing, which must be viewed as-it-is, a totality in itself, if knowledge of it is to be obtained. The

[1] Suhrawardī, *Opera II, p.* 15. The terms used here by Suhrawardī are not Peripatetic terms. The following comparison with the Stoic terms of the theory of λεκτόν should be made: the universal meaning *(al-ma'nā al-'āmm)* may be related to the Stoic common noun (κοινὴ ποιότης) ; the class name *(al-lafẓ al-'āmm)* to the Stoic προσηγορίαι the particular meaning *(al-ma'nā al-shākhiṣ)* to the Stoic individual noun (ἰδέα ποιότητος); and the proper name *(al-lafẓ al-shākhiṣ)* to the Stoic proper names (ὀνόματα).

[2] Shīrāzī, *Sharḥ II,* pp. 45:2-3: *kull ḥaqīqa, ay māhiyya siwā' kānat fī al-a'yān aw fī al-adhhān.*

[3] Suhrawardī's insistence on using *haqīqa* in place of *māhiyya* is in accordance with his "realist" position of equating what a thing is with its reality, i.e., *ḥaqīqa* is to be taken as *shay' kamā huwa.* Cf. the Stoic complete λεκτόν (αὐτοτελές) and deficient λεκτόν (ἐλλιπές) (Mates, *Stoic Logic,* p. 16). See also, Shīrāzi, *Sharḥ II,* p. 45: 3, ff.

[4] Cf. Shīrāzī, *Sharḥ II,* p. 45:13-16.

[5] Suhrawardī, *Opera II,* p. 15.

[6] Ibid., pp. 16-17. Cf. Shīrāzī, *Sharḥ II,* p. 47:12-49:2.

real thing, then, has specific concomitants which are attributed to it,[1] and the specific concomitant is said to be the essential *(al-dhātī)*. The accidental *(al-'araḍī)*, is separate from, or is a concomitant of, the reality of the thing, and is considered posterior to the reality of the thing when intellected. It may be a more general attribution or a specific one.[2] This section corresponds to the *Intimations:Logic*, I, 6, and to the *Paths and Havens:Logic*, I, 11.

In the Fifth Rule Suhrawardī deals with the universal *(al-ma'nā al-'āmm)*.[3] This "general meaning," or universal, is said not to have a reality outside the mind;[4] since to have a reality outside the mind is to have a specific quiddity by which it will be distinguished from something else, and thus become a specific thing *(shākiṣ)* and not a general meaning (nor universal). The general meaning is said to be either co-extensive *(mutasāwiq)* [5] or separate *(mutafāwit)*.[6] Following his semantic scheme in logic in this section, Suhrawardī defines synonymous *(mutarādifa)*, homonymous *(mushtaraka)*, and metaphorical *(majāziyya)* names.[7] This section

[1] Such as man *(al-insān)*, for which animality *(al-ḥayawāniyya)* is the attributed part.

[2] E.g., capability of walking is a more general accident of man (shared by animals, say) while capability of laughter is a specific accident, or coincidental, of man.

[3] Suhrawardī, *Opera II*, p. 17. The term used by Suhrawardī here is not the Peripatetic term *al-kullī*, but Shīrāzī considers the two terms to be identical *(Sharḥ II*, pp. 49:2-52:16). However, Suhrawardī chosed the terms he used very carefully, and I believe they support an alternate tradition of logic, perhaps of Stoic origin.

[4] Quṭb al-Dīn al-Shīrāzī considers the term *al-ma'nā al-'āmm* to be a "new" term used by Suhrawardī, and he takes it to be the same as *al-kullī (Sharḥ, II*, p. 49:3); but Mullā Ṣadrā considers Suhrawardī's use of the term *al-ma'nā al-'āmm* to be due to a confusion between *al-kullī al-'aqlī* and *al-kullī al-ṭabī'ī*. Only the former does not have a reality outside the mind *(Ta'līqāt: Sharḥ II*, p. 49, margin.).

[5] The usual Peripatetic term is *al-'āmm al-mutasāwī*. Alfarabi, however, uses both terms. See Alfarabi, *Utterances Employed in Logic*, ed. Muhsin Mahdi (Beirut: Dar El-Machreq, 1967), p. 61.

[6] Such as when the particulars or individuals differ with respect to meaning.

[7]Aristotle discusses only briefly things named equivocally, univocally, and derivatively *(Categories* I, 1-15). Philosophers in the Islamic period, on the other hand, treat this subject in considerable detail. Discussion of the "name" in relation to the thing named, is part of a well-defined theory of semantics. See Baghdādī, *al-Mu'tabar*, I, 8; Suhrawardī,

corresponds to the *Intimations:Logic,* I, 5, and to the *Paths and Havens:Logic,* I, 8.

The above mentioned first five rules (of a total of seven) of the *Philosophy of Illumination:Part One,* I, correspond to the first chapters of the logic of both the *Intimations* and the *Paths and Havens,* and so constitute that part of the logic of the *Philosophy of Illumination* related to the subject matter of the traditional *Isagoge* (e.g., the *Healing: Isagoge).*

In Rule six, Suhrawardī considers his two-fold division of knowledge, innate and acquired, as he had done in the introductory sections of the logic of both the *Intimations* and the *Paths and Havens.*[1] Here, too, Suhrawardī emphasizes that innate ideas serve as the grounds for knowledge; this is a basic view taken in the illuminationist reconstruction of philosophy when considering the fundamental epistemological question "How is knowledge obtained?"[2] The special significance of the question of the innate ideas in illuminationist epistemology, as had been indicated by Suhrawardī in the introductory sections of all of the major four works (cf. also *Healing: Isagoge,* I, 4), is the reason why he has included its discussion in this Rule of Part One of the book. The position taken here by Suhrawardī is based on a modified view of Aristotle's opening remarks in the *Posterior Analytics* I, 1; but the epistemological position given to this division of knowledge is part of Suhrawardī's own theory of Knowledge.

In the seventh Rule, Suhrawardī deals with definition and description, which corresponds to the subject matter of chapter two of both the

---

the *Flashes of Light,* p. 60; Sāwī, *al-Tabṣira [the Beacon],* pp. 13-16. For a discussion of Baghdādī's views on the relation between things known, their states in the mind and in the external reality, and the meaning *(al-m'ana,* translated by Pines as "thought-contents"), particular or universal, see Pines, "Studies in Abu'l-Barakāt al-Baghdādī's Poetics and Metaphysics," pp. 141-147.

[1] See Shīrāzī, *Sharḥ II,* pp. 50:16-52:15.

[2] The position here, that innate ideas have *a priori* rank, is also a major methodological position of Baghdādī. This has been discussed by S. Pines, in his studies on Baghdādī. See especially S. Pines, *Nouvelles études sur Awḥad al-Zaman Abu'l-Barakāt al-Baghdādī* (Paris: Librairie Durlaches, 1953), pp. 8, 17; idem, "Studies in Abu'l-Barakāt al-Baghdādī's Poetics and Metaphysics," pp. 127-128, where *a priori* cognition is said by Pines to be "the main theme" of Baghdādī's work.

Intimations and the *Paths and Havens.*[1] As we mentioned above, definition and description as logical problems are discussed in both the *Posterior Analytics* and the *Topics.* Suhrawardī's inclusion of the problems in his overall semantic theory is a marked departure from the standard structure of the *Organon.* The importance of this Rule may be readily ascertained when we examine the fact that Suhrawardī refutes the doctrine of definition, considered by the Peripatetics to be the first important step in science.

After refuting the Peripatetic position Suhrawardī presents an alternative view of the formal rules pertaining to definition, as well as of its epistemological position. This is one of the most important basic components of illuminationist theory of knowledge. The seventh Rule itself is divided into two parts, an introductory one, entitled "On Real Definitions" *(al-ḥudūd and ḥaqīqiyya),* and one entitled "Illuminationist Theorem" *(qā'ida ishrāqiyya),* in which Suhrawardī discusses what he considers to be the shortcomings of the Peripatetic formula for definition, and also presents his own alternative theory. In the introductory part, Suhrawardī deals with problems related to the rules governing definition. He posits that, in order for a thing to be known through a definition of it, either *all* or *some* of its units *(al-āḥād),* or the whole *(al-ijtimā')* of the thing to be defined must be specified. Suhrawardī further stipulates that, in constructing a definition, the thing must be defined in reference to something more apparent, or more evident *(aẓhar)* than the thing itself, known prior to it. In other words, that in reference to which a thing is defined, must be more evident and more prior in respect to it. Finally, Suhrawardī adds that definitions cannot be mere nominal substitutions *(tabdīl al-lafẓ).* In the section that follows, Suhrawardī considers real definition and description. He states his objections to the materialist view which considers reality to be only the corporeal *(al-ḥaqīqa al-jirmiyya).* He further states that when the Peripatetics desire

[1] Suhrawardī, *Opera II,* pp. 18-20. See below, Appendix B, where a translation of the *Philosophy of Illumination: Part One,* I, 7: "On Definition and its Conditions," has been provided. The topic of definition is one of the most important ones in Suhrawardī's logic as well as in his illuminationist philosophy. See Shīrāzī, *Sharḥ II,* p. 52-18-63:3; Baghdādī, *al-Mu'tabar,* I, 46-48, 50-64; Sāwī, *Tabṣira,* pp. 19-24; Suhrawardī, the *Flashes of Light,* pp. 64-66.

to know such a thing as man, they postulate something through which the idea "man" *(al-insāniyya)* is known, and this for them is said to be the definition of "man" as "rational animal." Suhrawardī objects to this definition on the grounds that defining x through y implicit in x is not a definition of it. Suhrawardī proposes an alternate way for knowing the idea "man," based on the individual's knowledge of his own ipseity first. As a result of the ensuing certainty based on, and because of, "self-knowledge," the subject can come to know the idea "man." This kind of knowledge, Suhrawardī argues, can never be achieved through mere constructed formulas of definitions.

In the next part entitled "Illuminationist Theorem," Suhrawardī states further objections to the Peripatetic formula of definition. According to the Peripatetics, the general and particular essentials *(al-dhātī al-'āmm wa'l-khāṣṣ)* of a thing to be defined must be specified. The general essential pertains to the universal reality *(al-ḥaqīqa al-kulliya)* of the thing and is called genus *(al-jins)*. The particular essential is called the differentia *(al-faṣl)* and pertains to the thing specifically. Suhrawardī objects to the Peripatetic view that a definition is made up of the genus and the differentia from two different points of view. Firstly, after having established that one obtains the unknown *(al-majhūl)* only through the known *(al-ma'lūm)*, and that the most prior known thing is innately known, he objects to the Peripatetic formula for definition on the grounds that the particular essential of the thing, i.e. its differentia, is just as *unknown* as the thing to be defined, nor is it more prior, and thus should not be used in combining a formula which supposedly is to define the thing. Secondly, in order to have certain knowledge *(al-ma'rifa al-mutayaqqina)* of a thing, the totality *(al-ijtimā'*, the organic sum) of the essentials *(al-jamī' al-dhātiyyāt)* must be known. This cannot be done by a mere process of discretely enumerating the essentials (i.e. the differentia) of the thing, since there may be a multiplicity of "hidden" *(ghayr ẓāhira)* attributes *(ṣifāt)* pertaining to the thing, thus making a complete enumeration impossible.

This means that Suhrawardī is considering that it is possible for a thing to have a large number, or an uncountable number, of essentials, i.e., that the sequence of all essentials of a thing not have a *real* lower or upper bound. This is not difficult to imagine when we think of a thing with many, non-countable, perhaps even infinite, attributes. Suhrawardī tells us that the Master of the Peripatetics (Aristotle) himself has admitted the difficulty of obtaining real definitions of things. Suhrawardī's alternate theory of definition, with which he deals in much greater detail later in his work, aims to specify the things specifically pertaining to the totality *(al-'ijtimā'*, organic whole) of the thing to be defined. The totality of the thing cannot be known by a mere formal method of enumerating a finite number of essential attributes of it, and can only be known by means of an alternate epistemological process. This, as we shall see later, is the illuminationist epistemological notion of knowledge of a thing based on "seeing" the thing as-it-is.

The second chapter of Part One of the *Philosophy of Illumination* is entitled "On Proofs and their Principles,"[1] and consists of seven Rules. Selected areas of three of the books of the traditional *Organon—On Interpretation, Prior Analytics,* and *Posterior Analytics*—are dealt with in this chapter.

The first Rule is devoted to a study of proposition *(qaḍiyya)* and syllogism *(qiyās)*.[2] Proposition is defined as a statement that can be said to be true or false. A syllogism is a statement composed of propositions. The simplest proposition is the predicative *(ḥamliyya)*, composed of a subject *(mawḍū')* and a predicate *(maḥmūl)*.[3] It is possible to combine two (or more) propositions into one by connecting the two. When the connection is by implication *(luzūm)*, the proposition is called connective conditional *(al-sharṭiyya al-muttaṣila)*.[4] The part that is connected to the protasis *(al-*

[1] *Fi'l-ḥujaj wa mabādīhā* , Suhrawardī, *Opera II*, pp. 22-45.

[2] Cf. Shīrāzī, *Sharḥ II*, pp. 63:4-70:1; Baghdādī, *al-Mu'tabar*, I, 69-74; Sāwī, *al-Tabṣira*, pp. 26-27. Both Baghdādī and Sāwī use the term *al-qawl al-jāzim* (λόγος ἀποφαντικός) synonymously with *al-qaḍiyya*. The two terms should be compared with ἀξίωμα, as well as with λόγος ἀποφαντικός. See Bochenski, *Ancient Formal Logic*, pp. 85-86.

[3] p (subject) is q (predicate).

[4] Also known as the "if, then" proposition, the connection by implication, or inference, *luzūm*, can be reduced to other types of connection, such as combinations of conjunction, disjunction, and negation. The basic form of this proposition is [x, p, q]: q(x) then p(x). The treatment of formal rules governing implication by Suhrawardī is to

shart) is called the antecedent *(al-muqaddam)*, and the part connected to the apodosis *(al-jazā')* is called the consequent *(al-ṭālī)*. When the connection between two propositions is by conflict *(al-'inād,* which may be translated as "disjunction"), the proposition is called the disjunctive (separative) conditional *(al-sharṭiyya al-munfaṣila)*.[1] Other propositions may be formed by connecting two or more such propositions. All conditional propositions are modifications of the predicative ones, though there is no attempt made here by Suhrawardī to show the manner of reducing one form of connection in propositions to another. This is followed by a discussion of the *modus ponens* and the *modus tollens*, and the fallacies as well as the valid inferences made from affirming/negating the antecedent or the consequent in the conditional and the disjunctive syllogisms. The subject matter of this Rule corresponds exactly to the first sections of chapter three in the logic of both the *Intimations* and the *Paths and Havens*.

The second Rule deals with universal and particular propositions.[2] Suhrawardī here introduces the temporal modals of always *(dā'iman)* and sometimes *(ba'ḍ al-awqāt)*. He then discusses types of inclusion *(al-istighrāq)*, the quantification sign *(sl-sūr)*,[3] the particular proposition *(al-shākhiṣa)*,[4] the universal definite proposition *(al-muhmala al-ba'ḍiyya)*,[5] and the universal indefinite *(al-muḥīṭa)*.[6] In each case, careful attention is given to a discussion of affirmation *('ījāb)* and negation *(salb)*. Suhrawardī next deals with a specific logical problem as relating to the Arabic language. The problem concerns the position of the copula, or connective *(al-rābiṭ)* in negation. The question is, how does negating a compound proposition

---

be compared to the Stoic. See Bochenski, *Ancient Formal Logic*, pp. 158-176; Mates, *Stoic Logic*, pp. 42-57.

[1] Also known as the "either, or" proposition, the connection by disjunction, *'inād*, can be reduced to other types of connection. The basic form of this proposition is [x, p, q]: q(x) or p(x). The two parts of this combined proposition, too, are called antecedent and consequent, respectively.

[2] Suhrawardī, *Opera II*, pp. 24-27. Cf. Shīrāzī, *Sharḥ II*, pp. 70:11-77:3; Baghdādī, *al-Mu'tabar*, I, 75-78; Sāwī, *Tabṣira*, pp. 30-32.

[3] A non-Aristotelian term. See Afnan, *A Philosophical Lexicon*, p. 131.

[4] p is q when p is a proper name.

[5] All p are q, e.g., "all men are animals," and negatively, "no man is stone."

[6] Some p are q, and some p are not q.

where the copula may be a conjunction, disjunction or implication, affect the form of the proposition? A distinction is made between the Arabic language and non-Arabic languages, and a generalized scheme is adopted. The effect of negation on both the particular and the universal propositions are examined.[1] The subject matter of this Rule is a selection of the problems dealt with in chapter three, sections 2-4, of the logic of the *Intimations*, and chapter three, sections 2-9, of the logic of the *Paths and Havens*. Thus Rules one and two of chapter two constitute an epitome of chapter three of the logic of both the *Intimations* and the *Paths and Havens*.

In the third Rule, Suhrawardī deals with the modal proposition *(al-qaḍiyya al-muwajjaha)* and derivatives.[2] The relation between the subject and the predicate of a predicative proposition is said to be necessary *(wājib)*, impossible *(mumtaniʿ)*, or possible *(mumkin)*. After examining the modal propositions, Suhrawardī analyzes the problem associated with an unrestricted usage of the universal quantifier by distinguishing among the terms "all" *(kull)*, "each and every" *(kull wāḥid wāḥid)*, and "totality" *(al-jamīʿ)*. Under the separate heading, "Illuminationist Wisdom" *(ḥikma ishrāqiyya)*, Suhrawardī attempts to reduce all propositions to one type, which he calls the "always necessary affirmative" *(al-mūjiba al-ḍarūriyya al-battāta)*.[3] This is among the important areas of formal logic where Suhrawardī has departed from the Peripatetics, (here specifically Avicenna), by combining temporal modalities with the mode necessary *(ḍarūra)*. This type of proposition is called the "always necessary," or "necessary at all

[1] The problem is presented as follows. Let C be the copula. To negate pCq one can either, in Arabic, say p¬Cy, or pC¬q, where ¬ stands for negation. In the case of universal propositions it is said all p are q, and ¬(all p are q) reduces to some p are q.

[2] Suhrawardī, *Opera II* , pp. 27-29. For a discussion of modal propositions see Hossein Ziai, "Modal Propositions in Islamic Philosophy," *Bulletin of the Iranian Mathematical Society*, no. 12 (1980). Cf. Shīrāzī, *Sharḥ II*, pp. 77:13-78:9; Baghdādī, *al-Muʿtabar*, I, 78-89; Sāwī, *Tabṣira*, pp. 32-44.

[3] This term seems to have been coined by Suhrawardī. M.T. Danesh Pajooh regards Suhrawardī's attempt to reduce all propositions to one type to be Aristotelian in origin (*Tabṣira*, p. 21). I have not found Aristotle saying anything to this effect anywhere, and his statement in the *Prior Analytics:* "For all propositions are convertible save only the particular negative" (*Prior Analytics* II, 52b 7-8) deals with the problem of "conversion" *(al-ʿaks fi'l-qaḍāyā)* and not with "reduction of propositions" *(radd al-qaḍāyā)*.

times," and is a derivative, or combines, the three modes with the temporal modalities "always" and "sometimes." With the exception of this special type of an itterated proposition, the subject matter of this section is an epitome of chapter four, sections 1-3, of the logic of the *Paths and Havens*.

In the fourth Rule, Suhrawardī deals with contradiction *(al-tanāquḍ)* in proposition, said to be the distinction made between two propositions in terms of negation or affirmation.[1]

In the fifth Rule, Suhrawardī deals with conversion of proposition *(al-'aks),* which is making the subject of a proposition the predicate and the predicate the subject while keeping the modality, the affirmative or negative nature, as well as the quantification of the proposition—in short, when the subject is made the predicate while the quality and the truth value of the proposition remain the same.[2] This section is a short epitome of chapter four, section 5, of the logic of the *Intimations,* and chapter four, sections 4-5, of the logic of the *Paths and Havens.*

Therefore, Rules 3-5 of chapter two of Part One of the *Philosophy of Illumination,* with the exception of the addition of the special temporal-modal proposition (in Rule 3), should be considered as an epitome of chapter four of the logic of the *Intimations* and of the same chapter of the logic of the *Paths and Havens.*

In Rule six Suhrawardī deals with syllogism.[3] The disjunctive syllogism *(al-qiyās al-istithnā'ī)* and the hypothetical syllogism *(al-qiyās al-iqtirānī),* together with the *modus ponens* and the *modus tollens* (dealt with in chapter two, Rule one), which form part of Suhrawardī's theory of the rules of inference, are defined. Further, "term" *(al-ḥadd)* as the subject of the premise *(al-muqaddima)* or predicate of the syllogism, and the middle term *(al-ḥadd al-awsaṭ)* are also defined. Next, under the separate

[1] Suhrawardī, *Opera II,* pp. 30-31.Cf. Shīrāzī, *Sharḥ II,* pp. 86:10-89:5; Baghdādī, *al-Mu'tabar,* I, 95-197; Sāwī, *Tabṣira,* pp. 44-51.

[2] Suhrawardī, *Opera II,* pp. 31-33. Cf. Shīrāzī, *Sharḥ II,* pp. 89:6-95:5; Sāwī, *Tabṣira,* pp. 51-59.

[3] Suhrawardī, *Opera II,* pp. 33-40. Cf. Shīrāzī, *Sharḥ II,* pp. 95:5-118:5; Baghdādī, *al-Mu'tabar,* I, 109-203; Sāwī, *Tabṣira,* pp. 91-119.

heading "Illuminationist Clarification" *(daqīqa ishrāqiyya),* Suhrawardī attempts to generalize the formal rules that govern negation. In the subsequent two sections, each entitled "Illuminationist Theorem," Suhrawardī attempts to show that the second figure *(al-shakl al-thānī)* and the third figure *(al-shakl al-thālith)* of syllogism are both only modifications of the first figure *(al-shakl al-awwal).* These sections,while of special significance for the study of the history of formal logic, are not of immediate pertinence for the study of illuminationist theory of knowledge *per se.* In the last two sections Suhrawardī deals with the conditionals *(al-sharṭiyyāt)* and reduction *ad impossible* in syllogism *(qiyās al-khulf).* The sixth Rule is a highly selective, short epitome of the first part of chapter five of the logic of the *Intimations,* and of chapter five of the logic of the *Paths and Havens,* and constitutes those elements of the *Prior Analytics* deemed important by Suhrawardī.

In the seventh Rule, Suhrawardī deals with the subject of demonstration *(al-burhān).*[1] There are four sections in this Rule. In the first section, which corresponds to the third part of chapter five of the logic of the *Intimations,* Suhrawardī deals quite extensively with the matter *(mādda, mawād)* of demonstration. He considers real sciences *(al-'ulūm al-ḥaqīqiyya)* to be constructed from demonstrations based on premises whose validity are certain *(al-muqaddamāt al-yaqīniyya),* and considers the following types of premises:

1- Primary premises *(al-awwaliyyāt).*[2] These are premises such as "whole is greater than the parts," "two things equal to a third are equal," etc.

2- Observed, or seen premises *(al-mushāhadāt)*—which are "seen" through the outer senses or the inner ones. Proofs based on "seen" premises are only valid for the person himself, and may be communicated only to someone else who has the same disposition *(mash'ar)* as the individual who has "seen" the object.

[1] Suhrawardī, *Opera II,* pp. 40-45. Cf. Shīrāzī, *Sharḥ II,* pp. 118:6-135:19; Baghdādī, *al-Mu'tabar,* I, 203-253; Sāwī, *Tabṣira,* pp. 91-119.

[2] Cf. the Aristotelian τὰ πρῶτα *(Posterior Analytics* I, 71b26).

3- Intuitive premises *(al-ḥadsiyyāt).*[1] These premises are of two types, the empirical *(al-mujarrabāt),* which are only valid if the frequency *(al-takrār)* of their occurrence is high, and the traditional. The intuitive premises are not obtained by induction *(istighrā'),* which is dispensed with by Suhrawardī as not a valid method of proof in the sciences. Proofs based on intuition are shared by those with the same intuitive capabilities only.

4- Generally accepted premises *(al-mashhūrāt).* These premises, we are told, cannot be used in the sciences.

5- A general class of premises which are called the imagined *(al-mukhayyalāt),* and which have no scientific value.

We note that Suhrawardī's discussion of the premises here is a modification of the *Intimations:Logic,* V, 3. In the last three sections of this Rule, Suhrawardī deals with analogy (which he does not consider to be part of scientific methodolgy), the "why" demonstration *(burhān lima),* the assertoric demonstration *(burhān anna),* and with the questions asked in science *(al-maṭālib).*[2] The seventh Rule as a whole constitutes Suhrawardī's selection of what he considers important problems from among the traditional subject matter of the *Posterior Analytics.*

[1] The intuitive premises play a fundamental role in the illuminationist construction of philosophy. These premises are to be found in Peripatetic philosophy as well. For example, Avicenna states that intuition is the "movement of striking upon the middle term" *(al-Najāt,* ed. al-Kurdī, p. 87); this is a paraphrase of Aristotle's definition of "quick wit" (ἀγχίνοια) *(Posterior Analytics* I, 89b 10). Sāwī stipulates the intuitive premises to be the "judgement of a powerful intellect" *(Tabṣira,* p. 152).

[2] The questions *mā, hal, 'ayyu, lima,* are considered the principle questions of science *(uṣūl al-maṭālib al-'ilmiyya),* with the secondary questions being: *kayf, kam, 'ayn, matā, man.* Suhrawardī's general non-Peripatetic scheme for the categories is as follows. The accidents are four: *kam* (quantity), *kayf* (quality), *iḍāfa* (relation), and *ḥaraka* (motion). See Suhrawardī, *Opera I,* p. 284 ff.; *Opera II,* p. 61-62. It should be noted that the term used by Suhrawardī for the equivalent of accident is *hay'a* and not the Peripatetic *'araḍ.* The great logician 'Umar ibn Sahlān al-Sāwī, whose *al-Baṣā'ir* Suhrawardī had studied, also reduces the categories—in this case to four: substance, quality, quantity, and relation—but does not include motion, nor does he discuss the essentially *ishrāqī* principle of motion-in-category. Therefore Sāwī cannot, in my view, be considered the immediate source of Suhrawardī, as is believed by S.J. Sajjādī. See Sajjādī, *Suhrawardī* (Tehran, 1984) pp. 98-99.

The third chapter of Part One of the *Philosophy of Illumination* is entitled "On Sophistical Refutations and some Judgements between the Illuminationist and the Peripatetic Doctrines,"[1] and is divided into three sections. The first two sections constitute an epitome of the *Sophistical Refutations,* which is generally more detailed than the corresponding sections in both the *Intimations:Logic,* VI, 5, and the *Paths and Havens:Logic,* IX. The third section is a highly argumentative section where Suhrawardī takes issue with the Peripatetics on major problems of physics and metaphysics. This section is divided into an introduction *(muqaddima)* and ten divisions, each called judgement *(ḥukūma).* The selected topics of this section cover those parts of foundations of illuminationist philosophy that differ with the Peripatetic.

4. Assessment

Having outlined the structure of the parts on logic in Suhrawardī's major works—*the Intimations,* the *Paths and Havens,* and the *Philosophy of Illumination* [2]—we are in a position to make the following assessment of Suhrawardī's logic.

The most significant differences between the structure of the traditional *Organon* and the structure of Suhrawardī's logic are : 1- there is no "book" of categories, nor are they discussed at all in any of Suhrawardī's logical works;[3] 2- there are no separate "books" of dialectics, rhetoric, or poetry, but there is discussion of their subject matters, and they are considered kinds of non-scientific syllogisms where the premises used are said to be non-scientific ones. Apart from these differences, Suhrawardī's logic is a selective epitome of logical problems within the *Organon,* which are at times treated with different emphasis. At other times there is an attempt on the part

[1] *Fi'l-mughālaṭāt wa ba'ḍ al-ḥukūmāt bayn aḥruf ishrāqiyya wa bayn aḥruf al-mashshā'īn,* Suhrawardī, *Opera II,* p.46.

[2] The structure of the logic of the *Apposites* coresoponds to that of the *Intimations.*

[3] Suhrawardī discusses the categories, which he considers not the invention of Aristotle, but of a certain Arkhuṭus, in his works on physics. Briefly, Suhrawardī's theory states that "intensity" *(shadda wa ḍa'f)* is predicated of all catergories, substance

of Suhrawardī to modify or change formal laws of Peripatetic logic, and there is a special emphasis placed upon the pragmatic use of logical rules—semantic, formal, and material—in philosophy. Logic is considered as a separate tool subordinate to philosophy.

The structure of all three works examined here is similar, considering the order in which logical subjects are dealt with. However, there are some differences to note. The logic of the *Intimations* consists of six chapters, while the logic of the *Paths and Havens* consists of nine, and this is a minor structural difference. The three parts of chapter five and the fifth section of chapter six of the logic of the *Intimations* are made into independent chapters in the logic of the *Paths and Havens*. The structure of the logic of the *Philosophy of Illumination* is, however, substantially different from the other two. The "new" structure of logic that emerges in the *Philosophy of Illumination* reflects Suhrawardī's reordering of logic into three broadly defined areas: 1- semantics (chapter I), which includes an epitome of the *Isagoge,* plus the problems of definition and description; 2- principles of proof (chapter II), which includes selective epitomes of *On Interpretations, Prior Analytics,* and *Posterior Analytics,* constituting Suhrawardī's own view of the rules governing both formal and material logic; and 3- errors of formal and material logic (chapter II, 1-2), which is structurally an epitome of the *Sophistical Refutations,* but is a section of logic where Suhrawardī attempts to refute many Peripatetic views while reformulating his own. This new structure reflects Suhrawardī's attempt to reorganize the traditional *Organon* in accordance with his general bipartite division of logic into expository propositions and proofs. (The errors of logic is a necessary corollary.)

Finally, we can point to areas and problems of logic especially pertinent to the philosophy of illumination. We may, to begin with, simply identify all of the Rules of logic in Part One of the *Philosophy of Illumination.* However true these Rules may be (Suhrawardī would not have included them in this work if this were not the case), such a general statement does not help us very much in our endeavor to answer the question "What is the

---

(jawhar), quality *(kayf)*, quantity *(kamm)*, relation *(nisba)*, and motion *(ḥaraka)*. See for example, *Opera I*, pp. 1-12; 146-148; *Opera III*, p. 113.

philosophy of illumination?" In fact, on closer examination we realize that, within the logic of the *Philosophy of Illumination,* Suhrawardī himself has indicated the special areas and problems by distinguishing them with special section headings, such as "Illuminationist Theorem," "Illuminationist Wisdom," etc. Among the host of special problems so designated by Suhrawardī, the following are of special importance : definition, negation, the special "always necessary universal affirmative" proposition, and the second and the third figures of syllogism. With the exception of definition, all of these are problems of formal logic. Definition plays an important role in the methodology of philosophy, and relates specifically to the question of the epistemological foundation of illuminationist knowledge. How it is obtained? And how it can be defined? We shall discuss this problem at length in the next chapter. The discussion of the purely formal problems of logic we leave for a more specialized study of Suhrawardī's logic.

Chapter Three

The Illuminationist Theory of Definition Formal Method and Knowledge

1. Terminology of Definition

I shall begin this chapter with a brief discussion of the terminology of definition used by Suhrawardī. My aim is to indicate the various possible types of definition, either explicitly referred to by a prescribed technical term or implicitly indicated by the use of a generic term.[1]

In Arabic and Persian philosophy and logic, all types of definition are grouped under the term *ta'rīf,* which basically means "making known" and is often translated as "definition." In certain instances, such a translation may not be a technically precise one, since it covers the essentialist, conceptualist, nominalist, and other types of definition, as well as any epistemological process by means of which something unknown "becomes" known in relation to something else. It is, therefore, important to bear in

[1] There are a number of recognized types of definitions. I cannot here attempt to enumerate them all, or to indicate the sources for the classification of definitions and their use in logic and philosophy, but shall simply specify a few major types. An important work on definition is Richard Robinson's *Definition* (Oxford: Clarendon Press, 1972). Robinson divides definition (Ch. 2) into two basic types: the thing-thing, or real definition, and the nominal definition. He further divides the nominal definition into the word-word definition and the word-thing definition which in turn is divided into the lexical and the stipulative definitions. The same author enumerates (Ch. 1) eighteen species of definition, which he classifies according to various authors' usage. A more philosophically precise classification of definition is given by Raziel Abelson, who classifies definition in respect to the adopted philosophical position, into three types: the essentialist or "E-type," the prescriptive or "P-type," and the linguistic or "L-type." Abelson does not consider this classification as an historical one, but simply a "useful schema." See Raziel Abelson, "Definition," *Encyclopedia of Philosophy,* ed. Paul Edwards (New York: Macmillan, 1967), II, 314-324.

mind the general sense of the term *ta'rīf*, as well as its restricted sense. Let us consider an important statement by Suhrawardī in the *Philosophy of Illumination*, which is made following his criticism of the Peripatetic formula for essentialist definition *(ḥadd):*

> It has been made clear that it is impossible to obtain an [essentialist] definition in the way the Peripatetics do [i.e., using the formula, proximate genus plus differentiæ], which is a difficulty even their [the Peripatetics'] master [Aristotle] admits. Therefore we [the illuminationists] only make definitions *(ta'rīfāt)* by recourse to things which specify the totality of a thing *(al-ijtimā'*, i.e.,"organic whole").[1]

In all works on Islamic philosophy that I have examined so far, both *ḥadd* and *ta'rīf* are translated as definition. This is not a precise philosophical translation. I prefer to use essentialist definition for *ḥadd*, and to use definition, in its unrestricted general sense, for *ta'rīf*. It is the aim of what follows to make a precise distinction between these terms, as well as among others.

1.1. Illuminationist Division of Logic and Definition

Let us turn our attention to Suhrawardī's classification of the kinds of definition. I previously had an occasion to say something regarding Suhrawardī's bi-partite division of logic into expository propositions *(al-qawl al-shāriḥ*, pl. *al-aqwāl al-shāriḥa)* and proofs *(ḥujja*, pl. *ḥujaj)*. This division of logic may at first appear somewhat puzzling, but if we are to understand its structural significance and its intended use, we must attempt to recover the meanings of the terms "proof" and "expository proposition."[2]

[1] Suhrawardī, *Opera II*, p. 21.

[2] The term, expository proposition had been used by philosophers before Suhrawardī, but not in the same way. Avicenna, and subsequent to him al-Ghazālī, used it as an equivocal term for essentialist definition *(ḥadd bi-al-tashkīk)*. See Avicenna, *al-Najāt*, p. 83; al-Ghazālī, *Mi'yār al-'Ilm*, ed. S. Dunya (Cairo, 1961), pp. 68, 271-275. The first philosopher in the Islamic period to emphasize the use of the expository proposition as a means for structurally dividing logic into two parts was the Persian philosopher 'Umar ibn Sahlān al-Sāwī. Consider, for example, Sāwī's statement: "Conception may be obtained by the method *(rāh)* referred to by the Arabic term *al-qawl al-shāriḥ*. This means [in Persian] *guft-i rawshan-kunanda* (i.e. expository proposition). [You should know that] some expository propositions are valid, and are called essentialist definition;

In the course of this chapter, we will examine this problem and also attempt to unravel the significance of the usage of the terms in question. Simply stated, "proof" as used by Suhrawardī, covers elements of both material and formal logic, and includes demonstration as well as other types of inferences. "Proof" also applies to mystical experiences.[1] The term "expository proposition" is a more technical term. Its meaning is indicated by Suhrawardī in the logic of the *Paths and Havens:*

> Know that the expository propositions are five: complete essentialist definition *(al-ḥadd al-tāmm);* [conceptualist definition, or] making the thing named known by means of the parts of the complete concept *(ta'rīf al-musammā bi-ajzā' al-mafhūm al-tāmm);* [2] incomplete essentialist definition *(al-ḥadd al-nāqiṣ);* complete description *(al-rasm al-tāmm);* and incomplete description *(al-rasm al-nāqiṣ).*[3]

From this statement we can infer that the term, expository proposition, signifies technical varieties of definition, and is to be distinguished from the general usage of the concepts "defining something" and thus "making it known." The term is applied to specified formulæ of definition such as the complete essentialist definition, and to other types.

It appears that the classification of the five types of definition is Suhrawardī's own, as examined explicitly in the *Paths and Havens.* However, the types mentioned, with the exception of the conceptualist type, were considered before him, though not as systematically. For example, the

---

some are partially valid *(nazdīk bi rāstī),* and are called description *(rasm)* . . . The [main] intention of logic has been shown to be the obtaining of knowledge concerning 1- expository propositions and 2- proofs." *(Tabṣira,* pp. 4-5). Cf. Avicenna, *Manṭiq al-Mashriqiyyīn [Logic of the Easterners]* (Cairo, 1910), p. 10, where one may discern the same view intimated by Avicenna.

[1] Proof *(ḥujja)* is usually divided into three kinds: syllogism *(qiyās),* induction *(istiqrā'),* and analogy *(tamthīl,* and *mithāl).* See Sāwī, *Tabṣira,* p. 5. Suhrawardī stipulates further that the proofs based on experience, inspiration and intuition have the same, if not higher, rank as proofs based on the Peripatetic demonstration. See, for example, *Opera II,* p. 13.

[2] Elsewhere the conceptualist definition is stated to be: "The formula indicating the concept of the thing *(al-qawl al-mu'arraf bi-ḥasab mafhūm al-shay'). Paths and Havens:Logic,* fol 15v.

[3] Ibid., fol. 14r.

essentialist and the descriptive types are mentioned by Aristotle in various parts of his works.[1] The term *qawl,* to be translated "statement," "proposition," or "formula" (perhaps even in some places "definition"), even "argument," depending on the context, is the term used by the Peripatetics prior to Suhrawardī to denote the same meaning as *al-qawl al-shāriḥ.*[2]

The term, expository proposition, as the second "pillar" of logic, is used by Suhrawardī to denote the relation between conception and assent at the very outset of the study of logic. At the beginning of the logic of the *Paths and Havens,* i.e., the first *"Mashra',"* (Path), entitled "On the *Isagoge,"* Suhrawardī states:

> You have learnt from the books [of logic] that everything sought in science is either a conception or an assent, and that the expository propositions and proofs connect the two.[3]

In the corresponding section of the logic of the *Intimations,* Suhrawardī states:

> That which connects conception to its idea is called expository proposition, be it an essentialist definition or something else, and that which connects assent to its

[1] See, for example, *Posterior Analytics* II. 3, 7, 10; *Topics* VIII.

[2] The term *qawl* has a number of meanings, the most basic of which is "compound utterance." See Avicenna, *al-Najāt,* p. 17. Cf. Goichon, *Lexique,* p. 319. As in the Greek term λογός, it is used in many senses. As an example of the uses of the term λογός in Plato, see G. Matthews, *Plato's Epistemology and Related Logical Problems* (London: Faber and Faber, 1972), p. 11. A strict Aristotelian sense of the term λογός (to be also said of the term *qawl)* is "formula," which is specifically used in relation to definition, e.g. in Aristotle, *Metaphysics* VII.4, 1030a7-9: "there is a definition (ὁρισμός) not where a word means the same as a formula (λογός) for in that case all formulæ would be definitions." It seems evident to me that the sense "formula" for *qawl* is the logically meaningful one. For various other senses of the term *qawl,* see Avicenna, *Livre des Directives et Remarques,* tr. A.-M. Goichon (Paris: J. Vrin, 1951), pp. 84, 193, 211. The concept underlying the expression "expository proposition" *(al-qawl al-shāriḥ)* is probably, however, not of Aristotelian origin, but may be compared to the Stoic ὁ ἐκθετικός λόγος and ὁ προφορικὸς λόγος. Cf. Afnan, *Lexicon,* p. 245; and E. Zeller, *The Stoics, Epicureans, and Sceptics,* tr. O.J. Reichel (New York: Russell and Russell, 1962), p. 73, n. 2.

[3] *Paths and Havens:Logic,* fol. 1v.

idea is called proof, be it a demonstration or something else. Expository propositions and proofs together constitute the method of science *(ṭarīq al-'ulūm).* [1]

From the two statements above we can readily infer the methodological significance of expository propositions in philosophy. This is why it is so crucial that we understand Suhrawardī's own theory as a step in our attempt at understanding the philosophy of illumination. Suhrawardī explicitly opens his study of logic by stating that definition has a fundamental position in the conceptual framework of science. He devotes special chapters in the logic of the *Intimations* and in the logic of the *Paths and Havens* (Chapter II in each case) to the study of definition; and in the *Philosophy of Illumination* (Part One, I, 7), he stresses the further significance of definition in illuminationist methodology by way of his own critique of the Peripatetic theory.

1.2 Typology of Definitions

Equipped with the knowledge that the expository proposition is the genus, so to speak, of various species of definition, we shall now consider the species in order to determine what types of definition are used by Suhrawardī to define things, words, or concepts. This is to distinguish the realist, nominalist , and conceptualist characteristics of definitions.[2]

The important type of definition in the works of Plato and Aristotle, as well as in the works of later Peripatetics in the Islamic period, is the real definition. The essentialist complete and the incomplete, as mentioned by Suhrawardī, are both real definitions.[3] These two types have a more or less clear history that goes back to Aristotle, in whose writings, however, the distinction between the complete and the incomplete type is not specified.[4]

[1] *Intimations:Logic,* p. 2.

[2] For a discussion of the distinction between realist and nominalist definition, see Robinson, *Definition,* Ch.VI. The distinction is made by both Plato and Aristotle, though not in a restricted sense. See Plato, *Theætetus,* 514b-515c, 547c-549c; Aristotle, *Categories* V, 2a19-3b24; VI, 6b-8a; *Posterior Analytics* I.22, II.3-10.

[3] Both kinds are formulæ that are said to specify the essence of the thing defined.

[4] The distinction made between the complete essentialist definition, as a formula combining the proximate genus and the differentia, indicating the essence, and the incomplete essentialist definition, is that the latter only partially signifies the essence.

The two kinds are real, and, in terms of modern philosophical terminology, essentialist definitions.[1]

In the case of these two types of definition, there is general agreement as to their Aristotelian origin, but the complete and incomplete "descriptive" types are of somewhat uncertain historical origin. The eminent contemporary historian of Islamic philosophy, Ibrahim Madkour, and A.-M. Goichon both indicate that the origin for the descriptive definition is to be found in the Galenic ὑπογραφή.[2] These two types are also real definitions, but they are not essentialist. We may think of them as types of ostensive definition, since they are said to distinguish a thing from another.[3]

Suhrawardī's fifth type of definition is a type of conceptualist definition, and seems to be clearly distinguished as a separate type only in his works. This type is the "formula that makes something known by means of its concept."[4]

The above five types of definition—the complete and incomplete essentialist, the complete and incomplete descriptive, and the conceptualist—comprise the central part of Suhrawardī's theory of definition. They are not, however, the only kinds of definition mentioned in his works. Scattered throughout most of his works that deal with logic, one finds a

---

This distinction is made by Avicenna (e.g. *al-Najāt,* p. 78), but for Aristotle the essentialist definition is supposed to reveal the essential nature *(Posterior Analytics* II, 90b24) *only* when the attributes of the thing are finite *(Posterior Analytics* I, 82b39, 84a27). The question of finitude of attributes and the problem of definition is an important one for Suhrawardī also.

[1] See Abelson, "Definition," s.v. *Encyclopedia of Philosophy.*

[2] See Avicenna, *Livre des Définitions,* ed. and tr. A.-M.Goichon (Cairo: Publi-cations de L'Institut Français d'Archéologie Orientale du Caire, 1963), p. 6 n.1. Cf. Avicenna, *Kitāb al-Ḥudūd,* tr. Muhammad M. Fouladvand (Tehran: Iranian Centre for the Study of Civilizations: Islamic Studies Series, 2), pp.58, 69. Less restricted equivalents, perhaps περιγραφή and διαγραφή, should also be considered.

[3] Description is considered to be a kind of definition by means of which a thing is distinguished *(mutamayyiz),* hence a kind of ostensive definition. See Suhrawardī, *Paths and Havens:Logic,* fol.17r.; Avicenna, *al-Najāt,* p. 79; idem, *Livre des Définitions,* p. 12; al-Ghazālī, *Mi'yār al-'Ilm,* p. 267.

[4] *Paths and Havens:Logic,* fol 15r.

discussion of types of nominalist, ostensive, and implicit definitions, concerning which we shall have occasion to say something later.

2. Definition and the Methodology of Philosophy

In a celebrated passage in Book II of the *Posterior Analytics,* Aristotle stipulates the position of definition to be that of the first step in science.[1] Also, from a formal point of view, definition is regarded as the premise in demonstration.[2] Therefore, once a definition is obtained, or constructed, one may proceed to scientific knowledge. Philosophers in the Islamic period up to and including Suhrawardī all agree with the Aristotelian method of demonstration, or scientific method, as well as with the formal position of definition in demonstration.[3] There are, however, a number of problems associated with Suhrawardī's critique of the Peripatetic formula of definition. These include the following questions: What constitutes the epistemological and ontological foundations of definition? What types of definition are thought to be valid? What is the formula of definition itself? What is the relation between definition and demonstration, and between definition and induction?

Before dealing with the major concern here, which is to analyze Suhrawardī's critique of the Peripatetics and then discuss his own view of definition, we shall briefly examine the possible background for an illuminationist theory of definition, i.e. Plato's and Aristotle's theories. We will do this in order to explain Suhrawardī's views within a broader philosophical context. At times, Suhrawardī agrees with the Aritotelian

[1] Aristotle, *Posterior Analytics* II. 3, 90b1-24.

[2] Ibid., 90b24. On Aristotle's view regarding the relation between definition and demonstration, see *Posterior Analytics* I. 2, 72a19-24; I. 8; I.10; I. 22; I. 33. This problem is treated at length by Anfinn Stigen in his philosophical study, *The Structure of Aristotle's Thought* (Oslo: Universitetsforlaget, 1966), Ch. IV, where Stigen shows "why, according to Aristotle, the problem of definition is central to any discussion of science" (p. 78, n.2.).

[3] See Suhrawardī, *Opera II,* p. 40: "Only demonstrations are used in the real sciences." Cf.idem, *Paths and Havens:Logic,* fol 98r.; idem, *Intimations:Logic,* p. 82; and Avicenna, *Livre des Directives et Remarques,* p. 47; idem, *Livres des Définitions,* pp. 2-11; idem, *al-Shifā':al-Jadal,* VI, 5.

position concerning the fomulæ of definition, and on other occasions with the Platonist view. Further, he constructs an alternate formula relying on both.[1] As we examine this problem, we must keep in mind two specific questions. Does Suhrawardī *accept* the Aristotelian method of obtaining a definition, of observing the world of existent entities and thereby abstracting certain categories and so arriving at a genus plus a number of differentiæ—a definition which, though it may or may not be demonstrated, does have a position in demonstration?[2] Or, is Suhrawardī's own view of definition finally more Platonic, one which considers definition to be the result of an all-embracing and harmonious philosophical investigation? This investigation would encompass a dialectical method whereby the participants come to obtain images of the most real things, Forms or Ideas, in their souls. Such a Platonic position considers definition the final *result* of a process whereby a

[1] The basic "formal" method of definition used by Plato is usually referred to as the method of dichotomy (or division). This method is specifically considered by Plato in *Phædrus,* 134a-c; *Sophist,* 580a-608d; and *Philebus,* 610d-613a. Aristotle also considers the method of dichotomy, usually in contrast to other methods of definition. See Aristotle, *Prior Analytics* II, 64-65; idem, *Posterior Analytics* II.5, 13; idem, *Topics* VI.6, 143b11-144a4; idem *Metaphysics* VII.12, 1037b28-1038a35; idem *Parts of Animals* I.2-4. Plotinus also makes use of the method of division or dichotomy in definition. See Plotinus, *The Enneads,* tr. S. MacKenna (New York: Pantheon, 1969), I.3.4, where he states: ". . . it employs the Platonic division and the discernment of the Ideal Forms"; and also ibid., VI.3.8-10: "The division into elements must, in short, be abandoned, especially in regard to Sensible Substance, known necessarily by sense rather than by reason;" and see Ibid., VI.3.16-18. A comprehensive study of Plato's method of dichotomy is done by Kenneth M. Sayre, who refers to the method as "Collection and Division." See Sayre, *Plato's Analytic Method* (Chicago: University of Chicago Press, 1969), Ch. IV.

[2] The basic "formal" method of definition used by Aristotle is usually referred to as definition by means of genera and differentiæ, sometimes called properties or attributes, both essential and non-essential. This method is extensively used by Aristotle in most of his works. See Aristotle, *Categories* III, V, XIII; idem, *Prior Analytics* I, 27; Idem, *Posterior Analytics* I.22, II.13-14; idem, *Topics* I.4-9, I.18, IV-VII; idem, *Physics* I.3; idem, *Metaphysics* III.1, III.3, *V*.3, VII.4, VIII.3; idem, *History of Animals* I.1, idem, *Parts of Animals* I.1, I.2.4. The combination of the method of dichotomy and the method of definition by genera and differentiæ is a possible basis for Suhrawardī's theory, which involves what must be called the method of "self-midwifery," after Plato. See Plato, *Theætetus,* 150b-d. Cf. Plotinus, *Enneads,* VI.3.1, 8-10, 16-18.

"teacher" plays a role in an individual's obtaining a totally personal (certainly *not* formally presentable) knowledge. Such alternate methodological positions should be considered first as we attempt to recover the intended meanings in some of the admittedly obscure passages in the works of Suhrawardī, and to formulate his illuminationist theory of definition.

2.1 The Methodology of Definition and its Position in Metaphysics

The methodology of definition should be considered as one of the basic components of a philosophical approach to the problem of metaphysics. It determines whether the approach is one of realism, idealism, nominalism, etc., by enabling the historian of philosophy to consider the way in which the philosopher under examination had used definition in his approach to metaphysics. Philosophy deals, among other things, with the question "what." The answer to this question, formulated as a definition, involves careful examination of both methodology and philosophical principles. For example, the answer to the question, "what is man?" when formulated as "rational animal" on the one hand, and as "self-conscious, self-subsistent ipseity," on the other, determines the philosophical position about what constitutes the foundation of metaphysics, to say nothing of the psychological principles involved. Just as a logicist "definition" of "what is number" reflects a fundamentally different view of the foundation of mathematics than does the intuitionist definition of number, so, too, illuminationist theory of definition reveals a different philosophical position than that of the Peripatetics.

Apart from questions pertaining to the epistemological foundation of definition in philosophy, we must consider how definition itself is to be formulated. Assume that we want to define a thing, X. This thing, we further assume, must be constituted in relation to its attributes, both essential and non-essential, concomitants, accidents, etc. Let us call all of them the constituents of X, and take them to be x_i. If the thing is simple, non-composite *(basīṭ)*, then X and x_i are one and the same.(The definition of simple things are a special case and will be discussed later.) We must attempt to clarify the philosophical position, in the case when the constituents of the thing are many, by deciding whether x_i are real or only ideally known, and how they may be known in relation to X. We have to decide further if the essential constituents of X, say x_j, are discrete, or continuous, in themselves or as part of X. Are x_i and x_j knowable in themselves, separately as well as a whole? Can x_i and x_j be exhaustively enumerated? What happens when x_i and x_j are not distinct from X, yet X is not simple? We must further indicate the nature of the inclusion *(indikhāl)* of x_i in X. Is the inclusion such that x_i are *not* distinguishable from X and are *not* ordered in it (this type of inclusion is called , *istighrāq)*; or such that x_i *are* distinguished from X, but *not* ordered in it (this type is called *shumūl)*; or yet, such that x_i *are* distinguishable in X and *are* ordered in it (this type is called *indirāj)*? Such questions are to be asked as necessary steps in determining just what position Suhrawardī takes in the *Grundlage* of the philosophy of illumination.

The next question pertinent in our examination of definition is that of priority *(taqaddum)*. Things are defined in relation to others that must be known prior to them for the definition to be more than a change of phrase *(tabdīl al-lafẓ*, in Suhrawardī's terms). That is, in order to define X we must be able to know a Y, itself consisting of y_i constituents, in relation to which X may be defined. And Y must be necessarily prior to X in respect to knowledge. Once again our philosophical position must be called upon since, depending on our view, Y may or may not be considered knowable if deductively, intuitively, or innately knowable, or in another way. Also, as with X, the question whether Y can be known through y_i will also have to be examined. Therefore, the definition of X will depend on the philosophical position concerning what is prior in knowledge, and most prior at that. What is the thing most prior in terms of knowledge for Suhrawardī? Is it a self-evident primary axiom, or some other evident thing? These questions will have to be fully examined if we are to understand illuminationist philosophy and Suhrawardī's philosophical position.

2.2 Two Approaches to Definition: Platonic and Aristotelian

The two main, well-formulated and well-documented philosophical methods known in the medieval Islamic period were the Platonic and the Aristotelian. (The Neoplatonist, though most influential in the development of philosophy in that period, was not as well-formulated.) The difference between the Platonic and the Aristotelian methods concerning the question of definition is best exemplified in the famous work of Alfarabi, *Harmonization of the Opinions of Plato and Aristotle,* where (§16) Alfarabi discusses the view of both Plato and Aristotle:

> Plato held the opinion that the only way to construct a true definition is by the method of division (dichotomy) *(qisma),* while Aristotle held the opinion that such a definition could only be obtained by the method of demonstration and synthesis *(tarkīb).* [1]

Alfarabi subsequently states emphatically that the two prevalent philosophical views do not disagree in principle, but only in approach. This characterization should be kept in mind as we evaluate Suhrawardī's position. We shall attempt also to determine how Suhrawardī viewed his own position in relation to that of Plato and Aristotle, and how he incorporated his own in the overall reconstructed illuminationist system.

What is quite certain is that when we define something, in the strict Aristotelian sense, we aim to know its essence (τί ἦν εἶναι), substance (οὐσία), and essential nature (τὸ τί ἐστι).[2] Thus the Aristotelian formula for definition cannot be separated from the ontological view held by the philosopher at the outset, prior to the act of constructing a definition by whatever method. Plato's view, on the other hand, regards definition both as an integral component of the method of philosophy *and* its end result.[3] Through dialectical means encompassing the method of synthesis and dichotomy (collection and division)[4] Plato aims to obtain an answer to the

[1] Alfarabi, *Kitāb al-Jam' bayn Ra'yay al-Ḥakīmayn [Harmonization of the Opinions of Plato and Aristotle],* ed. A.N. Nader (Beirut: Dar El-Machreq, 1968), pp. 87-88. Alfarabi's position is that the method of dichotomy (or division) and the method of demonstration and synthesis in definition are complementary.

[2] See A. Stigen, *The Structure of Aristotle's Thought,* pp. 138-139.

[3] The "Platonic definition" consists of the "formal" method of dichotomy plus the overall dialectical process such that the two methods are utilized in a dialogue together to recover the "definitions" of what is truly real, the timeless unchanging Forms which, if and when recovered, mark the culmination and the highest achievement of philosophy. See Sayre, *Plato's Analytic Method,* Ch. II, IV; Matthews, *Plato's Epistemology,* pp. 13-39.

[4] See above, §2

questions, "What is justice?" and "What is imitation?" (in the *Republic),* "What is courage?" (in the *Laches),* "What is knowledge?" and "What is logos?" (in the *Theætetus).*[1] The answers to these questions must be given as real definitions. The Platonic method employed is quite different from the Aristotelian real definition (the ὅρος and ὁρισμός) of the *Posterior Analytics, Topics, Metaphysics,* and *Parts of Animals.* The most fundamental difference between the two, in my view, is that the Aristotelian formula for definition is independent (at least formally) from the person who constructs it, while the Platonic method ultimately relies totally on the personal response of the individual, in the way in which he may come to realize in himself the Form of what is to be known. This distinction is a crucial one in our understanding of Suhrawardī. In light of this, we should be aware of the question concerning what part of Suhrawardī's theory of definition is the formal Aristotelian and what part the Platonic. In what way are the two methods synthesized into a coherent theory of illumination *(ishrāq).* In other words, what is the relation between the method of pure discourse and investigation *(baḥth)* and the method of intuition *(dhawq)?*

In addition, in terms of an illuminationist methodology of definition, we should consider the question: Is Suhrawardī's theory a combination of the Aristotelian formal method of definition and Platonic dialectic, or is Suhrawardī's theory essentially a "new" one?

Equipped with such questions, we shall now embark on the task of analyzing the illuminationist theory of definition. The first step shall be to present a short account of the theories of definition of both Plato and Aristotle.

2.3 Plato's Method of Definition Examined

The Aristotelian view of the Socratic definition may be summed up by saying that there are only two things which may justly be credited to Socrates: inductive argument and general definition.[2] However, according

[1] Cf. Robinson, *Definition,* p. 149.

[2] Aristotle, *Metaphysics* XII. 1078b27-30: "It is just to give credit to Socrates for two things, inductive arguments and defining universally; and both these are concerned

to the historian of Greek philosophy, W.K.C. Guthrie, Socrates had no adequate notion of essence, nor of how to define the real being of anything, and thus the comprehension of essence through definition is a methodological advance by Aristotle.[1]

The Socratic method of definition is sometimes called "persuasive definition," because it is a definition in which the author, instead of only attempting to clarify the usage of a word or concept, and so prevent misunderstanding, does in fact argue for that meaning which he himself approves. He believes this meaning to be the one which, when adopted, will lead the novice towards the right course of action.[2] This simply means that the philosopher himself has an "experience," or some other kind of first-hand knowledge of the thing, accepts its validity, and goes on to help induce it in the novice, i.e., the philosopher's intuition and "taste" for things determines his position vis-à-vis knowledge as well as method. To define something in this sense means that the person is attempting to convey, depending on the method, through formal means, dialectical means, gestures and intimations, his personal experiential understanding of a certain phenomenon, which could also be the result of "joint deliberation among several people for the purpose of arriving at a definition."[3] This is to be compared to Suhrawardī's own insistence of the significance of oral discourse in the "study" of illuminationist philosophy.[4]

From a strictly theoretical point of view, Plato continues to search for the Form of what is being investigated. In the dialogues, the search for the definition of a thing is intimately related to the theory of Forms, which states that there are eternal, unchanging Forms, which are the true objects of knowledge, while the many changing, perceptible particulars cannot be

---

with principles of science." Cf. Ibid., I.987a20-30; and W.K.C. Guthrie, *A History of Greek Philosophy* (Cambridge: Cambridge University Press, 1969), III, 425ff.

[1]Guthrie, *A History of Greek Philosophy*, III, 426.

[2] Ibid., p. 437

[3] Ibid., p. 440.

[4] See Suhrawardī, *Opera I*, p. 401; idem, *Paths and Havens:Logic*, fol. 15v.

known or defined independently.[1] And according to the so-called "Socratic fallacy," we cannot know a thing unless we can define it.[2]

In Platonic methodology, to "know" a thing, or to be able to "define" it, is seen from two points of view. The first is called the "recognitional sense." Laches, for example, will recognize and come to know courage when he meets it.[3] The reason why Laches recognizes courage is that he has in himself its Form. To anticipate Suhrawardī, the Form is innately *(bi'l-fiṭra)* in Laches. In the second sense, Plato is defining things through the method of dichotomy and synthesis, or division and collection as in Theætetus' definition of irrationals.[4] Plato, however, does not say that knowledge itself is so defineable, and the controversy as to whether he held that knowledge is or is not *identical* with true belief is well known and need not concern us here.[5] What *is* important, is that for Plato, definition is a "communion of Forms,"[6] and so, as in Suhrawardī's view, involves something more than a formal construction.

As clearly stated in the *Theætetus*, the problem is not being satisfied with anything less than knowledge as basis for knowledge.[7] It is clear that such requirements are not so evident in the Aristotelian formula,which is criticized by Suhrawardī.[8] But Plato, through a method of hypothesis, dichotomy and synthesis, which are integral components of his over-all

[1] See Matthews, *Plato's Epistemology*, p. 13.

[2] See Guthrie, A *History of Greek Philosophy*, IV, 242.

[3] Ibid., p. 243. The notion of a subject recognizing or "seeing" an object, hence knowing it, is also one of Suhrawardī's principle epistemological notions. See below, §3.5.

[4] See Matthews, *Plato's Epistemology*, p. 19; Sayre, *Plato's Analytic Method*, Ch. II, §11, Ch. III.

[5] See Matthews, *Plato's Epistemology*, pp. 12-29; Sayre, *Plato's Analytic Method*, Ch. II.

[6] See Matthews, *Plato's Epistemology*, p. 19: "If Plato accepted the thesis that knowledge is identical with true belief together with an account, then it seems advisable to look to the *Sophist*, and also to the *Politics* and *Philebus*, for further thoughts of definition and the communion of Forms."

[7] See Matthews, Ibid., pp. 136-211.

[8] See Suhrawardī, *Opera II*, pp. 20-21.

method,[1] arrives at a λὸγος, or definition, by formulating the conditions that are both necessary and sufficient for some kind of knowledge of the thing. This method provides us with a *means* of distinguishing belief from knowledge. In this overall method, along with the theoretical and somewhat formal process presented dialectically in the literary form of a dialogue, the role of psychological "midwifery" of the *Symposium* and the *Theætetus* should be stressed: together, they serve to bring about a definition.[2] In general, and we stress this point once again, many of Plato's dialogues take the unified form of a search for definition.[3]

According to Aristotle, Plato's preoccupation with definition is derived from the Socratic attempt to define ethical terms.[4] Also, the fact that Plato was impressed by the importance of definition in mathematics may provide us with a clue to some of the formal aspects of Suhrawardī's theory. For Plato definition could not be arbitrary and had to be informative. The corollary to this is that there does exist a right and a wrong answer to the questions, "What is justice?" and "What is knowledge?," and the correctness of the answer does not depend on how the *words* justice or knowledge would have been used by the Greeks. The equivalent of a word-thing relationship was considered arbitrary or conventional, and definition

[1] See Sayre, *Plato's Analytic Method,* Ch. IV; Matthews, *Plato's Epistemology,* pp. 36-40.

[2] E.g., Plato, *Theætetus,* 202b-c:"But in fact there is no formula in which any element can be expressed; it can only be named, for a name is all there is that belongs to it. But when we come to things composed of these elements, then, just as those things are complex, so the names are combined to make a description (the term here is also λόγος), a description being precisely a combination of names." Cf. R. Robinson, *Plato's Earlier Dialectic* (Oxford: Clarendon Press, 1970), pp. 1-49; Sayre, *Plato's Analytic Method,* pp. 230-238.

[3] Cf. W. Kneale and M. Kneale, *The Development of Logic,* pp. 21, 22.

[4] See Aristotle, *Metaphysics* I, 987b1-10: "Now Socrates was engaged in the study of ethical matters, but not at all in the study of nature as a whole, yet in ethical matters he sought the universal and was the first to fix his *thought* on definitions. Plato, on the other hand, taking into account the *thought* of Socrates, came to the belief that, because sensible things are always in a state of flux, such inquiries were concerned with other things and not with the sensibles; for there can be no common definition of sensible things when these are always changing. He called things of this sort Ideas and believed that sensible things exist apart from Ideas and are named according to Ideas."

in general was concerned with the thing to which the word refers rather than to the word itself.[1] Concerning the problem in the Platonic dialogues, W. and M. Kneale state: "What is defined is the Form or common nature present in many particular things."[2] Now such a view of definition is called "realist" and is historically connected to the phrase, "real definition" which had clearly influenced Aristotle, as seen in his account of definition and in his thinking in respect to logic in general. This is so in spite of the fact that he rejected the Platonic theory of Forms, as W. and M. Kneale state:

> Because of his [Aristotle's] Platonic training he expected to find as the ultimate object of intellect and the foundation of valid inference a system or chain of Forms whose interrelationships limit the possibilities of actual existence and determine the correctness or incorectness of scientific thought.[3]

It is quite clear, that like Plato, Aristotle also tried only to look at the thing and not at the word.

2.4 Aristotle's Method of Definition Examined

It should be clear by now that, for Plato, definition is an integral part of the problem of knowledge, a complex subject, and crucial to every aspect of inquiry. Aristotle summed up the problem of definition in a salient statement of the *Posterior Analytics:* "All sciences come into being through definition."[4]

As we look into Aristotle's discussion of definition, we are led to consider first his view of the history of the subject. According to Aristotle, the first to regard science as a problem of definition were the Pythagoreans, Democritus, and Socrates.[5] Socrates considered the problem of definition

[1] See Robinson, *Plato's Earlier Dialectic*, pp. 49ff; Robinson, *Definition*, pp. 12-27.

[2] Kneale and Kneale, *Development of Logic*, p. 21.

[3] Ibid.

[4] See Aristotle, *Posterior Analytics* II.17, 99a22-23. Cf. Stigen, *The Structure of Aristotle's Thought*, p. 78.

[5] See Aristotle, *Metaphysics* XIII.4, 1078b11-13: "Now Socrates occupied himself with the moral virtues, and in connection with these he was the first to seek universal definitions. For, of the physicists only Democritus touched upon the subject of definition

and its relation to inductive argument, but he was not, we are told by Aristotle, concerned with physical inquiry into things to be defined.[1]

According to Aristotle, Plato followed Socrates, and his definitions were not concerned with sensible things but with things of another kind, separate entities that are eternal and not subject to change (these things were called by him Ideas)—indeed, for him it is impossible to define sensible things.[2] In his critique of Plato, Aristotle goes on to state that Plato confused the problem of universal definition by introducing the Ideas, since every name would have to apply to two different things, the changing entities and the changeless Ideas, or Forms. The same names are now applied equivocally and could no longer be of any use in scientific discussions.[3]

Plato found a way of looking at reality on the basis of separate entities which were called Ideas, basically due to his view that knowledge of sensible, changing things is not possible, and for him definitions ultimately implied the Ideas. For Plato, science does not deal with sensible things; rather, as for Democritus before him, mathematics constitutes the ground for knowledge. For Aristotle, on the other hand, the sensible nature had also to be accounted for.[4] While Plato sought the principles and courses of things in the Forms, Aristotle concluded his investigation of physical entities in his portrayal of causes and definitions. Plato arrived at the Forms by speculating about the notion of knowledge itself and not the nature of things, and thus he allowed the principles of knowledge to determine the principle of things.(To anticipate Suhrawardī, the principles of knowledge

---

a little, and in some way he defined the hot and the cold; while the Pythagoreans before him considered definitions of a few things."

[1] See Aristotle, *Metaphysics* I.6, 987b1-4. See also above, §2.3. Cf. Stigen, *The Structure of Aristotle's Thought*, pp. 82-86.

[2] See Aristotle, *Metaphysics* I.6, 987b4-8: "But Socrates did not posit the universals as separate, nor the definitions. These thinkers [Socrates, Democritus, and the Pythagoreans], however, regarded them as being about other things, and called such things Ideas." Cf. Ibid., XIII.4, 1078b30-38.

[3] See Aristotle, *Metaphysics* XIII.4, 1078b30-1079a4.

[4] See Aristotle, *Metaphysics* IX.8, 1050b34-1051a2. Cf. Stigen, *The Structure of Aristotle's Thought*, pp. 78-103.

may be directly known as a result of a process called illumination. These principles then serve as the foundation for subsequent philosophical investigation and construction.)[1]

It should be emphasized that, in light of the above discussion, no Platonic theory of definition can be seen as distinct from the dialectical method of the dialogue. The Aristotelian theory of definition, on the other hand, can be incorporated into a number of formal rules, albeit rules not systematically developed by Aristotle in any one place in his works.[2]

I will only be concerned here with presenting a brief account of some of the salient features of Aristotle's theory. I aim to explain that part of the theory which is criticized by Suhrawardī, to consider the Aristotelian definition from an overall point of view, and also to discuss specifically its formulæ.

In Book II of the *Posterior Analytics,* Aristotle states his intention to discuss a theory of definition:

> Let us now state how essential nature is revealed and in what way it can be reduced to demonstration; what definition is and what things are defineable.[3]

Aristotle continues his discussion and raises questions concerning definition and its relation to demonstration.[4] The answer, given immediately, is that not every thing which is demonstrable is definable, but the premises of demonstrations themselves are definitions which may, in turn, be either indemonstrable primary truths or themselves demonstrations based on prior premises.[5] The point that needs to be stressed, therefore, is that any kind of

[1] See below, Ch. IV, §3.

[2] Though not systematically treated by Aristotle, a theory of definition is mentioned in the following: *Posterior Analytics* II. 3-10, 13; *Topics* VI-VII; *Metaphysics* VII.4-6, 10-17, VIII.2-3,6; *Parts of Animals* I.2-4.

[3] See Aristotle, *Posterior Analytics* II.2, 90a35.

[4] See Aristotle, *Posterior Analytics* II.3, 90b1-3.

[5] See Aristotle, *Posterior Analytics* II.3, 90b10-27. Cf. idem, *Posterior Analytics* II.4, 91a5-12: "So it emerges that not all the definable are demonstrable nor all the demonstrable definable; and we may draw the general conclusion that there is no identical object of which it is possible to possess both a definition and a demonstration. It follows obviously that definition and demonstration are neither identical nor contained either

definition, if it is to be scientific, has to depend on some knowledge which is prior to it, and the impression one gets from Aristotle here (in the *Posterior Analytics)* is that the most prior things in respect to knowledge are primary truths.

The importance of definition in philosophy is one of the main results of Chapter 4 of Book VII of the *Metaphysics,* where Aristotle states: "Thus there is an essence only of those things whose formulæ is a definition."[1]

Definition, therefore, determines what things science can treat, and it is the real definition which is the type so used. There are two basic types of definition that Aristotle talks about, the real and the nominal. The real is the most important; it is the type which is the object of Suhrawardī's critique, and we shall examine it fully shortly. The nominal definition is thought to have no value in science.[2] In the words of Aristotle, real definition may specify one of three things: essential nature,[3] substance,[4] or essence.[5] (There is one place where Aristotle states the relation between definition and both substance and essence.[6])

There are a number of formulæ for definition in the works of Aristotle, of which the most important is clearly the definition by genus and differentiæ. The most significant aspect of this formula is the manner in which the genus and differentia are said to signify the unity of the essence. This question, referred to as the "unity" of definition, is taken up by

---

within the other: if they were, their objects would be related either as identical or as whole and part."

[1] See Aristotle, *Metaphysics* VII.4, 1030a5.

[2] See Aristotle, *Posterior Analytics* II.9, 93b29-31.

[3] See Aristotle, *Posterior Analytics* II.9, 93b29; II.11, 94a11-17; II.7, 92b26.

[4] Ibid., 90b16; idem, *Topics* V.3, 130b25-26, VI.3, 140a34.

[5] See Aristotle, *Metaphysics* VII.5, 1031a11-12; idem, *Topics* I.2, 101b38; VII.5, 154a31-32.

[6] See Aristotle, *Posterior Analytics* II.3, 90b30-31, idem, *Metaphysics* IV.8, 1017b21-22, VII.1, 1042a17. In some cases Aristotle combines the term λόγος with οὐσία into λόγος τῆς οὐσίας, or with τὸ τί ἦν εἶναι into λόγος τοῦ τί ἦν εἶναι (Cf., e.g., idem, *Metaphysics* VII.4, 1029b20), or with τὸ τί ἐστι into λόγος τοῦ τί ἐστι (Cf., e.g., idem, *Posterior Analytics* II.10, 93b29). See also, Stigen, *The Structure of Aristotle's Thought,* p. 138.

Aristotle in the *Metaphysics,*[1] and is the most important aspect of Suhrawardī's critique. The question of the unity of definition touches upon the very foundation of philosophy, in relation to which differences between the Platonic methodology and the Aristotelian may be determined. For Plato, true philosophical inquiry must somehow involve the whole of philosophy, and only the whole may be called one. For example, any discussion of parts of the human body rests ultimately upon discussion of universal principles. This view may lead one to think that science is not possible. Aristotle's criticism here is based on distinguishing clearly between what is one in number and what is one in formula.[2] Such a distinction involves a careful examination of the universal and the particular. The relation between one and the whole, and the questions of what is one in number and what is one in formula, should be kept in mind as a possible basis for Suhrawardī's critique of the Aristotelian formula. What is one in formula can be found in many existent things, and what is one in number can be divided into what is many in formula, but that which is one in number—the individually existing thing—cannot be the subject of science.[3] Aristotle's solution to this problem is to combine what is one in number with what is one in form into a single formula, which he designates definition.[4] This corresponds to what is called "real definition."[5] The Aristotelian definition, which is one in form and one in number, becomes a unitary formula that signifies characteristics of things that may be known, and thus stated in science, which are either the thing's essence, essential nature, or substance.[6] The formula itself is one which brings together the genus and the differentiæ of the thing.[7]

[1] See Aristotle, *Metaphysics* VI.4, 1027b17-1028a6.

[2] See Aristotle, *Metaphysics* XIII.1, 1087b9-12. Cf. Stigen, *The Structure of Aristotle's Thought,* pp. 133-135.

[3] See Aristotle, *Metaphysics* XIII.8, 1084b2-23.

[4] Ibid., VII.4, 1030a7-11.

[5] See Aristotle, *Posterior Analytics* II.7, 92b26-34; II.10, 93b29-37; idem, *Metaphysics* VIII.6, 1045a17-25; VII.4, 1030b7-13.

[6] See Aristotle, *Metaphysics* IX.1, 1087b9-12; VII.15, 1039b20-1040a7; XIII.8, 1084b2-23. Cf. Ibid., VII.4, 1030a7-11: "Thus, there is an essence only of those things whose formula is a definition. However, there is a definition, not if a name and its

3. Suhrawardī's Theory of Definition: First Part of the Cycle

We have so far specified two approaches to the problem of definition, the Platonic and the Aristotelian, and we have mentioned that both were known by philosophers in the Islamic period. It should be further stated that the two approaches do have elements in common, that certain characteristics of the Platonic approach can be discerned in the Aristotelian, and certain Aristotelian components can be "read into" the Platonic approach (especially later in history, e.g. in medieval Islamic philosophy). The Platonic approach to definition seeks the unity of the thing defined in its Form, which though partially perceptible and definable in the multiple, is only fully defined by and in the person's ipseity as he realizes it in his own self-consciousness. There is no attempt to form a definition that would convey knowledge of multiplicity. The Aristotelian approach to definition seeks to formulate the multiple in a way adequately representative of the definiendum, and the unity is expressed in the formula; for example, the genus is a unity, and the genus plus the differentiæ is also a unity. We assume, without delving into an elaborate historical survey, that Suhrawardī was aware of the two approaches to this problem. It is in light of both theories that his own illuminationist theory and methodology, as well as his specific critique, should be examined.

It has been made clear above that, when examining a theory of definition, the most important considerations are: how the definition is obtained; if the definition is a formula, how the multiple elements, or constituents are combined so as to signify the unity of the thing defined; when obtained, what kind of truth value the definition has; and finally, the quality of the definition. Aristotle addressed himself to all of these throughout his writings, but as noted above, not systematically in any single work. The development of a systematic theory of definition was taken up by philosophers in the Islamic period.

---

formula merely have the same meaning (for then all formulæ will be definitions, since there can be a name having the same meaning as any given formula, and so even the Iliad would be a definition), but if the name and its formula signify something primary."

[7] See Aristotle, *Posterior Analytics* I.22, II.13-14; idem, *Topics* I.4-9, IV-VII.

Avicenna, in his main philosophical work, *al-Shifā'* (the *Healing*), divides the theoretical discussion of definition into two divisions, each of which is the characteristic component of one of the books of the *Organon*. The first division is characteristic of the *Posterior Analytics*, and is a study of basically two things: 1-how the definition is composed *(ta' līf al-ḥadd)*, and 2- how it is obtained *(iktisāb al-ḥadd)*. The second division is characteristic of the *Topics (al-Jadal* in *al-Shifā')*, and is a study of whether the definition obtained and composed according to the rules set down in the *Posterior Analytics* has indeed been so obtained and, if so, whether the conditions truly apply to the relation between the thing and the abstracted definition.[1] These divisions will serve as a helpful guide as we examine Suhrawardī's theory of definition, and will aid us to determine what characteristic component of the Aristotelian theory Suhrawardī criticizes.

I indicated in the previous chapter that Suhrawardī's overall and comprehensive view of logic is not totally different from that of the Peripatetics (though he does make changes in the traditional structure of logic as presented in the *Organon*), and certainly not in prime opposition to it. I also indicated that Suhrawardī's treatment of logic in the *Intimations*, the *Paths and Havens*, and the *Philosophy of Illumination*, differs in each work in terms of emphasis and terminology. In effect, the overall nature and content of Suhrawardī's logic is such that we can only indicate a designated "illuminationist logic," which is more a structural change than a conceptual one. The new structure is such that, unlike in the *Organon*, subjects pertaining to semiotics and to formal and material logic are treated in separate parts of illuminationist works on logic. However, there are also formal and other changes made by Suhrawardī in logic. He does isolate a number of problems, and attempts to define "new" rules governing them.[2] The nature of this attempt at refinement of certain parts of Peripatetic logic is characterized by Suhrawardī's intention to generalize formal rules. For example, we saw that Suhrawardī was concerned with formulating a

[1] Avicenna, *The Healing:Logic*, VI.4.1, p. 241: *al-ḥudūd qad nanẓur min amrihā fī annahā kayf tu'allaf wa kayf tuktasab . . . wa al-naẓar al-awwal fī kayfiyyat ījād al-ḥadd wa al-thānī fī kayf i'tibār al-ḥadd al-mawjūd.*

generalized form of the first figure of syllogism that would apply to the second and third as well.[1] He also was interested in defining a single form of a temporal modality in propositions, the iterated modality, that would serve as the form to which all others could be reduced.[2]

Of all the problems of logic which are of special significance for Suhrawardī, formal as well as material, conceptual *(taṣawwurī)* as well as pertaining to assent *(taṣdīqī)*, the most important is the problem of definition. Its significance lies not only in the problem itself, which, as noted above, determines the methodological position of the philosopher, but also in the manner in which Suhrawardī refutes the Peripatetic formula. And this centers on a special illuminationist view of the relation between the unity of essence and the multiplicity of a thing's essential attributes.

Since as the problem of definition is a central problem of knowledge, Suhrawardī's critique of the Peripatetic formula of definition, coupled with his own view, is a most significant methodological first step in illuminationist philosophy. Understanding Suhrawardī's theory of definition will also be the first major step in answering the question, "What is the philosophy of illumination?" In what follows, therefore, we shall examine Suhrawardī's view of the problem and attempt to ascertain if it points to a philosophical position in opposition to the Peripatetic's or complementary to it.

3.1 The *Intimations*

In the previous chapter I indicated that Suhrawardī deals with definition in a separate chapter in his works on logic, usually the second chapter, directly after his chapter on semantics; this corresponds to the traditional subject of the *Isagoge*. The "second chapter" of Suhrawardī's logical works is given the title,"On the expository proposition." The subject of this chapter combines parts of the *Posterior Analytics* with parts of the *Topics* pertaining to definition, which means that Suhrawardī deals with both the

---

[2] The intention of many post-Avicennan philosophers in compiling a "new" philosophy can be also exemplified by Ibn Kammūna's *al-Jadīd fi' l-Ḥikma*.

[1] See Suhrawardī, *Opera II*, pp. 36-39.

[2] Suhrawardī's iterated modal proposition takes on the form of "It is always necessary that."

composition, or coming into being (*ījād*, i.e.*ta'līf* plus *iktisāb*) of definitions as well as with conditions governing their use.

In the second chapter of the logic of the *Intimations*, Suhrawardī deals with definition in three sections.[1] The first section is devoted to a discussion of essentialist definition, the second to description, and the third to the errors concerning both the construction and usage of definition.

In the first section, Suhrawardī distinguishes two types of essentialist definition, the complete and the incomplete. The complete one is defined as:

> A formula (*qawl*) which indicates the essence of the thing and combines (*yajma'*) all of its constituent elements (*muqawwimāt*). In the case of the principle realities, it [the formula] is a synthesis (*tarkīb*) of their genera and differentiæ.[2]

This formula, though in conformity with the strict Aristotelian and with the later Peripatetic, has features which are seemingly Suhrawardī's own. These features can be best brought to the reader's attention by comparing them to Avicenna's formula. In the *Book of Definitions*, Avicenna states that, in accordance with what Aristotle has stated in the *Topics*, definition is:

> A formula which indicates the essence of the thing, i.e., the perfection of its essential being. This formula is obtained (*yataḥaṣṣal*) by [combining] the proximate genus and the differentia.[3]

This formula is the same as the one given in other Peripatetic works, and so may serve as an adequate basis for comparison with Suhrawardī's formula. There are two marked differences between the two formulæ. The first is that Suhrawardī requires that *all* of the constituents of a thing must be combined in the formula, a requirement not specified by the Peripatetic formula. (Any type of combination of elements that combines all of them must do so by a complete and exhaustive enumeration, or by some other way that will specify all.[4]) The second difference is that Suhrawardī's

[1] Suhrawardī, *Intimations:Logic*, p.14

[2] Ibid.

[3]See Avicenna, *Livre des Définitions*, §18. Cf. Avicenna, the *Healing:Logic:-Demonstration*, pp. 233-237.

[4] We may assume that an aspect of Suhrawardī's theory of definition is related to his critique of induction. He makes a distinction between complete and incomplete induction

formula insists on a method of synthesis *(tarkīb)* as a means for obtaining the unity of the definition through the multiple genera and differentiæ. This point, though mentioned by Avicenna in *al-Shifā' :al-Manṭiq:al-Burhān* (the *Healing:Logic:On Demonstration),* is not explicitly required by him in the formula.[1] The term, synthesis, is applied to composite real things, the only things for which there can be real definition, we are told by Suhrawardī.[2] The immediate corollary is that one cannot, strictly speaking, define substance, nor can one discretely enumerate all the essentials of a thing and thereby "define" it, which indicates that one cannot "know" anything without an *a priori* illuminationist basis for knowledge.

The next overall characteristic of this section of chapter two is Suhrawardī's distinction between real and nominal definitions. This distinction, as noted, is made by the Peripatetics, and goes back to Aristotle himself.[3] In no other work, with the exception of Avicenna's *Manṭiq al-Mashriqiyyin [Logic of the Easterners],*[4] is the distinction made so systematically, or in part of an independent chapter.

Suhrawardī starts his discussion of nominal and real definitions by stating that a single utterance, a word, is not an essentialist definition. The word "man," for example, is not a definition for the thing man. The incomplete essentialist definition is said to be composed of the *summum genus (al-jins al-ba'īd)* and a differentia, such as "rational substance."[5] However, Suhrawardī argues that such a definition is not valid because it seeks only to distinguish *(tamyīz)* the thing defined. This means that, for him, all such types of definition are ultimately a variety of the "ostensive." The real intention of definition, he further argues, is the conception of the

---

(al-istiqrā' al-tāmm wa'l-nāqiṣ). E.g., *Opera III,* p. 5. See William Kneale, *Probability and Induction* (Oxford: Clarendon Press, 1966), pp. 24-110.

[1] Avicenna, *al-Shifā' :al-Manṭiq: al-Burhān.* IV.4, 217-224

[2] See *Intimations:Logic,* p. 14: *mā lā tarkīb fīhi lā qawl dāll 'alayhi.*

[3] See Aristotle, *Posterior Analytics* I.22.

[4] See Avicenna, *Manṭiq al-Mashriqīyyin,* p. 34: "The thing which is called definition is either according to the name or according to the essence." Cf. idem, *al-Shifā' :al-Manṭiq:al-Burhān,* p. 217: "Among definition, some are real and according to essence, but some are metaphorical *(majāzī,)* and according to name (i.e., nominal)."

[5] Suhrawardī, *Intimations:Logic,* pp.14-15.

"core" of the thing, from which it will necessarily follow that the thing be distinguished as such.[1] The question to be raised at this point, a question which anticipates Suhrawardī's overall critique of definition as well as his specific arguments in the *Philosophy of Illumination* against the Peripatetic formula, is whether Suhrawardī regards any kind of formula of definition capable of providing knowledge of a thing. The answer, based on the logic of the *Intimations,* is that a complete essentialist definition that can combine *all* of the essentials does have truth-value, but no other definition does. Can there be such a formula? There is also the possibility, as Suhrawardī here intimates, that obtaining the unity of a definition through the multiple essentials is not possible through a formula, but that it may be acquired through a special mode of cognition pertaining specifically to the philosophy of illumination.

In Chapter II, §2, Suhrawardī discusses two kinds of description, complete and incomplete. The complete description is said to be: "A formula composed *(mu'allaf)* of the attributes and accidents of the thing."[2]This formula is more or less the same as the Peripatetic one.[3] It is considered *not* to be an essentialist definition, but an ostensive type, which distinguishes one thing from another.

Chapter II, §3 is devoted to explaining errors that occur in the construction and usage of definition. This section is significant in that Suhrawardī quotes Avicenna while attempting in earnest to reformulate the theory of definition.[4]

Let us make a brief assessment of what has been analyzed so far. The first thing we notice while examining the works of Suhrawardī is that, unlike most of the philosophical works written earlier, Suhrawardī's deal with definition as a separate part of logic. This represents a significant re-structuring of logic as it was traditionally presented in such works as the

[1] Ibid., p. 7: *taṣawwur kunh al-shay'.*

[2] Ibid, p. 15.

[3] Cf. Avicenna, *Livre des Définition,* §19.

[4] See, for example, *Intimations:Logic,* p.16: "And Porphyry has made it such that it is necessary that the genus be taken in the definition of the species, and the species in the

Posterior Analytics and the *Topics*. Second, of the various types of definitions mentioned by the Peripatetics, Suhrawardī considers the complete essentialist type to be the most important one. For this type of definition, he reconstructs a more complex formula, in which the unity of the definition is stipulated to be related to the the necessary enumeration of the complete sum of all the essentials of the thing to be defined. Suhrawardī's use of terms such as "all," *(kull)* "combination" *(jam')* and "synthesis" *(tarkīb)*, as applied to the manner in which the attributes or constituents of the thing to be defined are to come together in the formula of essentialist definition, indicate a new approach to the problem.[1] This new conception of a different methodology of definition insists that a Platonic component be added to the strict Aristotelian. It is simply the logical corollary to the problem of the necessity of a complete enumeration of attributes of the thing in essentialist definition, to the epistemological difficulty of such a requirement, and to the problem of induction.[2] We note that, in a work such as the *Intimations*, the differences between the Peripatetic methodology (incorporating the position of definition), and the illuminationist methodology is mentioned, if not fully developed.

There are two additional problems connected with definition: the relation between definition and demonstration, and the relation between definition and the four causes. The first problem is discussed in the *Posterior Analytics*, and the second problem in the *Metaphysics*.[3] The first has to do with two questions: Can definition be demonstrated? Does demonstration result in a definition? In the *Intimations*, Suhrawardī addresses himself briefly to these questions. In regard to the first one, he stipulates that the middle term of a demonstration, which is made of the essential causes of a thing, is a kind of definition.[4] He mentions the second problem in the same

---

definition of the genus and this is absurd." This statement is made by Avicenna in *Kitāb al-Ḥudūd*. See, *Livre des Définitions*, p.11.

[1] Suhrawardī's use of certain terms in his theory of definition, including mathematical ones, may best be fully understood in view of Baghdādī's work before him. See below, Appendix C, where the terms are analyzed.

[2] See Kneale, *Probability and Induction*, pp. 25-30.

[3] Aristotle, *Posterior Analytics* I, 76b35-77a4; idem, *Metaphysics* I.3.

[4] *Intimations:Logic*, p. 82.

section. He insists that the four causes, agent *(fā'iliyya),* material *(mādiyya),* formal *(ṣūriyya),* and final *(ghā'iyya),* must all be together *(tujma')* in the expository proposition (whatever kind of definition it may be). This is a strange condition, since only a composite definition as a kind of conclusion of a demonstration can satisfy it.[1]

3.2 The *Paths and Havens*

Paths and Havens:Logic, II is entitled, "On Expository Propositions." In this chapter, as in the *Intimations,* Suhrawardī examines the theory and application of definition. The discussion is much more elaborate, and in fact the longest single chapter devoted to an analysis of definition in all of Arabic and Persian philosophical works on logic up to that time.[2] In the course of the twelve sections of this chapter, Suhrawardī develops a comprehensive theory of definition. This theory is in part Peripatetic, and includes a critique of the Peripatetics' views as well. In what follows, we shall examine the salient features of Suhrawardī's criticism—criticism, for the most part, specifically directed against Avicenna.

In the first section,[3] Suhrawardī first introduces the five types of definition mentioned above, and subsequently devotes the entire discussion to the two types of essentialist definition, the complete and the incomplete. Two descriptions of the complete essentialist definition are given. The first is the standard, which is found in most Peripatetic logical works:

> A formula indicating the essence of the thing.[4]

And the second, which Suhrawardī attributes to the "later Peripatetics" *(al-Muta'khkhirūn)* is:

> A *differentiated* formula indicating the essence of the thing.[5]

[1] Ibid., pp. 82-82.

[2] See Paths and Havens:Logic, fols. 15v.-19r.

[3] Ibid., fol. 15v.

[4] *Paths and Havens:Logic,* fol 14v. Cf. Avicenna, *Livre des Définitions,* §18: *al-qawl al-dāll 'alā māhiyyat al-shay'.*

[5] *Paths and Havens:Logic,* fol. 14v.: *qawl mufaṣṣal dāll 'alā māhiyyat al-shay'.*

The second version of the essentialist definition is the one given by Avicenna in the *Logic of the Easterners* only.[1] The "differentiated formula" is explained by Suhrawardī to be the condition that is obtained when, in any formula of definition, each part of the formula corresponds exactly to a part of the reality of the thing to be defined.[2] Suhrawardī has taken upon himself to explain what he regards as enigmatic in the work of Avicenna, systematically from a semiotic point of view, by first analyzing two basic meanings of the term formula *(qawl)*. The first sense of the term refers to a formula composed of parts which correspond to, or indicate a meaning of, the utterance said of the thing. The second sense of the term refers to a formula which is basically indicative of a single meaning associated with a single utterance.

The most significant aspect of Suhrawardī's critique so far is the attempt to clarify exact meanings associated with the usage of the terms in relation to the overall theory of definition; and he has taken a conciliatory stance. However, once these preliminary semantic problems are dealt with, he begins a direct attack on Avicenna:

> The person who has added something to the essentialist definition and stated that it is a formula indicating the perfection of the essence of the thing, so as to avoid the incomplete essentialist definition, has erred.[3]

The statement which is here attacked by Suhrawardī, who does not mention its author, is a statement made by Avicenna in his *Book of Definitions* by way of explaining a statement made by Aristotle in the *Topics*.[4] In effect, Suhrawardī is attacking Avicenna and the Aristotelian philosophical position. His specific criticism of Avicenna is quite revealing. We begin to comprehend the perspective from which Suhrawardī's

[1] Cf. Avicenna, *Logic of the Easterners*, p. 34: *al-qawl al-mufaṣṣal al-mu'arraf li-al-dhāt bimāhiyyatihi.*

[2] *Paths and Havens:Logic*, fol. 14r.: *mufaṣṣal, ay kull juz' min al-lafẓ yadull 'alā juz' min ḥqīqat al-shay'.*

[3] *Paths and Havens:Logic*, fol. 14r: *al-ladhī zāda fi'l-ḥadd faqāla: innahu al-qawl al-dāll 'alā kamāl māhiyyat al-shay' iḥtirāzan 'an al-ḥadd al-nāqiṣ, akhta'a.*

[4] Avicenna, *Livre des Définitions*, §18: *mā dhakarahu al-ḥakīm fī kitāb Ṭūbiqā annahu al-qawl al-dall 'alā māhiyyat al-shay' ay 'alā kamāl wujūdihi al-dhātī wa huwa mā yataḥaṣṣal lahu min jinsihi al-qarīb wa faṣlihi.*

philosophical criticism is made. We can also determine the nature of the dispute. As Suhrawardī continues his refutation of the Peripatetic theory, he states the prevalent view of the incomplete essentialist definition:

> The incomplete essentialist definition is that in which a differentia of the thing is taken with the farthest genus *(genus longinquum, jins ba'īd)*.[1]

He then stipulates that this type of definition does not indicate the essence, and proceeds to give his reasons. His arguments here are based on semiotic considerations, developed earlier in his works, which relate to indication, or signification *(dalāla)*, of the meaning *(al-ma'na)*, or the idea, by the utterances *(al-lafẓ)* said of things *(al-ashyā')* to be defined.[2] The formulæ for the complete and the incomplete essentialist definitions are considered kinds of compound utterances, each of which signifies the essence according to one of the types of signification Suhrawardī had discussed in his theory of semiotics. A systematic combination of a theory of semiotics with a theory of definition marks a novel approach to the problem. The essence is signified by the incomplete essentialist definition only by concomitance *(dalālat al-iltizām)*, which is not considered a valid *(mu'tabar)* kind of signification. The complete essentialist definition, on the other hand, indicates the essence by way of implicit signification *(dalālat al-taḍammun)*.

Based on the semiotics of the problem, two components of Suhrawardī's critique of the Peripatetic notion of definition are noticed here. First, the incomplete type is not a valid definition and does not signify the essence of the thing which is defined and hence is not of any use in science or demonstration. Secondly, the complete type (bearing in mind that the specific requirement here is that *all* the multiple essentials of the thing be synthesized into one formula) does indicate the essence, but only implicitly, and.not according to the most valid type of signification. Such signification is stated to be by complete correspondence *(dalālat al-muṭābaqa)*. This means that, for a definition to be valid, its formula must correspond completely to the essence of the thing to be defined. Is this at all possible

[1] *Paths and Havens:Logic*, fol. 14v.

[2] See Suhrawardī, *Opera II*, p. 14; Shīrāzī, *Sharḥ II*, p. 35: 13-38; Baghdādī, *al-Mu'tabar*, I, 8; Sāwī, *Tabṣira*, p. 132; and Cf. *Intimations:Logic*, p. 3.

based on only the Peripatetic theory? The complete essentialist definition of things has to be examined in relation to implicit signification. What is obtained when we respond to the question "What is X?" by stating "the *summum genus* of X plus its differentiæ." "Rational animal," which is the Peripatetic formula for the complete essentialist definition of man, is regarded by Suhrawardī to indicate implicitly the essence of animal, and adds nothing to our knowledge of the idea "man" *(al-insāniyya)*. This is because, he argues, the formula *qua* formula does not indicate the idea, "animal" *(al-ḥayawāniyya)*, and the utterance "rational" only indicates "a thing that has a soul" By this Suhrawardī states, rationality only is established.[1] Suhrawardī examines further the formula "rational animal," and concludes that a single utterance, such as the word "animal," corresponds to the *thing* animal, but the formula (or compound statement) only implicitly signifies the species, which in any case is not the essence. An additional point made here by Suhrawardī is that there cannot be an indicative formula for a simple thing,[2] and only a compound formula can indicate the essence of something, which is here stated to be the sum of the constituents.[3]

Suhrawardī disagrees with the Peripatetics in respect to their purely formal and non-restricted usage of definition, whether the complete essentialist type or the incomplete type. The argument here rests on the fundamental philosophical problem of how the thing *as it exists externally* is related to the idea of it in the mind, and the thing may be defined so that the unity of its essence is preserved, and the multiplicity of its constituents is indicated at the same time. At this point Suhrawardī gives an example,

[1] *Paths and Havens:Logic*, fol.v.: *rubbamā yanqadiḥ fī sharḥ al-ḥadd al-madhkūr an yuqāl «qawlunā ḥayawān nāṭiq qawl dāll bi-al-taḍammun 'alā māhiyyat al-ḥayawān wa dalālat al-taḍammun mu'tabar». fa-hādhā al-qawl dāll 'alā māhiyyat al-ḥayawān wa laysa naḥidd lahu wajhahu daf'atan anna lafẓ al-ḥayawān dalla 'alā ḥaqiqat al-ḥayawān wa'l qawl bi-mā huwa qawl mā dalla 'alā al-ḥayawāniyya bal al-nāṭiq dalla 'alā shay' lahu nafs nāṭiqa, thumma na'lam min khārij annahu ḥayawān.*

[2] *Paths and Havens:Logic*, fol. 14v.: *al-shay' al-basīṭ al-ladhī lā juz' lahu lā qawl dāll 'alayhi.*

[3] Ibid.: *māhiyyat al-shay' majmū' muqawwimātihi.*

taken from mathematics, through which he points to the nature of the problem and to his own position (summarized in his *Philosophy of Illumination).*[1] In this example, he considers a surface, and states that the idea of its quantity is one and the same as the idea of its being surface *(saṭḥiyya)* as it is in the external world (outside the mind). This means that one cannot indicate the abstracted qualities in the real thing itself, which are qualities that exist necessarily in the mind.[2] Another example is used to further illustrate the same point. The idea "color" is a mental concept and cannot be determined outside the mind, thus it cannot have an independent differentia *(faṣl mustaqil)* separate from its being, in such a way that the differentia plus the essence (the thing as-it-is) become one thing, namely the thing "seen." Therefore, a real thing does not have separate parts which can be determined outside the mind independently of it, in which case the thing as it exists in the mind must also have separate parts, because the mental form *(al-ṣūra al-dhihniyya)* and the real thing *(al-'aynī)* must correspond.[3]

The conclusion Suhrawardī draws from his arguments, which should be considered fundamental to the philosophy of illumination, is that the constituents of a thing *(muqawwimāt al-shay')* are not separate from the thing, neither "really" *('aynan)* nor "mentally" *(dhihnan).* Therefore, a thing cannot have an essentialist definition—since that would mean that one has "separated" its constituents into genera and differentia—but can only be described as it is seen through the eye, which is then, and only then, the thing's determined reality. Thus, to define something, one must "see" it as-it-is.

Subsequent to his arguments concerning definition, Suhrawardī embarks on one of his most bitter attacks on Avicenna, with significant implications for the history of Islamic philosophy in general. The

[1] Cf., Suhrawardī, *Opera II*, p. 5.

[2] *Paths and Havens:Logic*, fol 15r.: *i'lam anna man i'tarafa bi-anna al-saṭḥ laysa miqdāran wa laysa akhaṣṣ mutaḥṣṣilan fi'l a'yān [akhṭa'a] bal miqdāriyyatuhu nafs saṭḥiyyatihi fi'l-a'ayān.*

[3] *Paths and Havens:Logic*, fol. 15v.: *laysa al-lawn fi'l-a'yān mutaḥaṣṣilan wa lahu faṣl mustaqill bi'l-wujūd majmū'uhumā sawād, bal huwa shay' wāḥid; wa idhā kāna lā juz' lahu fi'l-a'yān fa-lā juz' lahu fī al-dhihn li-anna al-ṣūra al-dhihniyya yajib an tuṭābiq al-'aynī.*

controversy conerns the question whether Avicenna is to be considered among the "Eastern" philosophers, as he so claims himself, or a pure Peripatetic. Suhrawardī first quotes Avicenna on a problem relating to the definition of simple things, and agrees with him that they can only be described and not defined.[1] The statement in question is said by Suhrawardī to have been made in a book entitled *Karārīs fi' l-Ḥikma [Quires on Philosophy]*, attributed by Avicenna to the method of "Easterners" in philosophy.[2] It is not clear what the *Quires* are, but the statement can be traced to Avicenna's *Logic of the Easterners.*[3]

Suhrawardī's attack on Avicenna is directed towards the matter of a distinction between Peripatetic philosophy and Eastern philosophy, initiated by Avicenna, who had stated that he has composed works based on the principles of the latter. Suhrawardī takes issue with Avicenna and states that while the *Quires are* attributed to the Easterners, they are, however, composed according to Peripatetic principles of philosophy *(qawā'id al-mashshā' īn)* and represent the established rules of *philosophia generalis (al-ḥikma al-'āmma).* According to Suhrawardī, Avicenna may have changed an expression or slightly modified a minor point, but he has not composed a work significantly different from his other works. The modifications made by Avicenna, do not establish him as one of the Eastern philosophers, who had prevailed in ancient times when the principles of Eastern philosophy *(al-aṣl al-mashriqī)* had been established by the Persian Khusrawāni sages.[4] We notice an important distinction made by Suhrawardī between *philosophia generalis* and *philosophia specialis,* here applied to the methodological differences between the Peripatetics and the

[1] *Paths and Havens:Logic,* fol. 15v.: *anna al-basā'iṭ tursam wa lā tuḥadd.*

[2] Ibid.: *ṣarraḥa al-shaykh Abū 'Alī, fī karārīs, yansubuhā ilā al-mashriqiyyīn.*

[3] See Avicenna, *Logic of the Easterners,* pp.1-4.

[4] *Paths and Havens:Logic,* fol 15r: *wa hādhihi'l-karārīs, wa in yansubuhā ila'l-mashriq fa-hiya bi-'aynihā qawā'id al-mashshā'īn wa'l-ḥikma al-'āmma, illā annahu ghayyara al-'ibāra, aw taṣarrafa fī ba'ḍ al-furū', taṣarrufan gharīban lā tubāyin kutubuhu al-ukhrā . . . wa lā yataqarraru bihi al-aṣl al-mashriqī al-muqarrar fī 'ahd al-'ulamā' al-Khusrawāniyya.* Corbin has discussed Suhrawardī's view of Khusrawānī philosophers and of ancient Iranian wisdom. See, for example, *Opera II,* p. vi; and ibid., *Prolégomèna,* pp. 24-26

illuminationists. *Philosophia specialis* is the domain only of the illuminationist philosophers. This distinction is made in a section of Suhrawardī's logic where the problem of definition is discussed, and this is a further indication of the methodological significance of the theory of definition to illuminationist principles of philosophy.

Up to this point, Suhrawardī has been mainly concerned with the critique of Peripatetic theory, and so has discussed the problem within a predominantly Peripatetic setting. He has modified the Peripatetic formulations, and has emphasized the notion of the unity of definition as well as other characteristic components of the theory, but he has worked within a Peripatetic conceptual and methodological framework. He stipulated: "In the *Paths and Havens* we intend only to complete the theorems and methods of the Peripatetics and to embellish them."[1] As we continue in the subsequent section of the *Paths and Havens,* the rudiments of the illuminationist theory gradually emerge.

In Chapter Two, §2,[2] Suhrawardī introduces his notion of a conceptualist definition. Although this type is not fully developed, he insists that it is the most correct type of definition. The formula associated with this type of definition stipulates the name *(ism)*, and if the person using the name means by it the collectivity of all the attributes of the thing which is to be signified, such a formulation stands for the most correct type.[3] There is a distinctly Platonic element (to which we referred as the recognitional sense) in such a definition; it is the person's inner comprehension of the name "man" or "virtue," for example, that leads to an adequate definition of the thing, "man," which may never be differentiated into a formula with multiple numbers. That is, the person recognizes the essence of "man" or "virtue" in himself, and only then may the formula for it, such as *m-a-n* or "rational animal," adequately convey knowledge of its essence. This view

[1] *Paths and Havens:Logic,* fol 15r: *wa naḥnu fī hādha'l-kitāb lā naqṣud illā tatmīm ṭarā'iq al-mashshā'īn wa ta'rīfahā wa tahdhībahā.*

[2] *Paths and Havens:Logic,* fol. 15r.

[3] *Paths and Havens:Logic,* fol. 15v: *a-fa'in 'uniya bi'l-ism nafs majmū' tilka al-ṣifāt, wa hādhā aṣaḥḥ al-ḥudūd.* This is, of course, possible if and only if the attributes of the thing to be difined are finite. Cf. Aristotle, *Posterior Analytics* I.22, 82b36-39; 84a27.

lays the groundwork for Suhrawardī's view on the theory of definition as developed in the *Philosophy of Illumination.* The discussion there is so terse that it can be only understood through the arguments presented previously in the *Intimations* and in the *Paths and Havens.* The core of Suhrawardī's critique here is that the collectivity of attributes *(jamī' al-ṣifāt, majmū' al-ṣifāt)* of a thing is never exhaustively formulated by a mere statement of the genera and differentiæ. This is because the thing and its essential attributes form a unity that has to be comprehended *as a unity.* It is a mistake to try to differentiate the multiple essentials in the hope that, through the multiplicity, the unity can be grasped. The unity must be recognized as-it-is, by the subject in himself, independently of the multiplicity. The unity is not deduced from anything other than itself, and in the illuminationist scheme, is known intuitively prior to any construction of a deductive system. This special mode of cognition is called illumination and vision *(ishrāq wa mushāhada)* by Suhrawardī.

We now proceed to briefly examine the remaining sections. In §3, Suhrawardī talks about linguistic philosophical problems associated with the use of technical terms is in science *(al-asmā' al-iṣṭilāḥiyya fi' l-'ilm).* Definitions of technical terms indicate their usage.[1]

In §4 Suhrawardī once again confronts the Avicennan position, regarding specifically the formula for essentialist definition. For the first time in this part of his logic, he quotes from Avicenna's book *Directives and Remarks,* where Avicenna stated that the essentialist definition is necessarily made up of the genus and the differentiæ.[2] This he considers to be an error because Avicenna has applied its use unrestrictively to anything, while it only applies to a thing that actually does have a genus and differentiæ.[3] Once again this critique leads Suhrawardī to consider the relation between the thing and its attributes. He states that, should a thing, not have a real genus and differentia, then the formula for the thing is either synthesized with its accidental attributes, or the thing itself is related to its

[1] *Paths and Havens:Logic,* fol. 15v: *al-asmā' al-iṣṭilāḥiyya fi' l-'ilm ḥudūduhā hiya al-aqwāl al-dālla 'alā ghayra mā iṣṭalaḥa 'alayhi.*

[2] Cf. Avicenna, *Kitāb al-Ishārāt wa al-Tanbīhāt,* pp. 11-12.

[3] *Paths and Havens:Logic,* fol 17v.

attributes, as an agent or form or material is related to the product. It should be noted that the the bulk of Suhrawardīs arguments here are taken from Avicenna's *Logic of the Easterners.*[1]

In §5, and §6, Suhrawardī develops a kind of definition we may designate ostensive. This kind of definition serves to distinguish among things, and is a perfectly adequate kind of definition for general use.[2]

In §7 Suhrawardī distinguishes between "rational" and the "capacity to reason" *(isti'dād al-nuṭq),* and he later uses this distinction in his formulation of an illuminationist theory of definition in the *Philosophy of Illumination.*[3] Suhrawardī analyzes the distinction by first considering that capacity to reason is the same as the activities of the intellect, i.e., thinking or cogitating *(ta'aqqul wa tafakkur).* He regards any kind of "capacity" as posterior to the "substantial reality" *(al-ḥaqā'iq al-jawhariyya).* He makes a further distinction between the "rational soul" *(al-nafs al-nāṭiqa),* which determines rationality, itself a determined, real essence, and the capacity of reason, which is a mental concept.[4]

From here, Suhrawardī goes on to consider some of the standard views regarding the notions of sameness and difference, their definitions and their use. And in §8-§12 such topics related to definition as description, nominal definition, definition by analogy, definition as subject of propositions, as well as the questions what is genus and what is differentia, are discussed by him, which need not concern us here. It should be noted, however, that most of the arguments are taken directly from Avicenna's *Logic of the Easterners,* or are based on it.[5]

So far we have concentrated on Chapter Two of the logic of the *Paths and Havens,* and have observed that this chapter, entirely devoted to definition, provides us with a host of problems related to Suhrawardī's critique of the Peripatetic formula for definition. Chapter Eight of the same book, which bears the traditional Peripatetic title, "On Demonstration," is

[1] Cf. Avicenna, *Logic of the Easterners,* pp. 42-44.

[2] *Paths and Havens:Logic,* fol. 16v-16r.

[3] *Paths and Havens:Logic,* fol. 16v. Cf. *Opera II,* p. 20.

[4] *Paths and havens: Logic,* fol. 16v.

[5] Cf. Avicenna, *Logic of the Easterners,* pp. 34-36.

basically a selective epitome of the *Posterior Analytics*, and corresponds to the structure of Avicenna's *Healing*.[1] This chapter contains sections that deal with some of the usual components associated with the problem of definition. Thus, for example, §7 deals with the relation between demonstration and definition; §10 deals with problems such as circular arguments and innate ideas as the grounds for knowledge; and §11-§13 deal with dichotomy, or division, in definition, i.e., with the Platonic method of definition, as well as with other problems. While most of the arguments in these sections are standard Peripatetic ones, they provide invaluable insight into Suhrawardī's own views, which ultimately culminate in the philosophy of illumination. Some of the issues raised here are also related to Chapter Two, and I shall attempt to analyze them with the intention of providing further information on Suhrawardī's new theory of the formulation of the essentialist definition.

The first important point is raised by Suhrawardī in §10, where he indicates that innate ideas are the basis for knowledge, and thus, from an epistemological point of view, they serve as the basis for any kind of definition. This means that there must be something most prior, with respect to knowledge, in relation to which things are to be defined. As examples of such innately known things, Suhrawardī cites the personal inspirtrions and mystical experiences of such philosophers as Avicenna and Abu'l-Barakāt al-Baghdādī. This is somewhat a change of heart on the part of Suhrawardī vis-à-vis Avicenna, whom at one point he had ridiculed for claiming to be one of the Eastern philosophers. From the standpoint of the history of philosophy in the Islamic period, it is interesting that Suhrawardī considers Baghdādī as a philosopher who established the methodology of Plato in certain areas of philosophy.[2]

For our understanding of Suhrawardī's theory, his §12 is most important. In this section he picks up the argument regarding the formula of definition which combines *all* the attributes of a thing, i.e., the type of

[1] *Paths and Havens:Logic,* fols. 88v-101r.

[2] *Paths and Havens:Logic,* fol. 97r. The term used by Suhrawardī is *madhhab al-Aflāṭūn.*

complete essentialist definition considered by him to be the only valid kind. He states:

> You cannot say "I will combine all the attributes and determine all of them," and then say "this is a formula that indicates the essence and so it is a [complete] essentialist definition." Because such a statement is a *petitio principii*.[1]

Suhrawardī indicates the impossibility of any formula of definition in which the multiplicity of the attributes (both essential and accidental) of the thing defined are combined (either simply enumerated, added, or synthesized) This is a puzzling problem. If the formula does not combine the attributes, it does not indicate the essence, yet for any formula to do this it must combine a large (possibly not countable) number of things, which may not be possible by complete, discrete, one-by-one enumeration. The solution rests on both the manner in which the multiplicity may be combined in a unitary formula, as well as on an alternate mode of cognition which would immediately strike upon the unity of the essence. Now, whether the alternative mode of cognition is a dialectical method which aims at allowing the subject to recover the timeless truths in his own self-consciousness, which then serves as the basis for formalized and demonstrated knowledge, or something else, remains to be seen. Does the definition of X simply rest on an intuition of it, or of something other than it, prior to an attempt at positioning its formula in some constructed structure? This problem will be discussed in the next chapter. I merely emphasize here, however, Suhrawardī's own insistence that only "the collectivity of the essentials of a thing is a valid definition of it," and leave the question as to what this collectivity is, and the method for obtaining it, for later consideration.

4. An Illuminationist Theory of Definition

Suhrawardī's terse philosophical style in the *Philosophy of Illumination* is quite perplexing to the reader who attempts to recover a coherent and consistent "theory" based on enigmatic and short statements.[2] Any attempt

[1] Ibid., fol. 98r.

[2] We note that Suhrawardī himself characterizes his style as metaphorical (*marmūza*, a term which means mysterious or secretive). Cf. Suhrawardī, *Paths and Havens:Logic*, fol. 15r.: *wa hiya ḥikmat al-khāṣṣiyya; wa'l-khaṭb al-'aẓīm marmūz fī kitābinā*

to examine this work alone will fail to uncover Suhrawardī's intended meaning. Therefore, we should keep in mind the results of our examination of Suhrawardī's views on definition in the *Intimations* and the *Paths and Havens* as we analyze his views in the *Philosophy of Illumination*. It should be clear that Suhrawardī is not satisfied with the Peripatetic theory of definition. This view is examined in the *Philosophy of Illumination,* but it is first discussed in the *Intimations,* and subsequently fully analyzed in the *Paths and Havens*. It should be equally clear that any attempt to study the philosophy of illumination cannot ignore illuminationist logic, as all studies up to now have done. The problem of definition leads us to understand what the philosophy of illumination is, and it is a problem that is fully dealt with only in logic.

The *Philosophy of Illumination,* Part One, I, 7 is entitled "On definition and its conditions."[1] This section consists of three parts, and is included in Suhrawardī's general scheme of semiotics. In this book, definition is only treated as part of semantics. In the first part of this section Suhrawardī discusses the conditions that have to be met for a definition of a thing to be meaningful, that is, for it to convey knowledge concerning the thing defined. Suhrawardī here fully formulates his own view of definition by stating that, in order to define something, either all of the units *(al-āḥād)* of that thing, or some of the units, or the thing's total whole *(al-ijtimā',* also implying the organic, undifferentiated whole), must be specified.[2] In

mushtamil 'alā'l-'uṣūl al-sharīfa al-musammā bi-Ḥikmat al-Ishrāq. We further note that the term *ramz* is used by him in his *Philosophy of Illumination* to characterize the philosophical style of the "ancients." Suhrawardī, *Opera II,* pp. 10-11

[1] This section, among the most significant ones in the work, has been translated so that the reader may consult it. See below, Appendix B.

[2] Both terms, *āḥād* and *ijtima',* are mathematical ones. See Baghdādī, the *Evidential,* I, 55-57. The term *ijtimā'* refers to a kind of "whole" which is called *jam' tarkībī,* in which the parts, or units, are not distinguishable from one another, and collectively they are not distinguishable from the whole. Cf. Aristotle, *Metaphysics* V.26, 1024a1-10. The Greek terms σύνολος, σύγκρισις, and σύστημα should be here compared to the term *ijtimā'*. See Thābit ibn Qurra, *al-Madkhal,* p. 299. Concerning the relation between *jamī'* and ὅλον, which is regarded as a kind of σύνθεσις see Ibid.; and Alfred Ivry, *al-Kindī's Metaphysics* (Albany: SUNY Press, 1974), p. 17. Cf. Aristotle, *Topics* VI.14, 151a30. In order to further comprehend the implications of the term *āḥād* it should be

this statement the term used for definition is *ta'rīf,* which includes both the essentialist type as well as the descriptive. This statement, taken by itself is quite enigmatic, but in light of what Suhrawardī had said in the *Intimations* and in the *Paths and Havens*—that the definition, to be valid, must combine all the attributes of the thing defined—the statement can be understood. The mathematical terminology used here by Suhrawardī is at first baffling, but upon further reflection and examination, the puzzle is solved and turns out to be fundamental in our overall understanding of illuminationist philosophy. The immediate source of Suhrawardī's mathematical terminology is Baghdādī's *Evidential,* I, I.13, where the use of mathematical rules in constructing definitions is elaborately detailed.[1] The importance of noting Baghdādī's mathematical rules for constructing definitions is indicated by Suhrawardī himself (as was noted above), who regards Baghdādī a contributor to the Platonizing elements of the theorems. It is crucial that we comprehend Suhrawardī's formula for definition and its relation to mathematical rules. Therefore, after a general account of the Seventh Rule, I shall return to this problem and analyze it in more detail.

The additional problems dealt with in §13 are concerned with two conditions (from among many given in the *Topics)* that must be met in order to render a definition meaningful. These are conditions that must be met in relation to the thing by means of which something else is defined. They are: 1- that by means of which another thing is defined has to be more

---

compared with the Greek μονάδες and μοναδιστί. The terms' significance in metaphysics can be seen in Baghdādī, *Evidential,* I, 55. And for the mathematical significance of the term and its implications in philosophy, see Thābit ibn Qurra, *al-Madkhal,* pp. 218, 222, 223, 299. It is important to bear in mind that the relation between units, *āḥād,* and the whole, *ijtimā',* depends on the notion of synthetic combination, *jam' tarkībī,* which constitutes the *ijtimā'* associated with the thing to be defined. This also means that the units, *āḥād,* cannot be determined in the reality outside the mind independently of the whole, *ijtimā'*. See below, Appendix C, where I analyze Baghdādi's mathematical rules governing definition. Suhrawardī's position may be summed up as follows: the one (the unit, the ordinal, the cardinal, the thing) cannot be known independently of many, nor vice versa. And in order to define "many," "one" must be defined first, the definition of which rests on a primary intuition of "number" and not on a formal definition based on whatever presuppositions about reality the knowing subject may wish to make.

[1] This section of Baghdādī's work is analyzed in Appendix C.

apparent *(aẓhar)* than the thing defined; and 2- it must be known prior to the thing defined. The implication of the two conditions is clear: namely, that in order for a thing to be known (by a definition of it, or otherwise) something must be known prior to it. This means that, ultimately, there must be something which is the *most apparent and most prior* in respect to knowledge, in relation to which everything else is to be known. The most prior known thing (which is also necessarily the most apparent) is, according to Suhrawardī, innate knowledge.[1] (As we shall see later on, innate knowledge is said to be "part" of the self-consciousness of man.) The most apparent thing in reality is, according to Suhrawardī, light *(nūr)*, which is known immediately and need not be defined. Now the terms "more apparent" and "more known" and "most apparent" and "most known" seem to be connected, and perhaps identical. The connection between "apparentness" and knowledge is a fundamental component of the philosophy of illumination. And the question as to what is most prior and most known is tied in with a psychological notion of self and consciousness. The basic epistemological position of Suhrawardī is a modification of the Aristotelian notion of "pre-existent," knowledge and the Platonic view of Ideas which are innate and have to be "recovered" in the subjects' own conscious, knowing being.

After setting down the conditions mentioned above, Suhrawardī distinguishes real definitions from nominal ones. He also considers a special kind of lexical definition *(tabdīl al-lafẓ)*, which he states to be useful for persons to whom the reality of a thing is known but the meaning of the utterance may be unknown.

In the second part, §14, of the Seventh Rule, Suhrawardī deals with the essentialist definition and with description. When introducing the essentialist definition, Suhrawardī is careful to attribute its formulation—stated to be the formula which indicates the essence of a thing—to a source to whom he

[1] See Suhrawardī, *Opera II*, p. 18. Cf. Baghdādī, *Evidential*, I, 8, 40-46; Sāwī, *Tabṣira*, p. 3; Aristotle, *Posterior Analytics* I, 1-3. The distinction between innate and acquired is a fundamental feature of Baghdadī's book. It was "established through personal reflection" by a philosopher whose knowledge was based upon *a priori* intuition. See S. Pines, *Nouvelles Études sur Awhad al-Zaman Abu'l-Barakāt al-Baghdādī*, pp 8-17.

refers as "some person."[1] The essentialist definition is marked as a type of definition which indicates the essentials *(al-dhātiyyāt)*, while description only makes known the externals *(al-khārijiyyāt)* of a thing. The distinction, therefore, is that the essentialist definition indicates the essential attributes of a thing, while description indicates its non-essential attributes. This distinction is crucial since, as noted above, Suhrawardī had insisted in his *Paths and Havens* that, for a definition to be a meaningful essentialist definition, it should combine into a formula all the attributes of a thing, which means both the essential and the non-essential attributes. It is clear that, for Suhrawardī, both the essentialist definition and description are real definitions, since they are to be used to define the thing "man" and not the word *man*; it seems that both types must be combined if the definition is to be valid. This indicates that knowledge of the thing rests ultimately upon a kind of perception of the idea of it, which in turn is only determined through the innate idea available to the subject *prior* to investigation by intuition. The Peripatetic formal use of definition is criticized by Suhrawardī because it does not convey *real* knowledge of the thing, but only indicates the combined abstract divisions of the mode of its existence.

Suhrawardī's arguments directed toward the Peripatetics are neither straightforward nor simple. In order to understand them we must have a comprehensive notion of the foundation of illuminationist philosophy. In §14, his arguments are as follows. There is a something in the objective reality of man, the *this* man and the *that* man, by which the idea, man (lit. man-ness, *al-insāniyya)*, is ascertained, and it serves as the foundation for our knowledge of man, whatever it is. The Peripatetics consider this "thing," states Suhrawardī, to be the essentialist definition of man as "rational animal."[2] However, Suhrawardī holds the view that capacity of reasoning is accidental and posterior to the reality of man, and hence "rational animal" does not signify the essence of man. This means that the formula for the essentialist definition of man is only formally valid, and only so according to the Peripatetics. In fact, this formula is a tautology,

[1] Most probably a reference to Avicenna, and probably to *al-Ishārat*. See Avicenna, *Kitāb al-Ishārāt*, pp. 11-13.

[2] See Suhrawardī, *Opera II*, pp. 19-20.

and without real value for one who seeks to know that by which the thing man, is known, i.e., the idea "man."

At this point, Suhrawardī briefly introduces into the argument what should be regarded as a fundamental component of his own view of knowledge, and states that, since the the soul is the origin of the thing by which the idea, man is ascertained, and since the soul is the "closest" *(aqrab)* thing to man, it is therefore through the soul that one may realize the essence of man and ultimately of all things.[1] Subsequently, and based on the subject's self-knowledge, the real sciences are constructed by employing the method of demonstration.[2] Suhrawardī shows a preference for a special method of obtaining the essence of things based on the knowing subject's primary intuition in the soul itself, which then serves as the basis for constructing definitions. Such "definitions" are ultimately used in elaborate constructions of further demonstrations.

In the last part of the Seventh Rule (§15), entitled "Illuminationist Theorem" and bearing the subtitle, "On the destruction of the Peripatetic theorem of definition," Suhrawardī first deals with the method by which the Peripatetics construct an essentialist definition, and shows how such a construction is an inadequate one for gaining knowledge of the essence of things. Suhrawardī commences by stating that the Peripatetics are content with merely "mentioning" the most general essential *(al-dhātī al-ʿāmm)* and the most specific essential *(al-dhātī al-khāṣṣ)*, and they call it an essentialist definition. Suhrawardī's emphasis is on the use of the word "mention," which is in opposition to his own formula, which requires, as we saw above, that the essentials be "synthesized" (or brought together in some other way) into a *unit*. This may only be possible in the subject's soul, and in relation to the object. Suhrawardī, in his usual philosophical style, goes on to explain the terms used. The most general essential of a thing, called the genus, is an essential that must be mutually exclusive of any other

[1] Suhrawardī's *Gedankenexperiment* concerning soul's knowledge of itself, though Avicennan in conception, indicates a more detailed analysis, and is incorporated fully into a comprehensive view of psychology. See *Opera III*, pp 10-14. Cf. Fazlur Rahman, *Avicenna's Psychology*. p. 31.

[2] Suhrawardī, *Opera II*, pp. 40-46.

general essential, and pertains to the universal reality *(al-ḥaqīqa al-kulliyya)* equated with the answer given to the question "What is it?" The specific essential, which is specific to the thing about which the question "What is it?" is asked, is called the differentia. The genus and differentiæ are the two basic components of Peripatetic essentialist definitions. Suhrawardī tells us that he adheres to a different way of ordering the genus and the differentiæ than the Peripatetics. This, he says, he has stated in his other books. The "other books" are the *Intimations* and the *Paths and Havens,* in which, as analyzed above, Suhrawardī has put forth the notion that the multiple genera and the differentiæ of a thing, and in general *all* of its attributes, should be combined into a formula in such a way as to convey the unity of the essence.

He goes on to state that the Peripatetics hold that the unknown may only be ascertained in relation to something known, a view which Suhrawardī regards as fundamental to the Peripatetic view of science. When the Peripatetics define something in relation to its essentials (which they have abstracted from it), they are allowing that the essential be more known than the thing they wish to define; while Suhrawardī holds that, at the outset, the essentials of a thing are as unknown as the thing itself. In effect, he is proposing that the relation among the thing taken totally, which is a unit, and the multiple essentials is an "organic" relation, in that the essentials cannot be separated from the whole thing and thus examined. Suhrawardī's arguments in this regard are as follows. We assume that a thing has a specific essential associated with it. Now this specific essential is either known *with* the thing itself or *in* something else (i.e., by means of knowing it as present in something else) or not known at all. The third possibility is of no concern. But if the essential is known *in* something else, it cannot be an essential of the thing, and if the essential is known *with* the thing itself, it is then a sensible, undifferentiated "part" of the sensed thing itself. Therefore a thing when sensed is known, and when known by means of sense-perception, its essentials are also known. Now obviously the mechanics of sense-perception become crucial, since they must be working in such a way as to provide for the "subject" a unified knowledge of the "object" at the moment of the act of perception. Such an act of perception, as we shall see, is one of the components of Suhrawardī's theory of illuminationist cognition:

> [One can obtain a definition only] by recourse to sensible or apparent things in another way [i.e., other than the Peripatetic formula of definition], and [only] if [and when] the thing pertains specifically to the sum total of the [sensible and apparent things] as an organic whole.[1]

Here, then, is both a special theory of cognition and a special theory of being, meant to explain knowledge of the whole of a thing as what it is.

In the last paragraph of §15, perhaps the quintessence of his critique of the Peripatetic theory, Suhrawardī attacks the Peripatetic formula of definition from yet another point of view. His attack is in part also related to his critique of induction.[2] Suhrawardī reiterates his fundamental position in regard definition by stating that, to know something by means of its essentials, one must be able to enumerate exhaustively *all* of them. He contends that the reality of a thing may only be known with certitude if and only if the sum total of the essentials is known.[3] Suhrawardī explicitly states for the first time that such knowledge of the total essentials by the method of enumeration is, however, not possible. This is because the thing to be defined may have a multiplicity of non-apparent *(ghayr ẓāhir)* attributes. Suhrawardī had previously said that a valid essentialist definition is one that combines all the attributes of the thing to be defined, but now he is saying that it is not possible to enumerate them exhaustively, nor to even know them all. He further asserts that it is not enough for someone to allege that he knows all the essentials and is able to enumerate them all, because there may always be one that he may never know, or that it would be impossible for him to recognize. There always remains an unknown element in an attempt to enumerate the constituents of a thing separately from the whole of what the thing is.

We may interpret Suhrawardī's words as follows. The set of essentials of a thing may be unbounded, and the elements of the set may not be

[1] Suhrawardī, *Opera II*, p. 21.

[2] See Suhrawardī, *Paths and Havens:Logic*, fol. 98v.; idem *Opera III*, p. 5.

[3] For a discussion of the relation among the "parts" and the "sum," see below, Appendix C.

discretely distinguishable from the set itself; knowledge of the set does imply knowledge of the elements, but it is not possible to know what the set itself is through knowing the elements separately. Suhrawardī's view, which holds that the essentials may only be ascertained when the thing itself is ascertained, is the basis for his critique of the Peripatetic theory. It serves as the impetus for his formulating an alternate theory. This he states thus:

> We only obtain a definition by means of things that pertain specifically to the totality (i.e., organic whole) of the thing.[1]

Finally, and at the very end of his critique, Suhrawardī states that the Peripatetics cannot, in the strictest scientific sense, define anything, and this undermines the very basis of demonstration. This is a dilemma which Suhrawardī traces to Aristotle himself.[2]

4.1 A Formulation of the Illuminationist Theory of Definition

So far we have been concerned mainly with presenting the various views of earlier philosophers and of Suhrawardī on the problem of definition. We have indicated Suhrawardīs arguments in specific sections of his major works. Now we are in a position to consider Suhrawardī's theory of definition from a broader theoretical and methodological perspective, and we shall also attempt to assess the implications of the theory.

It is evident that definition plays a crucial role in the construction of the philosophy of illumination. Any attempt to discuss the development of philosophy in the Islamic period without knowing the details of the theory and its epistemological significance, will be flawed if not openly misleading. Suhrawardī's theory of definition is a methodological as well as formal improvement on previous theories, and as such deserves a place in the history both of logic and of philosophy in general.

In the *Intimations*, the *Paths and Havens*, and the *Philosophy of Illumination*, several factors may be seen as parts of a unified theory of definition. Definition, which had been traditionally discussed in the

[1] Suhrawardī, *Opera II*, p. 21.

[2] Aristotle, *Posterior Analytics* II.3, 90b15: "never yet by defining anything—essential attribute or accident—did we get knowledge of it."

Posterior Analytics and the *Topics*, is treated by Suhrawardī in an independent "book" of his new structure of logic, which divides logic into semiotics, formal logic, and material logic. The formal rules governing definition are modified and expanded by Suhrawardī in all of the three works. We were not able to discern a distinctly Peripatetic formulation in the *Intimations* or in the *Paths and Havens* in contradistinction to a distinctly illuminationist formulation in the *Philosophy of Illumination*. A clear relationship exists among the works, to the extent that the critique of definition presented in the *Philosophy of Illumination* was only understood when we considered the *Intimations* as well as the *Paths and Havens*. We noticed that the *Intimations* contained a short introduction to the subject, followed by its detailed analysis in the *Paths and Havens*, which was formulated finally, but not detailed, in the *Philosophy of Illumination*.

From a formal point of view, Suhrawardī's theory is an improvement of the old theory. His expanded and more elaborate formula for the essentialist definition (both the complete as well as the incomplete), which insists that the essential attributes of the thing to be defined must be enumerated exhaustively and "combined" into a unitary formula, is a precise analysis of the problem of essentialist definition, and is a response to problems encountered with the Peripatetic formula. We observed Suhrawardī's systematic division of real definition into five types, which must be considered a contribution by him to the Peripatetic classification that divides the real definition into four types.[1] The formal theory elaborated by Suhrawardī combines the method of division and synthesis with the method of demonstration, and thus is more Platonic than any theory before him in the history of philosophy in Islam. But Suhrawardī's objections to the Peripatetics are themselves made within a Peripatetic conceptual and methodological framework. As Suhrawardī himself admits, illuminationist philosophy is not a method totally separate from Peripatetic philosophy.

We also observed that the critique of definition, which starts with formal rules, ultimately touches on fundamental epistemological questions. When Suhrawardī stipulates as a necessary requirement that we can only know a

[1] Cf. Avicenna, *The Healing:Logic:Demonstration* IV.4, pp. 217-224.

thing by knowing *all* its attributes, and that illuminationist definitions are achieved *only* by means of ascertaining the totality, or organic whole, of a thing, we can deduce that the core of the theory rests on two points: a Platonic attitude which insists that *only* knowledge can serve as the foundation for knowledge, and a fundamental point of methodology requiring that definition should ultimately strive to define the Forms, or to somehow get to know them through vision-illuminsion. Now, the condition that knowledge should stand as the basis of knowledge is met by Suhrawardī through the innate ideas, which serve as the foundation of knowledge and are "recoverable" in the subject's self-consciousness. But, there is the dilemma that from a purely formal view, the Forms cannot be defined, as Aristotle emphasizes. This dilemma leads Suhrawardī to formulate a symbolic mode of expression meant for a select group, by means of which a thing is shown *as-it-is* to the "student" (as it was to Meno, in Plato's eponymous dialogue), who is thus led to grasp the meaning of its essence by himself. Therefore, we may divide Suhrawardī's theory of definition into two complementary parts: the formal and the psychological or experiential. The formal part comprises a critique of the Peripatetic theory and the attempt to refine it from the Peripatetic standpoint itself. The psychological, or experiential part comprises several factors. From the basic condition required of the thing by means of which a definition is constructed, namely priority and intelligibility (the two most significant conditions according to Aristotle as well),[1] we are lead to what is *most* prior and *most* intelligible. This "thing" turns out to be "light," which is the fundamental basis of reality in illuminationist philosophy, and the very stuff of human self-consciousness. And light is its own definition; to "see" it is to know it:

> If, in reality, there exists a thing which need not be defined nor explained, then that thing is apparent, and since there is nothing more apparent than light, then more than anything, it is in no need of definition.[2]

[1] Aristotle, *Topics* VI.4, 141a23-142b.

[2] Suhrawardī, *Opera II,* p. 106.

The search for definition, for Suhrawardī, involves an additional factor. This is the endeavor by a "master," or teacher,[1] who leads the student through discourses based on both the discursive pillar of the philosophy of illumination as well as the intuitive. This is when the symbolic and metaphorical nature of illuminationist compositions is revealed to him, so that the student realizes the reality of the changeless, timeless truths, the Forms.

The theory of definition proposed by Suhrawardī seeks the answer to the question, "What is X?" in two complementary approaches. First, by means of a set of partial definitions of X, in terms of the essentials of X, a formal definition is constructed. This formal definition, let us call it d_1, is, however, only partial. Next, by a psychological method the subject is led to an understanding of X, based on d_1, which is realized by the subject, but may not be fully articulated. This higher level of knowledge of X is tantamount to a "new" definition of X. This process is continued in such a way that a new formal definition, d_2, is constructed, which, in turn, is complemented by an experience as an intuition of what X.is. In this manner a series of d_i definitions is obtained on the basis of which a valid definition of X, say a D that includes all d_i may be obtained. The dilemma is of course, whether D can be articulated in terms of d_i, or whether knowledge of X through D is only available to the subject in its self-consciousness. If so, D can only be expressed symbolically. Therefore, knowledge of X depends both on a set of partial formal definitions of X plus an experience of X as a primary intuition of that on which X rests. Formal methodology together with an experiential component constitutes the final symbolic mode of expression of the "results" of illumination, and this is a noted aim of Suhrawardī's reconstruction of philosophy.[2] Through the symbol or metaphor, the real knowledge of X, which exists "in" man, is recovered, hence known.

[1] The role of the Divine philosopher *(al-Ḥakīm al-Muta'allih)* in teaching the wisdom to be obtained through the study of illuminationist philosophy is most important. Such a teacher is compared to the ṣūfī *quṭb*. This person is referred to as the "upholder of the wisdom of illumination *(al-qayyim 'ala'l-ishrāq)*." See Suhrawardī, *Opera II*, pp. 10- 13, 244, 256, 260m.

Suhrawardī's critique of the Peripatetic formula points also to a view of being which must necessarily hold that the essence of a thing is *not* really separable from the attributes of that thing, i.e., the essences and attributes are one as seen in the external reality. Therefore, a real definition ultimately fails also, if the subject considers only the formal aspect but not the subjective experiential, or intuitively known, factors as well.

The dilemma faced by philosophy concerning real definition is a long-standing one. Among the more recent philosophers, Kant gave much attention to the problem of definition, and his thoughts regarding analytic and synthetic definition marks a departure from the purely Aristotelian formula for real definition.[1] In the twentieth century E.I.J. Brouwer's Intuitionist logic has opened a way into considering the question of the definition of number, and hence also of the methodology of definition in general, based on primary intuition.[2] It is beyond the scope of the present work to compare Suhrawardī's theory of definition with modern views on the subject, but it should be noted that the illuminationist theory is a novel view of the problem in relation to the strict Peripatetic.

Admittedly, one aspect of Suhrawardī's theory, namely the insistence on complete enumeration of the essentials of the thing synthesized in unitary formula, is, to say the least, enigmatic. However, if we consider the works of modern philosophers such as Bertrand Russell and Alfred J. Ayer, the fuzziness will be cleared to a great extent. Ayer distinguishes explicit definition from definition in use; he considers the former a kind of lexical definition, and argues that the Aristotelian definition *per genus et differentiam* yields only explicit definitions; and he considers the latter,

---

[2] Suhrawardī, *Opera I*, p. 401.

[1] See Immanuel Kant, *Logic*, tr. R. Hartman and W. Schwartz (New York: Library of Liberal Arts, 1974), pp. 141-146; N.K. Smith, *A Commentary to Kant's Critique of Pure Reason* (New York: Humanities Press, 1971), pp. 564-565; Lewis W. Beck, "Kant's Theory of Definition," in *The Philosophical Review*, vol. 65, 2 (374) (April, 1956), pp. 179-191.

[2] The Intuitionist foundation of mathematics has recently received much attention subsequent to Dummett's publication of *Elements of Intuitionism* (Oxford: Oxford UP, 1976). See, also, A. Heyting, *Intuitionism: An Introduction* (Amsterdam: North-Holland Publishing Company, 1956).

namely definition in use, a definition which reduces to a set of translatable symbols translated into equivalents.[1] Translatability of symbols into equivalents, must necessarily include, as an integral component, the experience of the truth underlying the symbol. Thus the symbol "man" is used, for which the Aristotelian essentialist definition "rational animal" is only an explicit definition. This definition is a tautology (in the strict non-mathematical sense). The essence of man (which is the truth underlying the symbol "man") is a thing which is *only* recoverable, according to the illuminationist theory, in the subject. This act of "recovery" is the translation of the symbol to its equivalent in the consciousness or the self of the subject. Russell's theory is reduced to a distinction between definition by "extension" (which is adefinition that seeks to enumerate the members of a "class")[2] and definition by "intention" (which is a definition that mentions a defining property, or a number of them).[3] The illuminationist theory can be seen as combining elements both of a definition by extension and of a definition by intention.

[1] Alfred J. Ayer, *Language, Truth and Logic* (London: Victor Gollanz Ltd., 1950), pp. 59-71. Cf. Paul T. Sagal, "Implicit Definition," in *The Monist,* vol. 57, no. 3, (July, 1973) pp. 443-450.

[2] Other terms, such as collection, set, aggregate, and manifold, are also used, and may mean what Suhrawardī intends by *al-ijtimā'*.

[3] Bertrand Russell, *Introduction to Mathematical Philosophy* (New York: Simon and Shuster, n.d.), p. 12. Cf. Irving Copi, *Symbolic Logic* (New York: The Macmillan Co., 1965), Ch. VI; Moritz Schlick, *General Theory of Knowledge* (New York and Wien: Springer-Verlag, 1975), pp. 31-39.

Chapter Four

Knowledge, Illumination and Cosmology

1. Is Knowledge Possible? Suhrawardī's Assessment of the Peripatetic View

I have shown in Chapter Three that Suhrawardī did not regard the Peripatetic method of definition to be a valid way for obtaining knowledge. We observed that the desired end of illuminationist epistemology is a kind of unqualified knowledge that is known with certitude *(yaqīn)*.[1] This kind of knowledge is knowledge of essence only, on the one hand, and on the other hand, it is knowledge which incorporates the timeless, changeless Forms. The stringent conditions which Suhrawardī sets for the possibility of knowledge are not entirely without precedent in philosophy. By means of discursive philosophy, according to Suhrawardī, formal validity is ascertained. But he distinguishes between discursive knowledge, and knowledge based on intuition, and considers the latter to have epistemological priority. This distinction is Suhrawardī's modification of Aristotle's view of science portrayed in the *Posterior Analytics*.[2] According to Suhrawardī's view, the most valid kind of knowledge is a kind of "experience" by the subject of what he calls "apocalyptic lights" *(al-ṣawāniḥ al-nūriyya)*. In general, this is a knowledge obtained by means of a mode of cognition referred to as

[1] Suhrawardī often uses the term *yaqīnī* or *mutayyaqqana* when he wants to modify knowledge with the attribute "certain." E.g., Suhrawardī, *Opera II*, p. 21. The term *yaqīnī* may be compared with ἐπιστήμη, e.g. Thābit ibn Qurra, *al-Madkhal*, pp. 4, 14, 185.

[2] The distinction between discursive reasoning and intuitive knowledge had been made by Aristotle. However, he does not allow for intuition to play a principle position in philosophical construction, as insisted by Suhrawrdī. For a discussion of Aristotle's views concerning this see Victor Kal, *On Intuition and Discursive Reasoning in Aristotle* (Leiden: E.J. Brill, 1988), especially pp. 44-53.

"mystical" experience. Suhrawardī considers such experiences the ground upon which a discursive philosophy may be systematically constructed by means of methods such as demonstration.

The validity of such discursive accounts depends ultimately upon the subject's experience. Suhrawardī attributes to mystical vision, intuition, and, in general, to the experiential mode of knowledge the same status as that of the primary, self-evident *(badīhī)* premises of demonstration. Suhrawardī uses a favorite analogy to describe his view of knowledge. He compares physical observation *(irṣād jismānī)* with spiritual observation *(irṣād rūḥānī)*, and states that the same kind of certitude, if not a higher level, as obtained from the world of sense-data *(al-maḥsūsāt)* is obtained from observing or "seeing" the non-corporeal.[1] He uses this analogy in its various forms in many places in his writings, and the commentators also use it to illustrate the fundamentals of the illuminationist theory of knowledge.[2]

For Suhrawardī, one does not proceed to know a thing by analyzing it (using the method of conception-assent, to which we will refer below), but by having an intuitive grasp of its total reality and then analyzing the intuition. This means that the philosophy of illumination is founded on visions and mystical experiences of the whole of reality and not on defining the multiple things *in* reality. Suhrawardī's theory of definition, as we saw in the preceding chapter, does in fact reflect this basic epistemological position.[3]

1.1 The Ontological Basis for the Lack of Certitude in Peripatetic Epistemology

Apart from the formal critique of the Peripatetic methodology, Suhrawardī attacks the Peripatetic view of knowledge on the basis of his

[1] Specific reference is made to the science of astronomy *(al-'ilm al-hay'a)*, with the implication that, just as one may predict astronomical occurrences in the future, one may make valid predictions concerning the unseen spiritual realm as well. See, for example, Suhrawardī,*Opera II*, p. 13.

[2] See Shīrāzī, *Sharḥ II;* Ibn al-Khaṭīb, *Rawḍat al-Ta'rīf*, II, pp. 564, 565.

[3] See above, Ch. III. §3-4.

own view of being as well. We shall discuss Suhrawardī's theory of being in more detail at the end of this chapter. Briefly, it is a theory according to which the real existence, or the essence of the "seen" (sensed or intellectually perceived) entity, is the foundation of being. It regards being in the univocal sense as purely abstract, or mental, or what may be called ideal. This ideal entity exists in the mind only, and cannot serve as the foundation for the being of things "seen." The essences of these entities determine what they are, and in the real world what we see is determined by them. Thus, essences of things are the most real and are thus the most knowable, and for Suhrawardī only the real essences of things—as basic and perceived ontic entities—form the foundation of an ontology that serves to explain the process of knowing things.

At the end of his general critique of the Peripatetic theory of being, Suhrawardī, in a famous and important Third Section of the *Philosophy of Illumination,I,*[1] devotes the second of his ten "judgements" *(ḥukūmāt),* §70, to an attack on the Peripatetic view of the foundation of knowledge. The section is entitled, "On explaining that the Peripatetic [position] makes it impossible that anything be known."[2] This section is divided into two parts; in the first, Suhrawardī enumerates his arguments against the Peripatetics, and in the second he provides an alternative illuminationist basis for knowledge. In his arguments against the Peripatetics, Suhrawardī addresses himself to six issues:

1- According to the Peripatetics, substances *(al-jawāhir)* have unknown differentiæ *(fuṣūl majhūla).*

2- Substantiality *(al-jawhariyya)* is known to the Peripatetics only by means of negative attribution, i.e., it does not indicate a thing's reality.

3- For the Peripatetics, the soul and the separate substances *(al-mufāraqāt),* i.e., all manner of substances such as the intellects, are unknown differentiæ.

[1] Suhrawardī, *Opera II,* pp. 61-105.

[2] Ibid., p. 73. Shīrāzī adds, "This [the impossibility of knowledge] is a necessary corollary of the Peripatetic theorems, and for this reason Suhrawardī has added 'they make necessary' "*(Sharḥ II,* p. 203:14-15).

4- For the Peripatetics, a thing's accidents and attributes, which are subsumed under various categories, are mere mental concepts. This means that, for example, the idea color *(al-lawniyya)* is a mental concept *(amr i'tibārī)* and does not have a being out there *(lā wujūd fi' l-a'yān);* this implies that the Peripatetics cannot "construct" basic conceptions of bodies *(ajsām)* or of accidents from things that are out there.[1]

5- The Peripatetics regard being in the univocal sense (as considered in the *metaphysica generalis),*[2] as the "most apparent" *(aẓhar)* thing. For Suhrawardī, being in the univocal sense is a mental concept which is not present in the real entities in the world out there. Notice that when examining Suhrawardī's theory of definition, we indicated that the most apparent thing serves as the basis of definition.[3] If being in the univocal sense is considered by the Peripatetics to be the most apparent thing,[4] then *it* must serve as the basis of definition. But such a definition cannot, according to Suhrawardī, be "scientific," because it would mean that an abstract concept, whose existence depends on the mind of the subject, be accepted as the basis for the real sciences, and this is absurd and contrary to illuminationist realism.

6- The concomitants *(al-lawāzim)* of a thing, i.e., properties and accidents or non-essential attributes, by means of which things are described by the Peripatetics, are also mental concepts. This means that such descriptions do not make anything known as it exists in the real world, which is the intention of illuminationist theory of knowledge.

[1] Suhrawardī, *Opera II,* p. 73.

[2] See Philip Merlan, *From Platonism to Neoplatonism,* 3rd ed. (The Hague: Martinus Nijhoff, 1968), pp. 160-220. In recent Persian philosophy, the distinction is made between 1-*metaphysica generalis (umūr 'āmma);* 2- substance and accidents; 3- theology or *metaphysica specialis (ilāhī bi-ma'nā-yi akhaṣṣ).* See, for example, Muḥammad H.F. Tūnī, *Ilāhiyyāt* (Tehran: Tehran University Press, 1333 A.H.), pp. 1-4. This distinction is also made by Suhrawardī, see above, Ch III.§3.2.

[3] Suhrawardī, *Opera II,* p. 18.

[4] In Peripatetic ontology, being is considered a general, self-evident concept *(mafhūm 'āmm badīhī).* See Tūnī, *Ilāhiyyāt,* p. 5; Sayyid Jalāl al-Dīn Ashtiyānī, *Hastī* (Mashhad: Khurāsān Press, 1379 A.H.), pp. 7-12; Maḥmūd Shahābī, *Būd va Namūd* (Tehran: Tehran University Press, 1335 A.H.), pp. 10-15.

Suhrawrdī's six points against the Peripatetics are all based on his illuminationist theory of being. This theory considers things and essences to be in themselves the source of their reality. In other words, "apparent" or "manifest" is an essential attribute which, if *in* the essence, will determine the degree to which the thing can be known. The more "seen" (sensed or intellectually perceived) a thing is, the better known it is. Suhrawardī's arguments against the Peripatetics show that he regards such a thing as "rationality" (by means of which the Peripatetics claim they know what "man" is) to be a mental abstraction that does not indicate at all what man is, for man's reality has to be "seen" in order that it may be known.

In the second part of this section (§70), Suhrawardī presents the rudiments of his own view of how knowledge is obtained. Simple things, i.e., things whose essences are one and not compounded of two or more elements, are things unknown to the Peripatetics, but are things that can be known to the practitioners of the philosophy of illumination. The principle emphasized by Suhrawardī is that, to be known, a thing has to be "seen" (use of *mushāhada)* as-it-is *(kamā huwa),* especially if it is simple *(basīṭ).*[1] The knowledge thus gained by the person who "sees" the thing as-it-is will allow him to dispense with definition *(istaghnā 'an al-ta'rīf).*[2] These arguments provide a transition between what we may call the mental approach to knowledge, and an approach that emphasizes a kind of direct "vision" of the essences of real things and insists that knowledge is valid only if the objects are "sensed."[3]

Let us examine Suhrawardī's arguments. He begins with an example. "Black," he argues, is a "simple unitary thing" *(shay' wāḥid basīṭ)* which, when known, is known as-it-is; it has no parts, some of which may or may not be known. "Black" cannot be defined at all for someone who does not see it as-it-is *(lā yumkin ta'rīfuhu li-man lā yushāhiduhu kamā huwa).* That is, if the simple thing "black" is "seen," it is known; if not, no definition of it will or can ever convey full or real knowledge of it. Suhrawardī's insistence that this is the case with simple, non compound entities is

[1] See Shīrāzī, *Sharḥ II,* p. 204:11-14.

[2] Ibid.

[3] See Suhrawardī, *Opera II,* pp. 42, 134-135.

concordant with the view of the Peripatetics.[1] But his view, which requires that the subject perceive the "whole" object for it to be known, is initiated with the general proposition that knowledge of things rests on a relation between an object and a knowing subject, and adds more. It demands that the knowing subject be in a position in which it perceives the thing *directly*, in a manner that corresponds to sight as an actual encounter between the seeing subject and the object seen, an encounter in which any obstacle between the two is lifted and what is obtained is a "relation" between them. It is this kind of "illuminationist relation" *(iḍāfa ishrāqiyya)* that characterizes Suhrawardī's view of the foundation of knowledge. Therefore, Suhrawardī stipulates that, "should a thing be seen, then one can dispense with its definition *(man shāhadahu [al-shay'] istaghnā 'an al-ta'rīf)*," and that in this case, "the form of the thing in the mind is the same as its form in sense-perception" *(ṣūratuhu fī'l-'aql ka-ṣūratihi fī'l-ḥiss)*.[2] This view of knowledge is a main principles in the foundation of the philosophy of illumination.[3]

Suhrawardī goes on to say that knowledge of compound things is obtained as a consequence of knowledge of simple entities. This he explains by first positing the existence of a relation between simple real things *(al-basā'iṭ al-ḥaqīqiyya)* and their simple mental counterparts *(al-basā'iṭ al-dhihniyya)* by means of sense-perception, such as knowledge of colors, sounds, shapes, tastes, smells, etc. He argues by generalizing this principle, one can create a basis for universal knowledge. Therefore, knowledge of simple things is by means of their own essences, while knowledge of compound things is by means of their essential attributes. The immediate corollary is that substance (a simple entity which, according to Suhrawardī, is a real thing) may be known by itself, but only by way of an

[1] Suhrawardī, *Paths and Havens:Logic*, fol. 15 v.

[2] Suhrawardī, *Opera II*, pp. 73-74.

[3] By *mushāhada*, Suhrawardī means a special mode of cognition that enables the person to have an immediate grasp of the essence of the object. Suhrawardī, *Kalimat al-Taṣawwuf* (MS Tehran: Majlis, *Majmū'a* 3071), p. 398: *al-mushāhada hiya shurūq al-anwār 'alā al-nafs bi-ḥaythu yanqaṭi' munāza'āt al-wahm*. Cf. Mullā Ṣadrā, *Ta'līqāt, Sharḥ II*, p. 204 (margin).

illuminationist relation to the perceiving subject, who "senses" or "sees" it as the essence of the attributes of that real thing.

For Suhrawardī, knowledge is fundamentally obtained by means of a special mode of perception, which is called "seeing" or "vision" *(mushāhada)*. This special mode of perception, which is said to be higher and more fundamental than predicative knowledge, emphasizes intuitive knowledge, where the subject has an immediate grasp of the object without the mediation of a predicate.[1] Thus, while for the Peripatetics, knowledge takes the form of a predicative proposition (X is Y), Suhrawardī's intuitive knowledge can be reduced to what is nowadays called an existential proposition (X is) where "is" signifies the essence.

We shall analyze this special mode of perception and knowledge in greater detail. But first, we shall examine briefly the divisions of knowledge into conception and assent, in order to elucidate the details of Suhrawardī's objections to Peripatetic epistemology. As will be made clear below, Suhrawardī's insistance on reformulating the standard Peripatetic view of conception and assent is indicative of an illuminationist epistemological

[1] I mean a kind of knowledge which is beyond ordinary knowledge. This kind of knowledge is "purely intuitive," writes Philip Merlan, "which grasps the object without the mediation of a predicate" (Merlan, *From Platonism to Neoplatonism,* p. 185). This is knowledge pertinent to things whose very nature dictates that they not have any predicates, such as God. This knowledge has to do with things "above being" and is called ἀγχίνοια by Aristotle (Merlan, Ibid., p. 186). It is usually translated as "intuition," or "quick wit." Cf. Aristotle, *Posterior Analytics* II. 34, 89b10 ff.: ἀγχίνοία ἐστιν εὐστοχία τις ἐν ἀσκέπτῳ χρόνῳ τοῦ μέσου. Cf. idem, *Nicomachean Ethics* VI.9, 1142b6 ff. Plotinus is considered the most significant Greek proponent of intuition (e.g. Cairo, *The Evolution of Theology in the Greek Philosophers* [Glasgow, 1923], vol. 1, pp. 220-221). "The essentials of the intuitionist theory are these: I have immediate or direct acquaintance with external reality in my sense-perceptions. I have immediate or direct acquaintance with internal reality, that is, with the process of mind, by introspection as the inner sense" (Leighton, *Man and Cosmos* [Appleton, 1922], p. 51). Cf. the distinction between πειθώ and ἀνάγκη (literally: persuasion vs. logical necessity, thus the distinction between discursive and immediate knowledge), in Plotinus *Enneads,* V. 3.6.

position in philosophy. It does not merely indicate preference in logical terminology, as interpreted by the commentator Shīrāzī.[1]

2. Conception and Assent: A First Epistemological Division

2.1 Suhrawardī's Objections to the Peripatetics

In the very first section of the *Paths and Havens,* Suhrawardī presents his position on the division of knowledge into conception and assent.This philosophical position differs from that of the Peripatetics with respect to three points. 1- The Peripatetics divide knowledge in general into conception and assent,[2] while for Suhrawardī it is every "object of quest" *(maṭlūb)*—i.e., problem or question—that must be so divided.[3] It is not clear why Suhrawardī insists on this point, except to indicate his belief that, in some cases, intuitive knowledge of an "object of quest" is a conception that includes assent, while in others assent may be separate from, and follow upon, conception. 2- The Peripatetics treat the division of knowledge at length, and discuss the various conditions that must be met by conception and assent in predication. Suhrawardī's discussion, in contrast, is a brief, primarily descriptive discussion, aimed at exposing the Peripatetics' errors.[4] 3- The definition of conception as "obtaining in the mind the form of things that are indicated by simple utterances," and of assent as "a judgement on two things as to whether the one is the other or not," are said to be wrong by Suhrawardī.[5]

Suhrawardī accepts the formal Peripatetic division of knowledge into conception and assent. But, for knowledge of anything to have more than purely formal validity, it must be founded on Divine inspiration. The illuminationist position stipulates that Divine assistance allows the person to

[1] See Shīrāzī, *Sharḥ II,* pp.41-42.

[2] Cf. Avicenna, *al-Shifā': al-Madkhal,* III, pp. 17-18; idem, *al-Shifā': al-Burhān,* I, pp. 51-53, III, p. 57; idem, *al-Shifā': al-Ilāhiyyāt,* I.1, pp. 29-36; idem, *al-Najāt,* pp. 3-4, 60; al-Ghazālī, *Mi'yār al-'Ilm,* pp. 67-68.

[3] Suhrawardī, *Paths and Havens:Logic,* fol. 1v.

[4] Ibid.

[5] Ibid., fol. 1r.

come to know the thing as-it-is.[1] The epistemological characteristic of knowledge founded on inspiration is that it is a knowledge by presence, and consists of conception of a thing together with its immediate assent. Knowledge by presence distinguishes illuminationist epistemology from the Peripatetic theory. Further, the division of knowledge into what is self-evident *(badīhī)*—also called primary *(awwalī)*—and speculative *(naẓarī)* or acquired *(muktasab)*, which is the Peripatetic division of both conception and assent, is abandoned by Suhrawardī in favor of the division of both into innate and acquired.[2] This division points to a different epistemological direction than that of the Peripatetics. Innately knowable things serve as the foundation of the special "sight" or "vision" *(mushāhada)* through which things are truly known.[3] Certitude in knowledge, which is the aim of science, is therefore based on innate visions and intuitions which, on the one hand, serve as the logical foundation for formal validity of science, and

[1] Suhrawardī, *Intimations:Logic*, p. 2: *yua'yyid ibn al-bashar bi-rūḥ qudsī yurih al-shay' kamā huwa.*"Divine assistance" is similar to the role of the Active Intellect in Peripatetic epistemology. The Holy Spirit, *rūḥ al-qudus*, and *ravān bakhsh*, which is the Persian equivalent, meaning *dator spiritus*, as the giver of Divine assistance, is identified by Suhrawardī in many instances with the the Active Intellect. It is also named the "giver of knowledge and Divine aid" *(wāhib al-'ilm wa'l-ta'yīd)*. Suhrawardī, *Opera II*, p. 201. Cf. idem, *Opera III*, p. 221: "...rays emanate from the Holy Spirit." The Holy Spirit is further identified as the *dator formarum (wāhib al-ṣuwar)* and with the archangel Gabriel. (idem, *Opera II*, p. 265). In illuminationist cosmology the equivalent of the Holy Spirit is an abstract (non-corporeal) light called Isfahbad al-Nāsūt who, in addition to acting as the Active Intellect and the *dator formarum*, has a special function (which is also a kind of pure self-consciousness), because it indicates its own essence by its own self: *wa huwa al-nūr al-mudabbir al-ladhī huwa Isfahbad al-Nāsūt wa huwa al-mushīr ilā nafsihi bi'l-anā'iyya.* Idem, *Opera II*, p. 201. For a detailed discussion of the role of the *dator formarum* in illuminationist epistemology as well as its position in physics, see Shīrāzī, *Sharḥ II*, pp. 263-269. Its "highest" function is said to be to give being *(wāhib al-ṣuwar yu'tī al-wujūd)*. Ibid., p. 268.

[2] Suhrawardī, *Intimations:Logic*, p. 2; idem, *Paths and Havens:Logic*, fol. 96r; idem, *Opera II*, p. 18. Cf. Baghdādī, *al-Mu'tabar*, I, 7-8.

[3] Suhrawardī, *Opera II*, pp. 18-19. Cf. Baghdādī, *al-Mu'tabar*, I, 4; III, 35-41.

on the other hand, serve as the psychological foundations of certitude in knowledge.[1]

Suhrawardī was opposed to the Peripatetic subordination of the scope and function of conception to assent because this restricts the highest form of knowledge (*'ilm*, or *ma'rifa*)[2] to the mere formula of essentialist definition.[3] Suhrawardī argues that such a method as that of the Peripatetics fails to lead to an adequate foundation of certitude in respect to knowledge. This knowledge, he maintains, is the true and higher correspondence (*muṭābaqa*) between the subject and the object resulting as a relation between the two *in* the self-consciousness (*anā'iyya*) of the subject.[4] This illuminationist position requires that assent is to be subordinated to conception (in the sense of intuitive knowledge). Also, Suhrawardī introduces a whole "group" of conceptions that carry assent with them which go beyond the self-evident conceptions in the Peripatetic scheme, and which include the ultimate knowledge of both the knowing "self" and the essence of things as they are.

[1] This illuminationist position in theory of knowledge may be indicative of a "Platonic" theory. Cf. F.E. Peters, *Aristotle and the Arabs* (New York: New York University Press, 1968), p. 173: "The weapon of *a priori* knowledge (*ma'rifa awwaliyya*) is used against the whole structure of Peripatetic psychology, and it is through his application of the same criterion that Abu'l-Barakāt arrives at Razian or, better, Platonic positions on absolute time and absolute space." See also Pines, "Studies in Abu'l-Barakāt al-Baghdādī's Poetics and Metaphysics," p.122.

[2] E.g. Avicenna, *al-Shifā' :al-Madkhal*, III, pp. 17-18. Both terms, *'ilm* and *ma'rifa*, are used by the Peripatetics to designate knowledge in the general sense, for which Suhrawardī uses the term *idrāk*, and this has the sense of perception or cognition as a process of knowledge. A possible exception is al-Ghazālī, who distinguishes between *ma'rifa* as pertinent to *taṣdīq*, and *'ilm* as pertinent to *taṣawwur* (al-Ghazāli, *Miḥak al-Naḥr*, ed. al-Na'sānī [Beirut: Dar al-Machreq, 1966], pp. 8-10.).

[3] Suhrawardī, *Paths and Havens:Logic*, fol. 100v.

[4] Ibid., fol. 100v, 100r. In this regard Plotinus' view of knowledge should be taken into account. Cf. P.V. Pistorius, *Plotinus and Neoplatonism* (Cambridge: Bowes and Bowes, 1952), p. 111: "Plotinus regards knowledge as the result of the imperfect human method of analysis and synthesis, while intuition is the perfection of self-knowledge, when there is complete identity between the subject and object of such knowledge." See Plotinus, *Enneads* V.3, 2-3.

Through his critique of the Peripatetics, Suhrawardī directs the reader's attention to a new formulation of the twofold division of knowledge. This, as we shall see, anticipates "illuminationist knowledge" *(al-'ilm al-ishrāqī),* a kind of knowledge based either solely on conception or on the state of the self in which conception and assent take place simultaneously.

2.2 The Illuminationist Division of Knowledge

Suhrawardī's criterion for true or certain knowledge is met only by a method through which a thing is "seen" thus known as-it-is. To "see" a thing in this sense is equal to the act of obtaining the essence of the thing. We observed that Suhrawardī holds the philosophical position that definition (as understood by the Peripatetics) does not lead to a valid conception, and hence neither to knowledge of the thing's essence.[1] So far, he has criticized the Peripatetics and, as we saw, stipulated the necessity for the aid of a Divine spirit in obtaining knowledge.[2] This, we further observed, simply indicates an alternative epistemological theory designated knowledge by presence *(al-'ilm al-ḥuḍūrī).*

We now begin to examine the *Philosophy of Illumination* on the question of the foundation of knowledge, and here the second rule (§8) of Part One, I, is of special significance. In this section, Suhrawardī picks up the question he had raised in the *Intimations* regarding the Peripatetic division of knowledge into conception and assent. Of particular interest also are the views of the commentators Shahrazūrī and Shīrāzī, to whom we shall make reference.[3]

The section we are examining bears the title "On the division [of knowledge] conception and assent" in Corbin's edition of the *Philosophy of Illumination.* This title is added by Corbin as well as by the commentator Shīrāzī, but is not given by Shahrazūrī in his commentary.[4] The terms "conception" and "assent" are not illuminationist terms; they are not used by

[1] See above, Ch. III.3.

[2] Suhrawardī, *Intimations:Logic,* p. 2.

[3] Shīrāzī, *Sharḥ II,* pp. 38:13-45:1.

[4] Suhrawardī, *Opera II,* p. 15. Shīrāzī, *Sharḥ II,* p. 38:13. Cf. Shahrazūrī, *Sharḥ,* fol. 27r.

Suhrawardī in the *Philosophy of Illumination.*[1] It was later commentators who, in their attempt to modify Suhrawardī's views in order to bring them into conformity with the traditional Peripatetic scheme, identified this section of Suhrawardī's work with the division of knowledge into "conception" and "assent." This, however, is an incorrect designation for the section, and has to be avoided. Shahrazūrī, whose *Commentary on the Philosophy of Illumination (Sharḥ Ḥikmat al-Ishrāq)* is more faithful to Suhrawardī's illuminationist intentions than the commentary by Shīrāzī, avoids the terms conception and assent. As we examine the section it will become clear that Suhrawardī is attempting to reformulate the Peripatetic theory and is quite deliberately avoiding the use of the terms conception and assent.

Suhrawardī begins the section by stipulating that "perception" *(idrāk),*[2] as the most general act of knowing an "absent thing" *(al-shay' al-ghā'ib),* occurs when the idea *(mithāl)* of the reality *(ḥaqīqa)*[3] of the thing is obtained by the person, i.e., *in* the knowing subject.[4] Suhrawardī considers this to be a more general view of knowledge than that signified by the

[1] In the only place where the term *taṣdīq* is used in the *Philosophy of Illumination,* it is used in the sense of "affirmation" in regard to propositions *(Opera II,* p. 57).

[2] Translation of the term *idrāk* (as used by Suhrawardī) into English poses some difficulties. The term "perception" is probably an adequate equivalent, but it should be understood in the most general sense of "apprehension." For the various shades of the meaning of the term "perception" as used in philosophy, see R.J. Hirst, "Perception," *Encyclopedia of Philosophy,* VI, 79-87. For various Greek equivalents of *idrāk* and its modifications such as *idrāk bi'l-'aql, idrāk bi'l-fahm, idrāk bi'l-ḥiss,* etc., see Afnan, *Lexicon,* pp. 98-99. Cf. F. Rahman, *Avicenna's De Anima* (London: Oxford University Press, 1959), p. 278; Avicenna, *al-Najāt,* pp. 277-279. For a history of "perception" in Greek philosophy, see D.W. Hamlyn, *Sensation and Perception* (London: Routledge & Kegan Paul, 1961), pp. 1-39.

[3] Suhrawardī uses the term *ḥaqīqa* to designate *māhiyya,* i.e., *quiddity. Opera II,* pp. 16-16. Cf. Shīrāzī, *Sharḥ* II, p. 45: 1-3.

[4] Suhrawardī, Opera II, p. 15: *huwa [idrāk] bi-ḥuṣūl mithāl ḥqīqatihi fīka.* Cf. idem, *Opera III,* pp. 2-3: *shinākht . . . .ān bāshad ki ṣūratī az ān-i ū dar tu ḥāṣil shavad.* The same statement is made by Suhrawardī in one of his mystical works, *Kalimat al-Taṣawwuf,* pp. 353-354.

Peripatetic's use of the terms *ma'rifa* and *'ilm*.[1] The term, *idrāk,* translated as "perception," indicates various ways or levels of knowing, including sense-perception *(idrāk ḥissī) and* intellectual perception *(idrāk 'aqlī)*,[2] as well as intuition and vision. In addition, for Suhrawardī, the term *idrāk* applies to a more restricted form of knowing than "realizing" or "obtaining" *(ḥuṣul),* a term which is used to describe, or designate, the act of knowing in the widest sense.

Suhrawardī reasons thus: to know an object (in the most general sense of knowing) means that the subject "obtains" the "idea" of the reality or *ḥaqīqa,* of the object. This proposition, the commentator Shīrāzī argues, signifies "knowledge based on illumination and presence" *(al-'ilm al-ishrāqī al-ḥuḍūrī),* by means of which an "illuminationist relation" *(iḍāfa ishrāqiyya)* is established between the subject and the object, resulting in knowledge of essence.[3] Illuminationist knowledge (in contrast to Peripatetic knowledge, which takes the form of conception, then later, assent) is non-predicative. It is based on the relation—obtained without a temporal extension—between the "present" object and the knowing subject, and it is held by Suhrawardī to be the most valid way to knowledge. This epistemological position is also the basis of Suhrawardī's critique of the Peripatetic theory of definition. To repeat, it is a kind of knowledge by means of which the essences of things (i.e., things as they are) may be "obtained." This kind of illuminationist knowledge is validated by the experience of the "presence" *(ḥuḍūr)* of the object, i.e., it does not require a conception and then (later in time) an assent, it is non-predicative, and it does not involve a temporal process. It is immediate; it occurs in a durationless instant *(ān).*

[1] The term *idrāk* as used by Suhrawardī is like a genus that covers a number of species, such as *'ilm, ma'rifa, ḥiss,* etc. al-Ghazāli divides *idrāk* into *'ilm* and *ma'rifa* (al-Ghazālī, *Miḥak al-Naẓar,* p. 102). In recent Persian philosophy, *idrāk,* which is taken synonymously with *shinākht* or *shināsā'ī,* is divided into *idrāk ḥissi; idrāk dhihnī; idrāk 'aqlī; shu'ūr* (both internal and external). See A.M. Mishkāt al-Dīnī, *Taḥqīq dar Ḥaqīqat-i 'Ilm* (Tehran: Terhran University Press, 1344 A.H.), pp. 2ff.

[2] See F. Rahman, *Avicenna's De Anima,* pp. 18-22, 25, 34; idem, *Avicenna's Psychology* (London: Oxford University Press, 1952), pp. 38-40.

[3] Shīrāzī, *Sharḥ II,* p. 39: 6-13. This kind of knowledge depends only on the presence *(mujarrad al-ḥuḍūr)* of the object.

The examples given by Shīrāzī of such illuminationist knowledge are the following: knowledge of God *('ilm al-bārī),* knowledge of incorporeal separate entities *('ilm al-mujarradāt al-mufāraqa),* and knowledge of oneself *('ilm bi-anfusinā).*[1] From the perspective of this illuminationist epistemological position, not all types of knowledge can be confined to the predicative conception-assent. This position further holds that "knowledge by presence" *(al-'ilm al-ḥuḍūrī,* presencing knowledge) is prior to "formal knowledge" *(al-'ilm al-ṣūrī).* But this priority can be "proven" only through illuminationist knowledge itself, when the illuminationist relation between the subject and object is so obtained.[2]

We have seen that Suhrawardī considers knowledge to be dependent on the relation between the subject and the object. His arguments in support of his view are as follows. Should the essence of a thing be obtained by the subject, then the thing is known; otherwise, the state *(ḥāl)* of the subject prior to knowledge and after it will be the same, in which case nothing can be said to have obtained. Therefore the state (the psychological response) of the subject to the object is one of the factors that determines whether knowledge is obtained or not. This subjective condition placed by Suhrawardī on knowledge by experience, by presence, and by intuition is not part of the fundamentally predicative and formal Peripatetic thoeoy of knowledge, as presented and emphasized by Suhrawardī.

One of the most significant statements made by Suhrawardī in this section is that there must be a complete correspondence between the "idea" obtained in the subject, and the object; only such a correspondence shows

[1] Shīrāzī, *Sharḥ II,* p. 38: 16-19: *al-'ilm al-ishrāqī al-ladhī yakfī fīhi mujarrad al-ḥuḍūr ka 'ilm al-bārī ta'ālā wa 'ilm al-mujarradāt al-mufāraqa wa 'ilminā bi-anfusinā.* Cf. Aristotle, *Metaphysics* I.2, 982b28-983a11; XII.7 1178b14-16. Suhrawardī develops the details of such concepts as *al-'ilm al-ishrāqi, ḥuḍūr, al-mushāhada al-ishrāqiyya,* etc. in his *Paths and Havens (Opera I,* pp. 480-496).

[2] See Shīrāzī, *Sharḥ II,* p. 38: 16-19. In general, any kind of knowledge which places an emphasis upon the intuitive mode of cognition is distinctly non-formal. Cf. Aristotle, *Metaphysics* VII.10, 1036a1-8; XII.9, 1075a5-7; Plotinus, *Enneads,* IV.3.18, V.3.3. Suhrawardī's concept of knowledge by presence may be compared to what Gilson calls "intuition of being." See Étienne Gilson, *Being and Some Philosophers* (Toronto: Pontifical Institute of Mediæval Studies, 1949), pp. 190-215.

that knowledge of the thing as-it-is has been obtained.[1] This means that to obtain knowledge, a kind of "unity" has to be established between the subject and the object, and the psychological state of the subject is a determining factor in establishing this unity. In anticipation of what will follow, we point out that for the Peripatetics, knowledge is ultimately established by a kind of "union" *(ittiḥād)* or "connection" *(ittiṣāl)* with the Active Intellect, after an initial separation or disjunction *(infiṣāl)*. The idea of union and/or connection with the Active Intellect is, as we shall see below, vehemently attacked by Suhrawardī. He argues that the unity of the subject and object is obtained in the knowing person by an act of self-realization, and that this can take place because there is no disjunction in reality, but only gradations of the manifestation of essence.

We conclude that Suhrawardī's position of what constitutes illuminationist knowledge is based on the unity of the subject and object by means of the "idea" of the object being obtained in the consciousness of the subject. It is crucial that we understand this fundamental illuminationist position. The subject's immediate experience of the "presence" of the object determines the validity of knowledge itself. Thus experience of such things as God, the self, separate entities, etc., is the same as knowledge of them.

3. Knowledge by Means of Illumination

3.1 Suhrawardī's Critique of the Peripatetic View of Knowledge as Union with the Active Intellect

In the *Intimations*, Suhrawardī identifies two views regarding knowledge in the general sense (i.e., *idrāk)*. The first view is stated as follows: "Some people hold the opinion that when someone knows something, this means that the subject and the object become one."[2] The second view is stated to be: "Some other people hold the opinion that when the soul knows [something], this means that it is united with the Active Intellect."[3]

[1] Suhrawardī, *Opera II*, p. 15. Cf. Shīrāzī, *Sharḥ II*, pp. 40:8- 41:5.

[2] Suhrawardī, *Opera I*, p. 68: *ba'ḍ al-nās ẓanna anna idrāk al-mudrik shay'an huwa an yaṣīra huwa huwa.*

[3] Ibid.: *ẓannū anna idrāk al-nafs huwa ittiḥāduhā bi'l-'aql al-fa''āl.*

Both views are rejected on the basis of arguments taken from physics, namely, that two things become one either by mixture *(imtizāj)*, connection *(ittiṣāl)*, or by synthetic combination *(tarkīb majmūʿī)*, all of which apply to bodies alone.[1] Suhrawardī thus rejects the classical view of union with the Active Intellect as grounds for knowledge.[2]

In the *Paths and Havens* Suhrawardī discusses the problem of knowledge and perception in a manner similar to that of the *Intimations*.[3] The discussion is, however, more elaborate and provides us with clear statements concerning the illuminationist theory of knowledge. In §201, Suhrawardī derides the opinion that knowledge in general obtains when the subject becomes one with the "form" *(ṣūra)* of the object.[4] The arguments against this opinion are again based on the physical impossibility of two different things becoming one.The argument presented here takes on an added dimension when Suhrawardī introduces the notion that man is a substance conscious of its own essence *(al-jawhar al-shāʿir bi-dhātihi)*. Therefore, he can dispense with union with the forms, and remain his own self (or, as he states, "you are you," *anta anta)* regardless of any act of perception or of knowledge.[5] This assumes that self-consciousness is the ultimate reality, a question to which we shall return later on.

[1] That connection and disjunction are only attributes of corporeal bodies is a metaphysical dictum put forth by Suhrawardī *(Opera I*, pp. 68, 475), but the arguments in support of the dictum are developed in physics. See Suhrawardī, *Kitāb al-Talwīḥāt [al-ʿilm al-thānī]* (MS. Berlin 5062) (hereafter cited as *Intimations:Physics)*, fol. 43r, v; See also idem, *Paths and Havens:Physics*, fol. 111r-112v, 115v.

[2] See Philip Merlan, *Monopsychism Mysticism Metaconsciousness* (The Hague: Martinus Nijhoff, 1963), pp. 85-113. Cf. Suhrawardī, *Opera I*, p. 69; Avicenna, *Mabdaʾ wa Maʿād*, tr. Mahmoud Shahābī (Tehran: Tehran University Press, 1332 A.H.), pp. 112-117. Merlan holds that Avicenna has criticized Porphyry for professing the doctrine of union, which may be due to a work attributed to Porphyry (Merlan, *Monopsychism*, pp. 25-26). Merlan, however, erroneously considers union a "distinctive mark" of Suhrawardī's "oriental philosophy" (Merlan, *Monopsychism*, p. 25).

[3] Suhrawardī, *Opera I*, pp. 474 ff; *Paths and Havens:Physics*, fol. 194v ff.

[4] Suhrawardī, *Opera I*, p. 474.

[5] Suhrawardī, *Opera I*, pp. 474-475. Cf. idem, *Opera III*, p. 23: *tu'ī-yi tu*, consciousness is thy thouness.

After further considering the Peripatetic view of knowledge and perception, which he rejects,[1] Suhrawardī goes on to state his own views (§208). He first refers the reader to the *Philosophy of Illumination*, wherein his own doctrine is to be found.[2] He further states that it is necessary for the reader to become familiar with the method of the *Intimations* before studying the *Philosophy of Illumination*. This method is obtained by Suhrawardī, he stipulates, in a "conversation" with Aristotle,[3] and is stated to be: "Man should first investigate the knowledge of his own essence and then ascend to what is higher."[4]

The reference is to Suhrawardī's famous dream-vision of Aristotle,[5] which is recounted in full by Suhrawardī in the *Intimations*,[6] but mentioned in other places as well.[7] In this dream-vision, analyzed below, Suhrawardī points to the significance of self-knowledge in the illuminationist view of knowledge and perception, as opposed to the Peripatetic view of knowledge based on union with the Active Intellect.

3.2 Suhrawardī's Dream-vision of Aristotle

The dream-vision, as discussed in the *Intimations*, is an allegory through which Suhrawardī expostulates his view of knowledge.[8] This story has a number of characteristic components which it is necessary to analyze.

1- The vision. The vision appears to Suhrawardī at night, during a period described as one in which he had been greatly preoccupied with

[1] Suhrawardī, *Opera I*, p. 475 ff. Cf. *Paths and Havens:Physics, fol.* 115v.

[2] Suhrawardī, *Opera I*, p. 483.

[3] Ibid., p. 484.

[4] Ibid.: *wa huwa an yabḥatha al-insān fī 'ilmihi bi-dhātihi thumma yartaqī ilā mā huwa a'lā.*

[5] The "Aristotle" of the dream-vision is thought by Majid Fakhry to be the "Aristotle" of the *Theologia*, (M. Fakhry, *A History of Islamic Philosophy* [New York: Columbia University Press, 1970], p. 330, n. 10. Cf. *Opera I*, p. 112 notes). But it seems more likely that Suhrawardī means the Peripatetic master of philosophy, i.e., the real Aristotle, and not anyone else.

[6] Suhrawardī, *Opera I*, pp. 70-74.

[7] Ibid., p. 484.

[8] Suhrawardī, *Opera I*, pp. 70-74.

thought and ascetic practices *(riyāḍāt)*. The vision is described as resembling sleep *(shibh nawm)* and one which induces ecstasy *(khalsa)*, a state accompanied by overwhelming pleasure *(ladhdha)*, flashes *(barq)*, and a glittering light, stated to be one of the intermediary stages of illuminationist visionary experience.[1] In the vision, Aristotle, "master of philosophy" and "one who comes to the aid of souls," appears to Suhrawardī, who is struck at first with great fear and awe. His fear turns to friendship when Aristotle greets and welcomes him effusively.

2- The problem posed in the vision. The question asked of Aristotle, one with which Suhrawardī had been preoccupied, is said to be the question of knowledge *(mas'alat al-'ilm)*. Aristotle is asked what is knowledge, how it is obtained, what does it constitute, and how is it recognized.

3- The solution. Aristotle's solution is: "return to your soul (or self)."[2] It is important to note that the solution to the problem of what is knowledge is through the subject's own soul, its ipseity. Self-knowledge is a fundamental component of the illuminationist theory of knowledge. Knowledge (as perception, *idrāk)* of the soul is essential and self-constituted, because an individual is cognizant of his essence by means of that essence itself.[3] Self-consciousness and the concept of "I," i.e., the self-as-self or its ipseity, are the grounds of knowledge. What is ultimately gained through the initial consciousness of one's essence is a way to knowledge, [4] called the "science based on 'presence, and vision'" *(al-'ilm al-ḥudūrī al-shuhūdī)*, which is said to be higher than the type of knowledge obtained by the philosophers for whom it is based on union with the Active Intellect.[5]

[1] There are fifteen states discussed in the description of the illuminationist visionary experience, and each of them is stated to be accompanied by an experience of a special kind of light. See Suhrawardī, *Opera II*, p. 252; idem, *Opera I*, pp. 108, 114.

[2] Suhrawardī, *Opera I*, p. 70: *irji' ilā nafsika.*

[3] Ibid. : *adraka dhātaka bi-dhātika*. The self-conscious, self-constituted subject is to be compared with Avicenna's so-called "l'homme volant" (Peters, *Aristotle and the Arabs*, p. 173). See Rahman, *Avicenna's Psychology*, pp. 8-20.

[4] Suhrawardī, *Opera I*, p. 75. Cf. ibid., p. 121.

[5] Ibid., pp. 74, 88, 90.

By relating the dream-vision of Aristotle, Suhrawardī presents a metaphor by means of which he aims to solve epistemological problems he had explicated and confronted in his critique of the Peripatetics. The solution to these problems is by means of self-knowledge, which constitutes the ground of knowledge. This type of knowledge, we are told, is obtained by the illuminationists as they progress up to the highest station *(maqām)* of psychological perfection, stated to be that of the Brethren of Abstraction *(Ikhwān al-Tajrīd)*.[1] The "state of abstraction" *(maqām al-tajrīd)*, or purity reminiscent of the ṣūfī states, is stated in the *Intimations* to be a state in which the individual dissociates himself from all material preoccupations. [2] In this state of being the person is able to "see" his own essence and recognize the "I" as that which necessarily knows his own ipseity *(dhāt)*, which knowledge then serves as the basis for subsequent acquired knowledge and philosophical construction.[3]

Let us now turn to an examination of the problem of self-knowledge and its origin and development in the works of Suhrawardī.

3.3 Illuminationist View of Self-Knowledge

In the fourth "book" of the physics of the *Intimations*, which corresponds to the *De Anima*, Suhrawardī devotes an entire chapter (Ch. IV)[4] to a special consideration of the individual's self-knowledge, knowledge of his own essence, and self-consciousness.

The problem is introduced by the question: "Is it not the case that you are never unconscious of your own essence *(dhātuka)* in both sleep and waking?"[5] The question is immediately answered as follows. If one postulates in the mind a human being who is instantaneously *(daf'atan)* created in a perfect state, not using his limbs or sense-perception, this

[1] See Suhrawardī, *Opera I*, pp. 73, 73n., 95, 103, 113; idem, *Opera II*, pp. 242, 252.

[2] Suhrawardī, *Opera I*, p. 115.

[3] Ibid., p. 116. Cf. *Paths and Havens:Physics*, fol. 198r-201v.

[4] Suhrawardī, *Intimations:Physics*, fol. 60r-69r.

[5] Suhrawardī, *Intimations:Physics*, fol. 60: *alyasa annaka lā taghīb 'an dhātika fī ḥalatay nawmika wa yaqḥatika?*

human being will not be conscious of anything except his own being *(inniyya)*.[1] Suhrawardī further elaborates that knowledge of one's essence is necessary *(wājib)*.[2] What Suhrawardī has said so far in the physics of the *Intimations* (IV.3.1) is an elaboration of what is basically an Avicennan doctrine that posits a kind of *cogito* which serves as the basis for the individual's knowledge of himself.[3]

In the following section (IV.3.2), Suhrawardī establishes the non-corporeality of the subject's own essence, and equates the non-corporeal part of the subject's being with the rational soul (IV.3.3). Apart from the special emphasis placed by Suhrawardī on the problem of self-consciousness, the rest of Chapter IV of the physics of the *Intimations* is an epitome of the *De Anima* as he knew it through Avicenna's work. In the physics of the *Paths and Havens*, too, the problem of self-consciousness is stressed by Suhrawardī as he discusses problems of the soul, and it is said to be a kind of objective ipseity, the thou *(anta)*, the I, the he, of the subject, and is equated with the subject's *act* of knowing its own essence.[4]

The psychology of self-knowledge is discussed in detail by Suhrawardī, in the physics of both the *Intimations*[5] and the *Paths and Havens*.[6] The important point is that by means of the position given to self-knowledge, Suhrawardī is able to establish the validity of knowledge, i.e., that knowledge of essence (not attainable by means of the essentialist definition) may be obtained through knowledge of the self by the self.

[1] Ibid. In this *Gedankenexperiment* Suhrawardī, though undoubtedly aware of Avicenna's similar idea of the "suspended" man, does not refer to him.

[2] Ibid.

[3] See Rahman, *Avicenna's Psychology*, p. 10; Peters, *Aristotle and the Arabs*, p. 173, n. 216.

[4] This problem is treated in great detail in the physics of the *Paths and Havens* VI.8 (part of the section corresponding to the *De Anima*), entitled *"Fi'l-idrāk wa'l-tajrīdāt wa barāhīn tajarrud al-nafs 'an al-mādda wa 'iqnā'ātihi," (Paths and Havens:Physics*, fol. 194v-198r).

[5] Suhrawardī, *Intimations:Physics*, fol. 63r-69r, especially III.2, fol. 65r-69r, entitled *"Fī taḥrīrāt wa barāhīn wa istibṣārāt 'alā tajarrud al-nafs."*

[6] Suhrawardī, *Paths and Havens:Physics*, fol. 191r ff.

Perhaps the most significant outcome of Suhrawardī's view of self-knowledge is the two-way identification made among various "levels" of consciousness. Consciousness of essences is identified as an essential component of the rational soul.[1] Further, it is stated in the *Philosophy of Illumination* that everything which is conscious of its own essence is an "abstract light" *(nūr mujarrad)*.[2] Still further an "abstract light" is said to be a "self-subsisting light."[3] Therefore, the rational soul, through an "activity" of self-consciousness is identified as, or equated with, the concept "abstract light," which links the cosmic order to the physical order via the intermediary principle of consciousness and its various levels of intensity; this will be detailed at the end of this chapter.[4]

The identification just made is crucial for an understanding of the philosophy of illumination. Self-consciousness, both as a cosmic principle and as a psychological principle, constitutes the foundation of illuminationist knowledge. Illuminationist knowledge, fundamentally based on an activity of the soul,[5] is realized through self-knowledge and is associated with the special mode of perception referred to as "sight" or "vision" *(mushāhada)*.[6] Again, the basic principle of illuminationist knowledge is the relation of the "I" *(ana,* ipseity of the subject) to the essence of anything by means of the "being" *(huwa,* objectified ipseity, the that-ness) of the thing, both conscious "of" themselves and "in" themselves, and cognizant of what they are, necessarily.[7] The principle of illuminationist vision *(al-mushāhada al-ishrāqiyya)* enables the subject to know a thing as-it-is, i.e., to know its essence.[8] Thus illuminationist knowledge *(al-'ilm al-ishrāqī)* depends on the experience of the "presence of the thing" *(ḥuḍūr al-shay')*, which is not a predicative type of knowledge, but due solely to the *relation* between the subject and the object—this knowledge is called the

[1] E.g., Suhrawardī, *Paths and Havens:Physics,* fol. 175r ff.

[2] Suhrawardī, *Opera II,* p. 110.

[3] Ibid.

[4] Ibid., cf. Shīrāzī, *Sharḥ II,* p. 290:3-17.

[5] Suhrawardī, *Opera I,* p. 485.

[6] Ibid.

[7] Ibid., p. 484.

[8] Ibid., p. 486.

"knowledge based on illumination and presence" *(al-'ilm al-ishrāqī al-ḥuḍūrī).*[1] The knowing subject, when related to the object, grasps the essence of the object because of its *Evidenz.*

This special mode of cognition, which is Suhrawardī's answer to the Peripatetics' "inability" to know anything, transcends the predicative mode of knowledge, and is an intuitive mode of cognition which depends solely on the illuminationist relation *(al-iḍāfa al-ishrāqiyya)* between the subject and the object. This mode of cognition entails an immediate, a-temporal, grasp of the essence of the object,[2] and is possible because of self-knowledge. When this type of knowledge has to do with "universals" *(kulliyāt),* it takes place through the "presence" of the "form," which is imprinted in the soul's essence. As for individuals, knowledge of them takes place through the "presence" of their essences combined with an illumination received by the soul *(ishrāq li-al-nafs).* This knowledge may also be obtained when their form is actualized in something (e.g. in the imaginary forms *[al-ṣuwar al-khayāliyya]*) that is present before the soul, which in turn is illuminated by the soul.[3]

3.4 Self-Consciousness and Illumination

Suhrawardī identifies every entity which is cognizant of its essence with an abstract light, and thus links the soul of an individual human being with the cosmic principles or lights.[4] As we now examine further the illuminationist theory of self-consciousness, we consider Suhrawardī's statement, in the *Philosophy of Illumination,* II.1.6, that the perception of one's own self-consciousness *(idrāk al-anā'iyya)* is the same as the direct perception of what a thing is in itself *(idrāk mā huwa huwa),* and not a perception by

[1] Ibid., 487.

[2] *Ibid.,* p. 486: *mushāhada ishrāqiyya li-al-nafs; ibid.,* p. 487: *al-'ilm al-ishrāqī lā bi-ṣūra wa athar, bal bi-mujarrad iḍāfa khāṣṣa, huwa ḥuḍūr al-shay' ḥuḍūran ishrāqiyyan kamā li-al-nafs.*

[3] Ibid., p. 487.

[4] Cf. Shīrāzī, *Sharḥ II,* pp. 290ff., e.g.: *man yudriku dhātahu, ka-al-nafs al-nāṭiqa mathalan , fa-huwa nūr mujarrad.*

means of an idea *(mithāl)* of self-consciousness.[1] This is true of all things that are self-constituted and cognizant of their own essence. "You," states Suhrawardī, "are never unconscious of your essence." He "proves" this by stipulating that self-consciousness cannot be validated by means of anything corporeal, which in turn indicates "that by means of which 'you are you' is a thing which knows it own essence, and that thing is your self-consciousness."[2] From this basic illuminationist principle of epistemology Suhrawardī draws a general conclusion, namely that everything which is conscious of its own essence shares consciousness with all other things of the same rank; thus consciousness becomes the principle of illuminationist knowledge which holds true of all self-conscious beings, starting with cosmic consciousness and progressing down to individual human consciousness.[3] He concludes further that self-consciousness is equivalent to being manifest, or apparent *(ẓāhir)*, identified with "pure light" *(nūr maḥḍ)*.[4] Self-consciousness is thus identified with "apparentness (or manifestation) and light-as-such" *(nafs al-ẓuhūr wa al-nūriyya)*.[5] Subsequently, Suhrawardī is able to formulate the illuminationist principle of self-knowledge and its connection to cosmic lights as follows:

> Everyone who perceives his own essence is a pure light. And every pure light is manifest to, and perceives, its own essence.[6]

This principle is supported by the following statement, which distinguishes Suhrawardī's position from that of the Peripatetics:

[1] Suhrawardī, *Opera II*, p. 111: *idrāk al-anā'iyya huwa bi-'aynihi idrāk mā huwa huwa.*

[2] Ibid., p. 112: *mā anta bihi anta . . . .huwa anā'iyyatuka.*

[3] Cf. Suhrawardī, *Opera III*, pp. 23, 37: *dhāt-i tu dhātīst qā'im bi khud mujarrad az mādda ki az khud ghā'ib nīst.* The idea of cosmic and human consciousness as a principle of metaphysics, by means of which the same principle is applied to corporeal as well as non-corporeal entities, is found in Plotinus. See Plotinus, *Enneads,* V.3, 2-3.

[4] Suhrawardī, *Opera II*, pp. 113-114.

[5] Ibid., p. 114.

[6] Ibid.: *kull man adraka dhātahu fa-huwa nūr maḥḍ, wa kull nūr maḥḍ ẓāhir li-dhātihi wa mudrik li-dhātihi.* Shīrāzī considers this to mean the union of the subject and the object. Shīrāzī, *Sharḥ II*, p. 297:2-3: *fa'l-mudrik wa'l-mudrak wa'l-idrāk hāhunā wāḥid.*

> A thing's perception of its own self is [the same as] its being manifest to its own essence, not its being abstracted from matter as is the Peripatetic theory.[1]

Suhrawardī reduces the Peripatetic theory that a thing perceives itself by becoming free from matter and corporeality, to an absurdity. The Peripatetic theory would necessarily imply that prime matter, which is not a form of something else and is free of any other matter, be conscious of its own essence, which is absurd.[2]

There are two important points which follow from this illuminationist theory of self-knowledge, and these are related to the question of manifestation and the nature of abstract lights. The most important point is that "abstract lights" do not differ with respect to essence (or to reality *[ḥaqīqa]*),[3] but only with respect to degrees of manifest "intensity" *(shadda)*.[4] In terms of consciousness, therefore, it can be said that every "I" is essentially the same as any other "I" because, in principle, each one is self-conscious. However, they may differ with respect to the degree of self-consciousness. What follows next is that, because "abstract lights" do not differ in respect to their reality, one from another, then they form a continuum. Thus the "whole"*(al-kull)*, too, Suhrawardī concludes, must also be conscious of its essence.[5]

The most significant "light" in the cosmology of the philosophy of illumination is the light called Isfahbad al-Nāsūt. This light, which is referred to as the "managing light" *(al-nūr al-mudabbir)*,[6] is an abstract light that "controls" what is below it in rank;[7] it controls the activities of individual animal bodies and the faculties of their souls,[8] it redirects the emanation given to it by the controlling lights *(al-anwār al-qāhira)* to the

[1] Ibid. This section (§119) bears the title *Ḥukūma,* and the description given is taken from Shīrāzī, *Sharḥ II* (p. 297: 5-8).

[2] Suhrawardī, *Opera II*, p. 115.

[3] Ibid., p. 120.

[4] Ibid., pp. 119, 126-127.

[5] Ibid., p. 120ff.

[6] Ibid., p. 201.

[7] Ibid., p. 147.

[8] Ibid., pp. 204-207.

human bodies,[1] and it further bestows both control *(qahr)*[2] and love *(maḥabba)*.[3] This light, which in its activity resembles the Active Intellect of the Peripatetic cosmology, and is so identified by Suhrawardī himself who refers to it as the Holy Spirit, *dator scientiæ (wāhib al-'ilm)* and *dator spiritus (ravān bakhsh)*. This "light" is further equated with the *dator formarum (wāhib al-'ilm)*,[4] and is the link between the human and the cosmic realms (i.e., between the corporeal and the non-corporeal). This light, Isfahbad al-Nāsūt, is said to point to its self by its own self - consciousness.[5] Thus the link between the cosmic and the human is the principle of self-consciousness and self-knowledge. The light Isfahbad al-Nāsūt is symbolized by multiple lights emanating from one source; these lights are called the Isfahbadiyya lights.[6] The multiple lights act in accordance to their "archetype" *(arbāb al-ṣanam)* at all levels, and since human self-consciousness itself is an "abstract light," there is no discontinuity between the cosmic and the human realm;[7] rather, they form a continuous whole. This theory is in marked contrast to the Peripatetic view of the Active Intellect, which is "one" and acts not in continuous multiple manifestations (as with the Isfahbbadiyya lights in relation to their "source"

[1] Ibid., pp. 218-219.

[2] *Qahr* is similar in principle to the Empedoclean νεῖκος See Fakhry, *A History of Islamic Philosophy*, p. 333.

[3] Suhrawardī, *Opera II*, pp. 224-225.

[4] Suhrawardī, *Opera II*, p. 201.

[5] Ibid.: *huwa mushīr ilā nafsihi bi'l-anā'iyya.*

[6] Ibid., pp. 226-228, 237.

[7] In the illuminationist cosmology, what is "emanated," or simply obtained, from the Source of light, designated Light of Lights *(Nūr al-Anwār)*, is not separate from it, but.is continuous *with* it; nor are the emanated lights discrete. E.g., Suhrawardī, *Opera II*, p. 128: *wujūd nūr min Nūr al-Anwār laysa bi-an yanfaṣil minhu shay';* ibid., p. 137: *ishrāq Nūr al-Nūr 'alā al-anwār al-mujarrada laysa bi-infiṣāl shay' minhu.* Cf. ibid., p. 146: *al-nūr al-mujarrad lā yaqbal al-ittiṣāl wa'l-infiṣāl.* The Light of Lights and what emanates from it form a continuum, and thus, unlike Peripatetic cosmology, non-corporeal, separate entities are not discrete. The metaphor of "light" and its properties in propagating from one source describes the illuminationist cosmology very adequately.

the light Isfahbad al-Nāsūt), but as the *one* ultimate perfection of the intellect. [1]

Suhrawardī's search for certitude in knowledge leads him to see the foundation of knowledge as a multiplicity of experiences of essences (of the subject as well as of the object), which is considered by him to constitute both the grounds of man's immediate experience of the object as-it-is as well as the ground for the cosmic principles of self-consciousness and self-manifestation. We observed that the particular illuminationist mode of perception and knowledge depends on 1- the subject: its experience of essence; 2- the object: its apparentness or manifestation *(ẓuhūr,* similar to Husserl's *Evidenz)* and presence *(ḥuḍūr);* 3- the illuminationist relation *(al-iḍāfa al-ishrāqiyya)* between the subject and the object, active when the subject and the object are "present" and "manifest" to their own essence, and thus to each other. This, then, constitutes the grounds for the reconstructed illuminationist theory of knowledge, wherein the inadequacy of the Peripatetic essentialist definition is overcome. We shall now examine the actual "processes" that constitute illuminationist epistemology. This is the process that commences with and in the knowing subject and results in knowledge of the object, and is characterized by an activity in the subject's self-consciousness. He may intuit something, deduce something, or in some other way become acquainted with something unknown to him prior to when the process is triggered.

[1] I do not wish to discuss the problem of the Active Intellect in peripatetic philosophy in detail here. Briefly, in the common Peripatetic scheme, the Active Intellect *(al-'aql al-fa''āl)* serves both as *dator formarum* and as "link" with the acquired intellect *(al-'aql al-mustafād).* But the significant difference between the Peripatetic Active Intellect and Suhrawardī's Isfahbad al-Nāsūt is that the latter is a continuous part of both what is below it in rank as well as what is above it. And unlike the Peripatetic Active Intellect, which is the tenth intellect in a "mechanical" cosmological scheme where the intellects are numbered, the Isfahbad al-Nāsūt is *itself* a multiplicity of abstract lights, for which it serves as *one* archetype. For a discussion of the Active Intellect, see F. Rahman, *Prophecy in Islam* (London: George Allen and Unwin Ltd., 1958), Ch II. Cf. Aristotle, *De Anima* III.5, 430^{a}10ff., where νοῦς ποιητικός is to be compared with *al-'aql al-fa''āl;* Avicenna, al-Najāt, II.6; Alfarabi, *Ārā' Ahl al-Madīna al-Fāḍila,* ed. M. Kurdī (Cairo, 1948), pp. 10ff; Suhrawardī, *Opera III,* pp. 53-55.

3.5 Illuminationist Epistemology: The Processes of Intuition and Vision-Illumination

3.5.1 Intuition.

There are a number of places in the various works of Suhrawardī where what are called "judgements of intuition" *(aḥkām al-ḥads, ḥukm al-ḥads)* are used as valid forms of inference.[1] In each instance, the validity of the judgement of intuition is unquestioned and is given the rank of demonstration, in that in a valid inference based on such intuitive judgements one can dispense with constructing demonstrations.[2] Intuition, in the sense used here by Suhrawardī, is most probably an elaboration of the Aristotelian "quick wit" (ἀγχίνοια),[3] but Suhrawardī incorporates this particular type of inference into the epistemology of the philosophy of illumination. Using a modified Peripatetic technical terminology, he identifies intuition first as an activity of the habitual intellect *('aql bi' l-malaka)*[4] and, secondly, as the activity of the holy intellect *(al-'aql al-qudsī)*;[5] but he considers the most important "act" of intuition to be the subject's ability to perceive most of the intelligibles in a short time without a teacher.[6] In such a case intuition moves to grasp the middle term *(al-ḥadd al-awsaṭ)* of syllogism, which is tantamount to an immediate (without temporal extension) grasp of an essentialist definition, i.e., of the thing's essence.

3.5.2 Vision-Illumination.

The two-fold process of vision-illumination *(mushāhada-ishrāq)* acts on all levels of reality. It begins on the human level, in outward sense-

[1] Suhrawardī, *Intimations:Physics,* fol. 64v; idem, *Opera I,* pp. 57, 440; idem, *Opera II,* p. 109.

[2] E.g., Suhrawardī, *Opera I,* p. 57: *al-ḥads al-ṣaḥīḥ yaḥkum bi-hādhā dūna ḥājja ilā burhān.*

[3] See Aristotle, *Posterior Analytics I*.33, 89b10-20, and above, n.17. Cf. Aristotle, Nicomachean Ethics VI.9, 1142b5-6: ἔτι ἡ ἀγχίνοια ἕτερον καὶ ἡ εὐβουλία· ἔστι δ' εὐστοχία τις ἡ ἀγχίνοια Cf. Suhrawardī, *Intimations:Physics,* fol. 69r; idem, *Paths and Havens:Physics,* fol. 201v.

[4] E.g., Suhrawardī, *Intimations:Physics,* fol 69r.

[5] E.g., ibid., fol. 65v, 69r.

[6] Ibid.

perception, as sight *(ibṣār)*. The eye *(al-baṣar,* or the seeing subject, *al-bāṣir)*, when capable of seeing, sees an object *(al-mubṣar)* when the object itself is illuminated *(mustanīr)* by the sun in the sky.[1] On the cosmic level, every "abstract light" "sees" the "lights" that are above it in rank, while the higher "lights" instantaneously, at the moment of vision, illuminate the lower in rank. The Light of Lights *(Nūr al-anwār)* illuminates everything, and the Heavenly Sun, the "Great Hūrakhsh," enables the vision to take place. In effect, knowledge is obtained through this "coupled" activity of vision-illumination, and the impetus underlying the operation of this principle is self-consciousness. Thus every being comes to know its own degree of perfection, an act of self-knowledge which induces a desire *(shawq)* to "see" the being just above it in perfection, and this act of "seeing" triggers the process of illumination.[2] By means of the process of illumination, "light" is propagated from its highest origin to the lowest elements.[3]

Illumination is also the principle by means of which celestial motion is regulated.[4] Through illumination, the very source of reality, the Light of Lights, may ultimately be "seen," because everything is a degree of its intensity and thus "connected" to it. The emanation of the "abstract lights" from it does not involve a disjunction *(infiṣāl)* from the source.[5] Illumination is propagated from the Light of Lights to the human level by means of certain intermediary principles. These are the "controlling lights" *(al-anwār al-ghāhira)* and the "managing lights" *(al-anwār al-mudabbira)*.[6] Among the "managing lights" the principle lights which directly effect the human soul are the Isfahbad lights.[7] In general, all higher lights control and illuminate the lower ones which, in turn, are capable of

[1] Suhrawardī, *Opera II*, p. 134.

[2] Ibid., pp. 139-141: *wa kull wāḥid yushāhid Nūr al-Anwār.*

[3] Ibid., pp. 142-143.

[4] Ibid., pp. 142, 147-148, 175, 184-185.

[5] Ibid., p. 137, 146.

[6] Ibid., pp. 139-140, 166-175, 185-186. Note that the managing lights function on the human level, as *al-anwār al-insiyya (Opera II*, p. 201), as well as on the cosmic level, as *al-anwār al-falakiyya (Opera II*, p. 236).

[7] Ibid., pp. 201, 213-215.

"seeing" the higher ones. The Light of Lights controls everything.[1] It is the most apparent to itself, and thus it is the most self-conscious being in the universe.[2] All "abstract lights" are illuminated directly by the Light of Lights, whose luminosity *(nūriyya)*, essence *(dhāt)*, and power, are all one and the same.[3] The Light of Lights is self-emanating *(fayyaḍ bi-al-dhāt)*, and its attributes and essence are one.[4] When the "heavenly illuminations" *(al-ishrāqāt al-'ulwiyya)* reach man's soul through the intervention of the Isfahbad lights, all knowledge is given to him. Such moments are the visions of the "apocalyptic lights" *(al-anwār al-sāniḥa)*, which thus serve as the foundation for visionary experience, and for obtaining unrestricted knowledge.[5] Human souls who have experienced the "apocalyptic lights" are called "abstract souls" *(al-nufūs al-mujarrada)*, because they have torn away from the physical bondage of body. They obtain an "idea of the light of God" *(mithāl min nūr Allah)*, which the faculty of imagination imprints upon the "tablet of the *sensus communis*" *(lawḥ al-ḥiss al-mushtarak)*. By means of this idea, they obtain control over a "creative light" *(al-nūr al-khāliq)* which ultimately gives them power to know.[6] The moment of illumination, which is experienced by the Brethren of Abstraction *(ikhwān al-tajrīd)*[7] and the Masters of Vision *(aṣḥāb al-mushāhada)*,[8] is described by Suhrawardī as a gradual experience of "light" in fifteen steps, starting with the experience of the "flashing pleasurable light" *(al-nūr al-bāriq al-*

[1] Ibid., pp. 122, 135-136, 197.

[2] Ibid., p. 124.

[3] Ibid., pp. 121-124.

[4] Ibid., p. 150

[5] Ibid., pp. 141, 204-205. Cf. ibid., p. 13: *al-ishrāqiyyūn lā yantaẓim amruhum dūna sawāniḥ nūriyya.*

[6] This is when the knowing subject, as the self-conscious monad, becomes the creative subject.

[7] Ibid., p. 252. These "brethren" enjoy the highest possible human rank, which is the rank of "creation," by means of which they are able to bring into being (the term used is *ījād*, which can be translated as "create") any form they wish. Cf. ibid., p. 242: *wa li-ikhwān al-tajrīd maqām khāṣṣ fīhi yaqdirūn 'alā ījād muthul qā'ima 'alā ayyi ṣūrat arādū, wa dhālika mā yusammā maqām kun.*

[8] Ibid., pp. 156, 162.

ladhīdh) and ending with the experience of a "light" so violent that it may tear the body apart at the joints.[1]

Suhrawardī's theory of vision is thus one of the two main components of his illuminationist theory of knowledge. The principles of this theory are developed by Suhrawardī in such a way as to apply to external vision, i.e., sight, as well as to "internal" vision. Therefor, his theory applies to physics as well as to metaphysics. The analysis of the theory begins with a discussion of external vision *(ibṣār)*, what is called "vision, or seeing, by means of external senses" *(mushāhada bi'l-ḥiss al-ẓāhir)*, in both the sections on physics as well as in sections on metaphysics of Suhrawardī's works. In physics, Suhrawardī rejects the corporeality of rays *(jismiyyat al-shu'ā')*[2] and the view that holds rays to be colors *(lawniyyat al-shu'ā')*.[3] Next, he rejects the theory of external vision which holds that "vision *(ibṣār)* takes place solely because rays leave the eye and meet *(yulāqī)* the objects of sight."[4] Suhrawardī also rejects the view which holds that the act of sight *(ru'ya)* takes place when the form of the thing *(ṣūrat al-shay')* is imprinted in the "vitreous humour" *(al-ruṭūba al-jalīdiyya)*.[5] This is because the form of large objects cannot be imprinted in the humour. In order to fully analyze Suhrawardī's theory of vision, showing deep phenomenological understanding on his part, it is necessary to place this theory in its historical context, and to give a brief account of the theories he has rejected.

The philosophical view of sight presented by Suhrawardī is among the most significant principles of illuminationist philosophy, and this view is applied to the principle of illuminationist vision as well. Almost all questions relating to illuminationist epistemology, as well as the question of being in the philosophy of illumination, can only be fully understood when a careful analysis of the illuminationist principles of sight and vision are

[1] Ibid., pp. 252-254.
[2] Ibid. p. 97.
[3] Ibid., p. 98.
[4] Ibid., p. 99.
[5] Ibid., p. 100.

presented. How does vision take place?[1] How does it act? What is this thing called light without which vision cannot take place? These, and similar questions, must be kept in mind when analyzing the illuminationist theory.

Aristotle, at the beginning of the *Metaphysics,* considers sight to be the highest in rank in sense-perception. For Suhrawardī, the fact that vision has no temporal extension and that there is no need for a material relation *(rābiṭa)* between the "seer" and the thing seen, makes sight or vison prior to thinking and superior to it. This is because any enumeration of essential attributes, of the genera and the differentiæ requires time. The construction of dialectical syllogism and induction also take time. Vision, however, takes place in a durationless instant *(ān),* and this is the "moment" of illumination. We may infer why the allegory "light" is so significant in illuminationist philosophy. A knowing subject—the "luminous, self-conscious I"—as well as an object both possess the quality of apparentness *(ẓuhūr*, or *Evidenz),* which are measured in degrees of light intensity. Further, there must be "light" for vision to take place; whether the light is the outward, manifest light *(al-nūr)* necessary for sight, or the abstract light *(al-nūr al-mujarrad)* necessary for vision.

The theories of vision rejected by Suhrawardī include the Aristotelian the Platonic as well as the Euclidean. I do not aim to give a detailed account of the history of this problem here, but we may safely assume that the summary of the problem given by Alfarabi was known to Suhrawardī. The eighth problem in Alfarabi's *Harmonization Between the Opinions of the two Philosophers Plato and Aristotle,* is devoted to the problem of vision.[2] Alfarabi states the principle of Aristotle's opinion to be: "[He] holds the opinion that sight takes place by an action that occurs to the eye;"[3] and

[1] By vision here, I mean a principle that incorporates both sight *(ibṣār)* and vision in the broader sense *(mushāhada).*

[2] Alfarabi, *Kitāb al-jam' bayna ra'yay al-ḥakīmayn,* ed. N. Nader (Beirut, 1968), pp. 91ff. An indication that this work is significant for the study of illuminationist philosophy is that it is printed on the margins of Shīrāzī's *Sharḥ Ḥikmat al-Ishrāq*.

[3] Ibid. Aristotle has discussed the problem of sight in many places in his works, including the *Topics* (114aff.) where he discusses the relation between the thing known, the sense-perceived, and the object of sight. It seems that the most important discussion of the problem is to be found in his *De Anima* (418aff.). Ḥunayn ibn Isḥāq's treatise,

of Plato: "[He] believes that sight takes place by a thing leaving the eye and colliding with the the thing seen."[1] Alfarabi himself states that the followers of Aristotle and Plato did not understand the true meaning of the two philosophers, and thus thought that a corporeal *thing* was meant to leave the eye, as did the mathematicians *(al-aṣḥāb al-ta'ālīm)* who were followers of Euclid. They argue that the thing that leaves the eye must be either air *(hawā')* or light-ray *(ḍaw')* or fire or smoke, all of which were rejected by them.[2]

The positive theory of vision, as developed by Suhrawardī and portrayed in the metaphysics of the *Philosophy of Illumination,* is an application of the general theory of knowledge to which we have referred above. Suhrawardī begins by restating the conclusions reached in the physics:

> Theorem: [On Vision] You have now learnt that sight does not consist of the imprint of the form of the object in the eye, nor of something that goes out from the eye. Therefore it can only take place when the luminous object *(al-mustanīr)* encounters *(muqābala)* a sound [healthy] eye.[3]

Thus, external vision takes place in accordance with Suhrawardī's general theory of knowledge, namely that the subject (the sound eye) and

---

entitled *Fi'l-ḍaw' wa ḥaqīqatihi* (Published in *al-Machreq,* 1899, pp. 1105-1113), is an epitome of Aristotle's views on the subject. Ḥunayn considers Aristotle's opinions to be the best. Aristotle held that light could not be corporeal, since the movement of corporeal bodies takes time, but light's movement does not. Also, what is predicated of body is accident, and light is not an accident, hence it is not corporeal. Also, bodies when next to each other become dense, but the multiplicity of light does not make it dense. Thus light is not a body.

[1] Alfarabi, *Kitāb al-Jam',* p. 92. Flūṭirkhus, in his *al-Ārā' al-ṭabī'iyya* (published in *Arisṭū fī al-nafs,* ed. A. Badawi , Beirut, 1954, pp. 95-188), states that Plato does not believe that a thing *(shay')* leaves the eye, but that a ray *(shu'ā')* leaves it. Also Plato in his *Timæus* (45b-46a) does not consider sight to be based on a thing leaving the eye, and he considers three kinds of light as the grounds of sight: an abstract light that emanates from the sun, an abstract light that leaves the eye and collides with the thing seen, and the color of the thing seen, that emanates from it and is abstract also.

[2] See Alexander of Aphrodisias, *Fī al-radd 'alā man yaqūl anna al-ibṣār yakūn bi al-shu'ā'āt al-khārija 'inda khurūjihā min al-baṣar,* in *Shurūḥ 'alā Arasṭū mafqūda fi'l-Yūnāniyya,* ed. A. Badawi, (Beirut, 1969) pp. 26-30.

[3] Suhrawardī, *Opera II,* p. 134

the object (the luminous thing) are both present, and their presence together necessitates the act of vision.[1] There are a number of conditions that have to be met, however, for the act of vision to be consummated. These conditions are: 1- The presence of light, which as we shall presently see, is due to the propagation of light from the source of light, i.e., the Light of Lights. 2- The absence of any obstacle or "veil" *(ḥijāb)* between the subject and the object.[2] 3- The illumination of the object as well as the subject. The object is illuminated because illumination carries the light of the Light of Lights all the way down from the source to the elemental level. The subject is illuminated by the the same principles, but the "mechanism" which allows for the subject to be illuminated is a complicated one, and involves a certain activity on the part of the faculty of imagination. When an object is seen, the subject has acted in two ways: an act of vision and an act of illumination. Thus, vision-illumination is actualized when no obstacle intervenes between the subject and the object.

To sum up, one of the principles in the foundations of the philosophy of illumination is that the "laws" governing sight and vision are based on the same rule. The rule has three components: the existence of light, the act of vision *(mushāhada* or *ibṣār)*, and the act of illumination *(ishrāq)*. Sight takes place as the result of the encounter between the sound eye and the luminous object. Whenever light exists, the eye will see. Sight and the illumination of light on both the object as well as the subject takes place in a durationless instant, at the "moment" when the subject and the object are present before one another. Vision, too, works in the same manner, but the "instrument" is no longer the eye but the creative acts of the illuminated subject's imagination, and the light that illuminates the object seen is noncorporeal light; it is the abstract light of illuminationist cosmology. Vision takes place when there are no obstacles between the subject and the object (obstacles indicate either "opaque," *ḥājiz,* things, or the absence of light). Everything, therefore, depends on the existence of light, which is explained in the illuminationist theory of emanation, or propagation, of light

[1] Ibid., p. 150

[2] Ibid., pp. 134-135. Both excessive proximity *(ghurb mufraṭ)* and excessive distance *(bu'd mufraṭ)* are considered to be obstacles that block the actualization of "sight."

4. Illumination and Emanation

Suhrawardī's theory of illumination is a special form of the theory of emanation as developed by the Neoplatonists. The basic features of a theory of emanation, all of which are incorporated by Suhrawardī in the philosophy of illumination, are: 1- A necessary "downward" movement, from the "higher" to the "lower," i.e., the necessary emanation of Nous from the Plotinian One, or the self-emanation of the Light of Lights. 2- Exclusion of creation: the world is not created or made *ex nihilo* either in time or at once; there is no "maker," no demiurgus who gives order to a primordial chaos or gives "forms" to an external matter; and there is no divine "will."[1] 3- Eternity of the world.[2] 4- Non-temporal relationship between the higher and the lower beings. There is a fifth feature of the general theory of emanation which is not included in Suhrawardī's theory: the "law of mean terms."[3] This law—which was introduced by the later Neoplatonists[4]—demands that some thing partly nameable and partly unnameable (partly finite and partly infinite) serve as the link between the infinite and the finite.

It is evident that the germ of the Plotinian doctrine of emanation is to be found in Plato's account of Eros (the urge toward the good, as it is expressed in philosophical knowledge, which proceeds from the sensed world to the Ideas).[5] It is equally evident that it was Plotinus who made the

[1] The Light of Lights does not differ "in reality" *(fi'l-ḥaqīqa)* from other lights, and it does not have a will, on the basis of which it would have emanated starting from a chosen time onward (Suhrawardī, *Opera II*, p. 122).

[2] While Suhrawardī never explicitly declares the world to be eternal, it is a necessary corollary to his view that emanation is eternal *(al-fayḍ abadī)*. (Cf. ibid., p. 181.) Eternity itself is a concept which is essentially part of the Light of Light's emanation, because this "act" of emanation is not a change *(taghyīr)*, nor does it include non-being *('adam)*. The world continues eternally to be (as it has been), with the continuity of the Light of Lights (Ibid., pp. 177-183).

[3] The only difference between the Light of Lights and the other lights is a degree of perfection, and this is depicted in the variations of intensity in the "lights." This means that there is no "gap" or principle of mediation between the Light of Lights and the other lights. Cf. Suhrawardī, *Opera II*, pp. 126-127.

[4] J.M. Rist, *Plotinus: the Road to Reality*, p. 36.

[5] Ibid., pp. 66-69.

moral rule "Being good means doing good" into a cosmic law of emanation.[1] It is also evident that Suhrawardī's theory of emanation and his doctrine of the Light of Lights bears a resemblance to Plotinus' theory of emanation and cosmology as presented in the *Enneads*.[2] Suhrawardī's "model" for the process of emanation, however, is (as we shall presently see) in Plato's *Timæus*. But, if we bear in mind the metaphor of heat and fire in the *Enneads* (heat emanates from fire because fire is what it is) and ponder the question asked by J.M. Rist, "What is the One, that it emanates Nous and Being?"[3] we may be led to a more comprehensive understanding of the Light of Lights and its activity.

The Light of Lights emanates "light" because of what it is, and the "rays" thus propagated ultimately reach the entire cosmos; it is through these rays that the cosmos is held together and movement and change are regulated.[4] The existence (self-consciousness) of the Light of Lights is not separate from its activity (illumination), and both are emanated and ultimately reach the elemental realm. Unlike the Plotinian One, from which Nous appears, from the Light of Lights another "light" is obtained which is not *essentially* different from it. (As in the Plotinian model, the source is not effected by emanation.) In effect, that the Light of Lights *is* what it is and that it *does* what it does, is one and the same. Thus, that the Light of Lights *exists* becomes a first axiom from which the whole of reality may be deduced.

In any theory of emanation, the relation between the infinite and the finite has to be explained. There is an infinity which is infinite in many ways, if not in infinite ways—an infinite order infinity. Next, there is an infinity which is restricted—in Rist's term, a "lesser infinity"—a finite order infinity. Plotinus' Nous and Suhrawardī's First Light *(al-nūr al-awwal)* are

[1] Ibid., p. 66.

[2] See ibid., Ch. III, IV, VI.

[3] Ibid., p. 69.

[4] The Light of Lights is self-emanating *(fayyāḍ bi-al-dhāt)* and is the "active knower" *(al-darrāk al-fa''āl)* (Suhrawardī, *Opera II*, p. 117). Since any act of "knowing" *(idrāk)* is self-manifestation, self-knowledge, and self-consciousness (Ibid., pp. 110-113), the Light of Lights is pure self-consciousness and unchanging, eternal emanation (Cf. ibid., pp. 121-122, 152, 175).

such an infinity.[1] Infinity is a concept introduced to Greek philosophy by Plotinus; it is accepted that "Perfect Being for the Greeks meant limitation and finitude."[2] Rist, who regards the Plotinian One to be infinite, holds that this notion of infinity marks a development in Greek thought, and states: "One beyond Being means for Plotinus simply to place it beyond finitude, to make it intrinsically infinite."[3] It is in regard to such a view of the One's infinity that the real difference between Plato and Plotinus may be seen. Similarly, it is in view of the addition of the infinitesimal that the difference between Plotinus and Suhrawardī may be seen: the infinitesimal as the moment *(laḥẓa* or *ān)* of illumination-vision serves as the link between the infinite and the finite.[4]

Illumination and emanation, as delineated by Suhrawardī in the *Philosophy of Illumination,* combines two processes. The first process is the emanation of the First Light—also called the Closest Light *(al-nūr al-aqrab)*[5] from the Light of Lights. The First Light is simply obtained *(yaḥṣul).*[6] The only difference between this light and the Light of Lights is

[1] The First Light is determined, and thus "finite," yet it has an "infinity" of qualities which is received by it and is emanated from it. The very fact that the First Light transmits the essence of the Light of Lights must mean that it is infinite, but a determined infinite.

[2] Joseph Owens, *The Doctrine of Being in the Aristotelian Metaphysics* (Toronto: Pontifical Institute of Mediæval Studies, 1963), pp. 35-63, 467-468.

[3] Rist, *Plotinus: The Road to Reality,* p. 24. Cf. Owens, *The Doctrine of Being in Aristotelian Metaphysics,* p. 39n.

[4] Every lower light, though controlled and dominated by the higher one, may "see" the higher, and the "moment" of vision is when any lower light is linked with any higher, and ultimately with the highest. See Suhrawardī, *Opera II,* pp. 135-136. The terms *ān* and *laḥẓa* indicate a sense of an infinitesimal temporal extionsion, or moment. They also indicate the idea of durationlessness as a "measure" for indicating the "when" of linkage between the finite and the infinite, in short, the "moments" of vision and illumination.

[5] Ibid., pp. 126-127, 132.

[6] Ibid., pp. 125, 138-139. Suhrawardī does not use the more common terms *ṣudūr* or *fayḍ* to describe the emanation of light from the Light of Lights. The term used, *ḥuṣūl,* which means "to obtain," is less restricted than the other terms and conveys more of a "natural" process of propagation of light than a "desired" or "willed" emanation from the Source.

in their relative degree of intensity *(shadda)*, which is a measure of perfection, the Light of Lights being the most intense light simply.[1] There is no difference between these two lights regarding their modalities (necessity or possibility), and the obtaining of the First Light in no way disjoins it from the Light of Lights; it is *continuous* with the Light of Lights. This is also true of *all* the "abstract lights"; they, too, differ from one another and from the Light of Lights only in respect to intensity. The First Light (a) *exists* as an abstract light;[2] (b) has a twofold movement: it "loves" *(yuḥibbu)* and "sees" *(yushāhidu)* the Light of Lights above it and controls *(yaqharu)* and illuminates *(ashraqa)* what is below it;[3] (c) has a "rest," and this rest implies something like "matter," called *barzakh*, which has a "shape" *(hay'a)*—and together the "matter" and "shape" serve as a receptacle for light;[4] and (d) in addition, this first Light has something like a "quality" or an attribute: it is "rich" *(ghanī)* in relation to the lower lights and "poor" *(faqīr)* in relation to the Light of Lights.[5] The "richness" and "poverty" of a light corresponds to the degree of its perfection and its degree of intensity, and seems to parallel the the distinction between Sameness and Difference made in Plato's methodology. This scheme is true of all lights. Through seeing the Light of Lights, and motivated by love and sameness, another "abstract light" is obtained from the First Light.[6] When the First Light "sees" its own poverty, its own "matter" and shape are obtained. As this process continues, the spheres and the elemental world all come to be.[7] These lights, so obtained, are the principal abstract lights, and they are multifarious.

The second process is not separate from the first, but is the result of the activity of the abstract lights. This process itself is the coupled process of illumination and vision. When the First Light is obtained, it has an immediate vision of the Light of Lights in a durationless, discrete

[1] Ibid., pp. 119, 126-127.
[2] Ibid., p. 126.
[3] Ibid., pp. 135-137.
[4] Ibid., pp. 132-134.
[5] Ibid., pp. 133, 145-147.
[6] Ibid., pp. 138-143.
[7] Ibid., p. 138.

"moment," whereupon the Light of Lights instantaneously illuminates it and thus "lights up" the "matter" and the shape associated with the First Light.[1] The light that comes to reside in the first abstract light is an "apocalyptic light" *(al-nūr al-ṣāniḥ)* and is the most receptive of all lights.[2] The process continues and the second light receives two lights: one light from the illumination of the Light of Lights directly, and one light from the First Light, the First Light having received it from the Light of Lights and now passing it on because of this light's transparency.[3] In the same manner, the third light receives four lights: one directly from the Light of Lights, one from the First Light, and the lights of the second light. The process continues and the fourth light receives eight lights, the fifth sixteen lights, and so on. The result is that the number of lights (and with it the activity, intensity, and the very essence of the Light of Lights, which is self-consciousness—symbolized as abstract light) increases according to the sequence 2^{n-1}, the Closest Light being the first member of this sequence.[4] Of these multiple lights, the essence of each of which is self-consciousness, some are the "controlling lights" *(al-anwār al-ghāhira)* and some the "managing lights" *(al-anwār al-mudabbira)*.[5] The controlling lights themselves are either the lofty or "exalted controlling lights" *(al-anwār al-qāhira al-a'lūn)*, or the "formal masters of the idols" *(anwār qāhira ṣūriyya arbāb al-aṣnām)* that are the "archetypal lights."[6]

5. Being and Light

5.1 Being and its Primary Determinants

Having set forth Suhrawardī's theory of knowledge and shown its relation to his cosmology, I am now in a position to comment on his theory of being. Illuminationist ontology has been a subject of controversy, and it

[1] Ibid., pp. 139-140.

[2] Ibid., pp. 138, 140.

[3] Ibid., pp. 190-191, 195.

[4] Ibid., pp. 138-141. The series 2^{n-1}, together with the series 3^{n-1} are the two series that serve as the basis of the harmony of Plato's World-Soul. See F.M. Cornford, *Plato's Cosmology* (New York: Bobbs-Merril, n.d.), p. 49.

[5] Suhrawardī, *Opera II*, pp. 132, 139-140, 153-156, 170-178, 223.

[6] Ibid., p. 143.

has been attacked by many philosophers, notably Ṣadr al-Dīn al-Shīrāzī known as Mullā Ṣadrā.[1] Most philosophers have attacked that part of Suhrawardī's theory which has been given the name "primacy of essence" *(aṣālat al-māhiyya)*. This is an ontological position characterized by Mullā Ṣadrā as one which regards the "essence" or the "quiddity" *(māhiyya)* of things as their real being, and their "existence" *(wujūd)* as a derived and abstracted concept which cannot exist independently of the mind or of the individual. In opposition to this view, Mullā Ṣadrā presents his own view of being, as follows.

As we examine the contingent world, Mullā Ṣadrā stated, we observe a sequence of existent entities as stone, tree, horse, man, etc. We observe that these entities share one thing, which is their "existence." When it is said that "X exists" or "X is" (X *mawjūd)*, then we ask, is the existence of X the same thing as "what" X is itself as it is determined out there? Or, is the existence of X "additional" to "what" X is as it is determined out there? The theory of being which is characterized as the one which adheres to the "primacy of existence" *(aṣālat al-wujūd)* regards existence as the real being, i.e., this being is not something that is purely in the mind. This theory holds that this X here has a being, but what "limits" the existence of this X is its essence.[2]

As we examine the illuminationist view of being, we may first infer that it seems that Suhrawardī's position is opposited to Mullā Ṣadrā's ontological theory. It is true that the he holds that "existence" *(wujūd)* is said univocally *(bi-m'nā wāḥid)* of many things (i.e., X, Y, Z exist), and that such existence can only be so predicated of many different things if it is purely a mental concept. Suhrawardī considers that, since X, Y, Z are determined outside the mind, "what" they themselves are (their *dhawāt)* is most real, and is the basis of any derived or abstracted concept. Thus all beings that have a common element, which is "existence," differ with

[1] E.g. see Mullā Ṣadrā, *Ta'līqāt* (Shīrāzī, *Sharḥ II)*, pp. 170-206 marg.; idem, *Kitāb al-Mashā'ir*, ed. H. Corbin (Tehran: Institut Franco-Iranien, 1964). Mullā Ṣadrā devotes the First Book of his major work, *al-Asfār al-Arba'a,* to the study of being.

[2] For a detailed discussion of Mullā Ṣadrā's theory of being see Jalāl Āshtiyānī, *Hastī* (Mashhad: Khurāsān Press, 1960), pp. 28-32, 69-103.

respect to one "essential" *(dhātī)* element. This differentiating element is the one we indicate when we answer the question "What is the existent entity?" *(mā huwa al-shay')*. The answer is "that by which the thing is what it is in itself." By means of this difference we are able to perceive the form of one being as stone, of another as tree, of another as horse, and of yet another as man. It is customary to call this element the "essence" or "quiddity" (or the "what-ness," or the "what-is") of a thing.[1]

"Existence" *(wujūd)* and "thingness" *(shay'iyya)*, in so far as they are mental concepts *(mafhūm*, pl. *mafāhīm)*, do not have a genus or a differentia, and thus cannot be defined or described. This is how Suhrawardī begins the metaphysics of the *Intimations*.[2] This first tenet of the theory of being, as delineated by Suhrawardī, is in full agreement with the basic tenet of *metaphysica generalis*,[3] and so is Suhrawardī's position that this notion of being is self-evident *(badīhī)* and innate.[4] As a first attempt, however, to present a view of being that differs from the traditional Peripatetic one, Suhrawardī stipulates that "thingness" is predicated of things in a manner that is not "original" or "primary" *(tuḥmal 'ala'l-ashyā' ghayr muta'aṣṣila)*, and further, that there is no "thing" in an unrestricted sense *(lā shay' muṭlaq)*. Thus the common predicate of many things is "posterior to" or "dependent upon" *(ṭābi'a)* the determined essences *(al-māhiyyāt)*. This is so in any act of thinking *(ta'aqqul)*, when the mind abstracts and separates the common predicates as concepts out of real things.

5.2 Being and Cosmology

In Part One of the *Philosophy of Illumination*, Suhrawardī "proves" that existence in the univocal sense (as homonymous being, i.e., predicative being) is a mental concept that depends for its existence on the individual

[1] Suhrawardī's theory of being is developed throughout his works; there is no one special section in which it is systematically discussed. See especially Suhrawardī, *Opera I*, pp. 19, 152-153; idem, *Opera II*, p. 20.

[2] Suhrawardī, *Opera I*, pp. 4ff. See also idem, *Opera I*, pp. 125ff., 199ff.

[3] See Merlan, *From Platonism to Neoplatonism*, pp. 160-220. Cf. Suhrawardī, *Opera II*, p. 173.

[4] Suhrawardī, *Opera I*, pp. 4, 199-200.

essences of things. Such a univocal being is predicated of various things, e.g., "the necessary exists," "substance exists," "accident exists." But the "difference" between the necessary, substance, and accident, cannot be determined in relation only to their common predicate. Only the essence of things as they are may serve to distinguish the things out there. On the other hand, Suhrawardī does treat being in an "equivocal" sense, i.e., the being which corresponds to the differences that are apparent in things out there. But Suhrawardī calls this being "light," and his "science of lights" *('ilm al-anwār)*[1] examines the essence *(dhāt)* of things out there, and their gradation in terms of intensity and priority. Since the most intense and prior "light" for Suhrawardī is that which corresponds to pure self-consciousness, it is the degree of self-consciousness that determines the rank as well as order of being in the equivocal sense.

The most important distinction between Avicennan ontology and Suhrawardī's theory of being, as it is finally presented in the *Philosophy of Illumination,* concerns the primary divisions of being. For Avicenna, the three modes of possibility, impossibility, and necessity, as embodied in the beings out there, are "static," while the corresponding modes in the illuminationist theory, "richness" *(ghinā')* and "poverty" *(faqr),* are embodied in the beings out there as a gradation of light that is continuous, and thus consist of a series of successive stages. The upper limit (the being of the absolutely rich *[al-ghanī al-muṭlaq]),* corresponds to the Necessary Existent of Avicennan ontology, and the lower limit (the being which is absolutely poor *[al-faghīr al-muṭlaq]),* corresponds to the non-existent *[ma'dūm]* of the Avicennan ontology. The upper and lower limits are both members of the continuous reality.[2]

Thus a thing *(shay'),* which in Avicenna's ontology is either necessary *(wājib),* possible *(mumkin),* or impossible *(mumtani'),* is, in illuminationist ontology, either a light in itself *(nūr fī ḥaqīqat nafsihi)* or not, i.e., "rich" or "poor."[3] That which is light in itself is divided into 1- light which is a "form" or "shape" *(hay'a)* of some thing else, and this is called

[1] Suhrawardī, *Opera II,* p. 10.

[2] Ibid., pp. 107, 121-124.

[3] Ibid., pp. 107-109.

accidental light *(al-nūr al-āriḍ)*, e.g., the light of the sun and fire; and 2- pure light *(al-nūr al-maḥḍ)*, which is a self-subsisting light, e.g., the Light of Lights, all other abstract lights, and everything else that is self-conscious. That which is not a light in itself is divided into three kinds: 1- Something which is free of place *(mā huwa mustaghnī 'an al-maḥall)*, called "dark substance" *(jawhar ghāsiq)*; 2- That which is a shape or form for something else, called "dark form" *(hay'a ẓulmāniyya)*; 3- That which is "intermediary" *(barzakh)*, which is body. Bodies are of three types: 1- A body which remains in a dark state when light is taken away from it; 2- A body which remains dark, but self-subsistent, when light is taken away from it; and 3- A body which is never separated from light.[1] This is an ontology which regards the real being of things out there to be a continuous whole, composed of what we may call self-conscious and self-subsistent "monads," not separate from the whole, and known in themselves by themselves. These "monads" are light-entities conscious of their "I"'s *(anā'iyya)*, and collectively they constitute a whole cosmos that is also conscious of itself.[2]

Mullā Ṣadrā's account of Suhrawardī's view of being is that, in the illuminationist theory, primary being is "essence" *(māhiyya)*, while "existence" *(wujūd)* is a derived, mental concept. Mullā Ṣadrā himself adheres to the view that primary being is "existence," while "essence" is a derived, mental concept. My account of Suhrawardī's theory of knowledge and its relation to illuminationist cosmology in this chapter raises the question whether the terms "essence" and "existence" are being used in the same sense by Mullā Ṣadrā when applied to Suhrawardī's view and to his own.

What Suhrawardī considers to be a derived, mental concept is "existence" in the "univocal sense" *(bi-ma'nā wāḥid)*, i.e., as predicated of everything in identically the same sense. He reserves the term "existence" *(wujūd)* for this univocal sense of being and this univocal sense only. For what Mullā Ṣadrā understands to be primary being, i.e., being in an "equivocal sense" *(bi-al-tashkīk)*, which Mullā Ṣadrā calls "existence,"

[1] Ibid., pp. 187-190.

[2] Ibid., pp. 110, 112, 114. Cf. Suhrawardī, *Opera I*, pp. 115-116, 186-188.

Suhrawardī uses the term "light," avoiding the term "existence." But this "light" is not "essence" as Mullā Ṣadrā understands it, i.e., it is not a derived, mental concept for Suhrawardī, but is the being of things out there, and is characterized by intensity, priority, nobility, and perfection.

Appendix A

Translation of Suhrawardī's "Introduction" to the *Philosophy of Illumination*

§1 In the name of God the Merciful the Comassionate. O God! Remembrence of thy name is exalted, and thy Majesty is great, and what thou bestowest is lofty, and thy glory is beyond all! Prayer and salutation be upon thy chosen, and upon thy Messengers all, and specifically upon Muḥammad "the chosen" the lord of humankind, and the interceder for all on judgement day. Peace be upon him and upon them. Enable us, with thy light, to become one of the triumphant ones, and [be counted] among those who remember thee, and are thankful for thy bounty.

§2 Know, my brethren, that your frequent demands for writing down the philosophy of illumination have weakened my resolution to refrain, and have eliminated my desire not to comply. Were it not for an incumbent obligation, a message that has appeared, and a command given from a place disobedience of which will lead to going astray from the path, I would not have felt obliged to step forward and openly reveal [the philosophy of illumination]; for you do know how difficult it is. But you went on, all of you my friends—may God direct you toward what He loves and approves of—begging me to write for you a book in which I mention what I have obtained by my intuition *(dhawq)* during my retreats *(khalawāt)* and moments of revelation *(munāzalāt)*. In every seeking soul there is a portion, be it little or great, of the light of God, and every endeavoring person has intuition, be it perfect or imperfect. Knowledge does not rest only among a particular group of people, so that the doors of Heaven be shut behind them and the rest of the world be denied the possibility of obtaining more, but rather the *dator scientiæ* *(wāhib al-'ilm)*,[1] who stands

[1] Shīrāzī regards *wāhib al-'ilm* to be *al-'aql al-fa''āl (Sharḥ II,* p. 14.)

by the "clear horizon" (Qur'ān: LXXI/23) is not stingy with the unseen *(al-ghayb)*. The most evil age is the one which is lacking in personal endeavor, in which the movement of thought is interrupted, the door of revelations *(al-mukāshafāt)* is locked, and the way of visions *(al-mushāhadāt)* is closed.

§3 I have composed for you, before this work and during its composition (when certain obstacles interrupted me) books according to the Peripatetic method in which I have summarized their theorems. Among these works is the short epitome called the *Intimations*, which includes many theorems which were summarized in it despite its brevity. Below this work there is my book the *Flashes of Light*. I have composed other works, among them books I had written in my youth. This work *[Philosophy of Illumination]* however, is another method and a shorter way to [knowledge] than that other way [of the Peripatetics], and is more orderly and precise, and less painful to study. I did not obtain it at first through cogitation *(bi'l-fikr)*, but rather it was arrived at through another thing. Subsequently I sought proofs *(al-ḥujja)* for it. So that should I, for example, stop having the vision, no one could make me doubt [the certainty of what I had obtained].

§4 In all that I have mentioned in regards the "science of lights" and everything that is constructed upon it, I have been assisted by all those wayfarers in the path of God. [What has guided me] has been the very intuition of the leader of philosophy *(imām al-ḥikma)* whose master is Plato, the "possessor of Divine support and light" *(ṣāḥib al-ayd wa'l-nūr)*. Likewise [the "science of lights" is based on the intuition of philosophers] before Plato, from the time of Hermes the "father of philosophers" *(wālid al-ḥukamā')* up to Plato's time, including such great philosophers as Empedocles, Pythagoras, and others. The language of the early philosophers was metaphorical and symbolic, so that what has been said against them, even though it may have been directed against their manifest statements, had not been directed against their intentions, because one cannot refute a metaphore nor symbol. This is also the basis of the Eastern theorem of light and darkness, which was the method of the Persian philosophers such as Jāmāsf, Farshāwashtar, Buzurjmihr, and others before them. This theorem, however is not the theorem of the infidel magus, the heterodoxy of Mani, and whatever leads to associating other deities with God, who is to be exalted above anthropomorphic attributes.

Do not imagine that philosophy exists in this short period alone. The world has never been without philosophy, nor without a person who is in charge of its wisdom, possessing proofs and explanations. Such a person is God's vicegerent on earth; and this will be the situation so long as there are heavens and earth. The difference among the earlier and the later philosophers is only with respect to their use of language as well as in respect to their divergent habits in stating explicitly their doctrines or only hinting at them. All philosophers agree that there are three realms [of being],[1] and agree on the unity of God; there is no dispute among them concerning the principles of [philosophical] problems. Even though the First Teacher [Aristotle] has an eminent position, a high rank, penetrating insight, and perfect speculative capabilities, it is not permissible that one exaggerate about him in such way as to end with contempt for his two masters [Socrates and Plato]. The group [of philosophers] include the "messengers" *(ahl al-sifāra)* and the "lawgivers" *(al-shāri'ūn)*, such as Agathodæmon, Hermes, Asclepius, and others.

§5 The rank of [philosophers] are many, and they fall into classes, as follows: a Divine philosopher *(ḥakīm ilāhī)* who is proficient in theosophy *(ta'alluh)* but lacks discursive philosophy *(baḥth)*; a discursive philosopher who lacks theosophy; a Divine philosopher proficient in both theosophy and discursive philosophy; a Divine philosopher proficient in theosophy, but of middle ability or weak in discursive philosophy; a philosopher proficient in discursive philosophy, but of middle ability or weak in theosophy; a student [lit. "seeker"] of both theosophy and discursive philosophy; a student of only theosophy; and a student of only discursive philosophy. Should it happen that, in some period, there be a philosopher proficient in both theosophy and discursive philosophy, he will have the leadership *(al-ri'āsa)*, and [such a philosopher] is God's vicegerent. Should it happen that this be not the case, then a philosopher proficient in theosophy, but of

[1] The three realms are: *'ālam al-'aql; 'ālam al-nafs; 'ālam al-jirm,* i.e., intellect, soul, and matter. Cf. Shīrāzī, *Sharḥ II,* p. 20.

middle ability in discursive philosophy, [will have the leadership]. Should it happen that even this is not the case, then a philosopher who is proficient in theosophy, but who lacks discursive philosophy, then he is God's vicegerent. The earth will never be without a philosopher proficient in theosophy. Leadership on earth will never be given to the proficient discursive philosopher who has not become proficient in theosophy. So, the world is never without a proficient theosopher, who is more worthy than he who is only a discursive philosopher; for, inevitably, vicegerency must be held [by someone]. By this leadership I do not mean [only] temporal control. Rather, the *imām*-theosopher may be openly in command; or, he may be in occultation—to whom the multitude refer as "the pole" *(al-quṭb)*—he will have the leadership even if it is in utmost concealment. When earthly rule *(al-siyāsa)* is in such a philosopher's hands, the age will be a luminous one; but if the age is without Divine management *(tadbīr ilāhī)*, darkness will be triumphant. The best student is the seeker of theosophy *and* discursive philosophy; next [in rank] is the student of theosophy; and then the student of discursive philosophy.

§6 This book of ours is [meant] for the student of theosophy *and* discursive philosophy. There is nothing in it for the discursive philosopher not given to, and not in search of theosophy. We only discuss this book and its metaphores and symbols with the person who has made a serious effort in theosophy, or else the one who seeks it. The reader of this book must have at least reached the stage in which the Divine Light *(al-bāriq al-ilāhī)* has appeared to him, and its appearance has become a firm state [in his soul]. Any other person will not benefit at all from this book. So, whoever wishes to learn only discursive philosophy, let him follow the Peripatetic method, which, for discursive philosophy alone, is fine and sound. We have nothing to say to such a person, nor do we discuss with such a person our "illuminationist theorems" *(al-qawā'id al-ishrāqiyya)*.[1] Indeed the

[1] These theorems cover specific areas of illuminationist doctrine and form section headings in the *Philosophy of Illumination.* (Cf. Suhrawardḍ, *Opera II*, pp. 220, 36, 37, 135). Parts of theorems, such as "lemmas," are called *daqīqa ishrāqiyya* (ibid., p. 34), and in one case a general theorem is called *ḥikma ishrāqiyya* (ibid., p. 29). Other terms

affair of the illuminationists *(al-ishrāqiyyūn)* remains in disorder without [the guidance of] apocalyptic lights *(sawāniḥ nūriyya)*. For, some of these [illuminationist] theorems are based upon these lights, so that if a doubt should befall the illuminationists in regards to the principles, they will overcome it by recourse to the admitted, unrestricted premise *(al-sullam al-mukhalla'a)*.[1] Just as we have observed the sense-data *(al-maḥsūsāt)* and are certain in regards to some of their conditions, and subsequently construct true sciences *('ulīum ṣaḥīḥa)* upon them—such as astronomy, etc—likewise we observe [lit. "see"] certain spiritual things, and subsequently construct [the philosophy of illumination] upon *them*. He who does not follow this way does not count as far as wisdom is concerned and will be a plaything in the hands of doubts.

---

such as *nukat ishrāqiyya* and *sunnat al-ishrāq*, are used in a less restricted sense and serve to identify special topics in illuminationist philosophy.

[1] Such premises have the same rank as the "primary" ones, and are said to be obtained by a "soul separated from body, which has a vision of the intellectual principles *(al-mabādi' al-'aqliyya)* and the apocalyptic lights." (Shīrāzī, *Sharḥ II*, p. 26.)

Appendix B

Translation of the *Philosophy of Illumination* Part One, I The Seventh Rule

[On definition and its conditions]

§13 When something is to be made known to someone who does not know [it], the definition of that thing should be [constructed] through things that pertain to the thing specifically, so as to specify [all] the units [of the thing], or specify some of them, or [to specify] the aggregate, organic whole. It is necessary that a definition be [constructed] by means of things that are more apparent than the thing defined, and not by means of things that are of only the same clarity, or more obscure than it, or by means of such things that may not themselves be known except by means of the thing that they make known. Therefore, the statement of someone who defines "father" as "that which has a son" is wrong, because "father" and "son" are equal with respect to knowledge and lack of it, and whoever knows one knows the other. Another condition for that by means of which a thing is defined is that it be known prior to the thing defined and not concurrently with it. [For example, it is incorrect] to say "Fire is an element that resembles the soul," because the soul is something less known than fire. Likewise [it is incorrect] when they say "The sun is a star that rises in daytime," because the day may only be known by the period of time which marks the rising sun. Defining the reality [of a thing] cannot take place merely be means of substitution of terms [lexical definition], because such a substitution is only useful to someone who knows the reality but is uncertain about the meaning of the term [used]. The definition of the correlatives should mention the cause that brings about the relation, and the definition of the derivatives should mention that from which the derivation is made together with something else which, in turn, depends on the types of derivatives.

§14 *Section* [On real definitions]. Some people give the technical name "[essentialist] definition" to a formula which indicates the essence of a thing. Such a formula indicates the essentials of all things that are *internal* in respect to the reality of a thing. The name given to the [kind of definition] which makes known the *externals* in respect to the reality of a thing is "description." For example, know that when some people affirm that the body has parts [i.e. the Peripatetics who regard body to be made of two parts, form and matter], others doubt this [i.e., the Atomists who regard body to be made of individual atoms], and yet others deny the parts altogether [i.e., the ancient natural philosophers who regard body to be absolute quantity]—you will later learn what the "part" is. The multitude do not learn about [the existence] of such parts from [merely] the concept of the thing named. Indeed, the name only signifies the sum total of the concomitants of the thing conceived.

Further, if for example it is established that both water and air have non-sensible parts [i.e., form, matter, or atoms] some people will deny [their existence], and the parts. According to them, the parts have nothing to do with what they understand from [the names water and air]. When a body—as we explained it to be—is part of a corporeal reality [and has a name] people only conceive whatever appears to them [of that body], which are the things intended by the name [given to it conventionally] both by the name-giver and by them. Now if this is the situation with sensible things, how much more will the [difficulty] be of something of which nothing can be sensed at all! Further, given that there is something possessed by man by means of which his human-ness [i.e., essence] is determined—this thing is unknown to the multitude as well as to the initiate among the Peripatetics when the latter define it as "rational animal." [This is because] the capacity for reasoning is accidental and posterior to the reality [of man]. [In opposition to the Peripatetic formulation, we hold that] the soul—which is the principle of all of these things [i.e., the essentials]—can only be known through the concomitants and the accidents. Now there is nothing closer to man than his soul, [and this is how the case stands with regard to it]. How much more difficult will be the [knowledge] of other things? However, we will say what is necessary about this question.

§**15** *Illuminationist Theorem* [On the destruction of the Peripatetic theorem of definition]. The Peripatetics admit that, in [constructing an essentialist] definition of a thing, one has to mention the general and specific essentials of the thing. The general essential—i.e., that which is not part of another general essential—which belongs to the universal reality and by which one expresses the answer to the question "What is it?," is called "genus"; and the particular essential of the thing they call the "differentia." Now in respect to constructing definitions there is a different order [for the genus and differentiæ] which we have mentioned elsewhere in our books. Further, the Peripatetics admit that the unknown can only be obtained through the known. But [we observe] that the specific essential of a thing is not well-known to one who does not know it [already] from some other place. But, if the specific essential is known through something other than the thing defined, it will not be specific to the thing defined. If the essential is specific to the thing, but not apparent to sense and not well-known, they both will remain unknown. And if [we assume] that the specific essential is defined, but by means of general things rather than what is specific to it, then this will not be a definition of the essential. (We have previously mentioned the state of [knowledge] of the specific part [of a thing]). So, one can only obtain [a definition] by recourse to sensible or apparent things in another way [i.e, other than the Peripatetic formula of definition], provided when we are able to specify the sum total [of the parts] which specify the thing by [specifying the] aggregate, organic whole of it. You shall learn the core of this [new method] in what follows.

Whoever enumerates [all of] the essentials he knows, cannot be confident of not having neglected the existence of another essential, and the person who wants to clarify or contest the statement may ask him about it [the essentials that may have remained undetected]. The person who is constructing a definition cannot, at that point, rightfully say "Were there other attributes [of a thing], I would know them"; for there are numerous attributes that are hidden [and he may have neglected to note them]. And it is not sufficient to say "Should the thing have another essential [hidden to us], we will still be able to know the essence without it." The answer is: "The reality [of a thing] is known only when the sum total of the essentials of it are known." This means that if it is ever possible that [the thing] have another essential that is not perceived, knowledge of the reality of the thing cannot be certain. So, it has been made clear that it is impossible to obtain an [essentialist] definition in the way the Peripatetics do [i.e., the formula proximate genus plus differentiæ], which is a difficulty even their [the Peripatetics'] master [Aristotle] admits. Therefore we [the illuminationists] only make definition by means of things that specify the aggregate, organic whole.

Appendix C

Analysis of Abu'l-Barakāt al-Baghdādī's *Evidential: Logic*, I.13

Section 13 of al-Baghdādī's *Isagoge* of the logic of the *Evidential,* is curious in that it has no counterparts in Arabic works on philosophy before him. Having noted Suhrawardī's theory of definition, this section of al-Baghdādī's work may be seen to have had a distinct influence on the illuminationist theory.

The section is devoted entirely to an analysis of mathematical rules that may be used in constructing definitions. The title of the section is: "On division *(qisma)* analysis *(taḥlīl)*, combination *(jam')*, and synthesis *(tarkīb),* useful in obtaining definitions."

There is a basic distinction made between that which is apparent, or out side the mind, and that which is only in the mind, i.e., a distinction between the real and the mental. The term used for the real is *wujūdī* and is further connected with sense perception; and the term used for the mental, or ideal, is *dhihnī* or, sometimes, *'aqlī.*

The following is a list of the mathematical rules that are explained:

1. Combination (jam'). There are two kinds of combinations. (a) A combination in which the units *(āḥād)* are distinguished *(mutamayyiz)* in the whole, i.e., the units may be discretely enumerated and the sum is a simple addition of the units. This kind of combination is called combination by composition *(jam' ta'līfī).* An example of such a combination is an army made up or composed of men. (b) A combination in which the units are mixed *(takhtaliṭ)* and connected *(tattaḥid)* in such a way that the whole is not distinguished from the parts, i.e., the units of the whole together make up a continuous whole. The name given to this combination is combination by synthesis *(jam' tarkībī).* An example of such a combination is the body of man which is made up of the various humours which in turn are made up of elements.

2. *Composition (ta'līf)*. There are two kinds of composition. (a) Mental composition *(ta'līf dhihnī)* an example of which is the ideal composition of a universal meaning composed of its particulars, such as genus composed of species and species composed of individuals. (b) Real composition *(ta'līf wujūdī)* such as the thing's composition of its parts, e.g. body composed of limbs, flesh, heat, hands, feet, etc.

3. *Synthesis (tarkīb)*. There are two kinds of synthesis: (a) Mental synthesis *(tarkīb dhihnī)*, such as when the genera and the differentiæ are synthesized in a definition; (b) Real synthesis *(tarkīb wujūdī)*, which, in turn, is divided into natural *(ṭabī'ī)*, e.g., the body of the animal "naturally" synthesized from the biles, elements, and principles; and artificial *(ṣinā'ī)*, e.g., the drink Sikanjibīn made of vinegar and honey.

The remaining parts of the section are devoted to the study of rules that govern subtraction *(tafrīq)*, division *(qisma)*, and analysis *(taḥlīl)*, and they need not concern us here.

The point that has to be emphasized is that in general, in any kind of combination which is by synthesis, the units and the whole together make up an "organic" entity such that the parts cannot be distinguished from the whole, while is a combination by composition of units that may be distinguished in themselves as well as from the whole.

Glossary of Terms
Arabic English

āla, tool.

ān, duration-less instant.

āḥād, units.

ahl al-sifāra, messengers.

ajsām, bodies.

amr-i'tibārī, mental concept.

anta anta, you are you (thou-ness).

anta, thou.

anwār qāhira, controlling lights.

anwār sāniḥa, apocalyptic lights.

anā'iyya, self-consciousness.

arbāb al-ṣanam, archetype.

aqrab, closest.

ashyā', things.

asmā' iṣṭilāḥiyya fi'l-'ilm, technical terms in science.

asmā' mushtaraka, homonymous names.

asmā' mutarādifa, synonymous names.

athar, affection.

awwaliyyāt, primary premises.

aḥkām al-ḥads, judgements of intuition.

aṣālat al-māhiyya, primacy of essence.

aṣālat al-wujūd, primacy of existence.

aṣḥāb al-ta'ālīm, mathematicians.

aṣḥāb al-mushāhada, mastersrs of vision.

aẓhar, more evident, most apparent.

'ayd, confirmation.

'adamī, non-being.

'aks, conversion (of syllogism).

'ana, the "I."

'aql fa''āl, Active Intellect.

'aql bi'l-malaka, habitual intellect.

'aql qudsī, holy intellect.

'araḍī, accidental.

'awāriḍ lāzima, concomitant accidents.

'awāriḍ mufāraqa, separate accidents.

'aynī, real thing.

ba'ḍ al-awqāt, sometimes (the mode).

badīhī, self-evident.

barzakh, intermediary.

barzakh, matter (iluminationist term).

basā'iṭ dhihniyya, simple mental counterparts.

basā'iṭ ḥaqīqiyya, simple real things.

basīṭ, non-composite, singular.

baṣar, eye.

bi-al-tashkīk, equivocal sense (of being).

bi-m'nā wāḥid, univocally (said of being).

burhān 'anna, assertoric demonstration.

burhān lima, why demonstration.

Burhān, Posterior Analytics.

burhān, demonstration.

bāriq ilāhī, nūr ilāhī, light of God.

bāṣir, seeing subject.

dā'iman, always (the mode).

daf'atan, instantaneously.

dalāla, signification.

dalālat al-iltizām, signification of concomitance.

dalālat al-muṭābaqa, signification of correspondence.

dalālat al-qaṣd, signification of intention.

dalālat al-taḍammun, signification by implication.

dalālat al-ḥīṭa, implicit signification.

dalālat taṭafful, concomitant signification.

dhāt, essence.

dhāt, ipseity (illuminationist usage).

dhātiyyāt, essentials.

dhātī al-'āmm, general essential.

dhātī al-khāṣṣ, particular essential, specific essential.

dhātī, essential.

ḍarūra, necessary (the mode).

ḍaw', light-ray.

ḍawābiṭ 'arshiyya, Heavenly Rules.

ḍawābiṭ lawḥiyya, Rules of the Tablet.

ḍawābiṭ, rules.

faqr, poverty.

faqīr, poor.

fayyaḍ bi-al-dhāt, self-emanating.

fayḍ, emanation.

faṣl mustaqil, independent differentia.

faṣl, differentia.

Fi' l-'Ibāra, On Interpretation.

fi' l-a'yān, reality out there.

fikr, tafakkur, cogitation, thought.

firāsa, insight.

fiṭrī, innate.

fuṣūl majhūla, unknown differentiæ.

fuṣūl, sections.

ghanī, rich.

ghayb, unseen.

ghayr basīṭa, non-simple.

ghayr fiṭrī, acquired.

ghayr ẓāhir, non-apparent, hidden.

ghinā', richness.

ghā'iyya, final (cause).

harj, chaos.

hawā', air.

hay'a ẓulmāniyya, dark form.

hay'a, shape.

huwa, objectified ipseity.

ḥājiz, opaque.

ḥāl, state.

ḥadd awsaṭ, middle term.

ḥadd nāqiṣ, incomplete essentialist definition.

ḥadd, term (of syllogism).

ḥadd, essentialist definition.

ḥadsiyyāt, intuitive (premises).

ḥakīm muta'llih, ḥakīm ilāhī. Divine philosopher.

ḥaqā'iq jawhariyya, substantial realities.

ḥaqā'iq, truths.

ḥaqīqa jirmiyya, corporeal reality.

ḥaqīqa kulliya, universal reality.

ḥikma 'āmma, philosophia generalis.

ḥikma baḥthiyya, discursive philosophy.

ḥikma dhawqiyya, intuitive philosophy.

ḥikma ishrāqiyya, illuminationist wisdom.

ḥikma muta'alliha, Divine philosophy.

ḥudūd ḥaqīqiyya, real definitions.

ḥujja, proof.

ḥukm, judgement.

ḥuḍūr al-shay', presence of the thing.

ḥuḍūr, presence.

ḥuṣul, realizing or obtaining.

ibṣār, external vision (sight).

idrāk 'aqlī, intellectual perception.

idrāk al-anā'iyya, perception of one's own self-consciousness.

idrāk mā huwa huwa, perception of what a thing is in itself.

idrāk ḥissī, sense-perception.

idrāk, perception.

ijtimā', organic whole, totality, whole.

ikhwān al-tajrīd, Brethren of Abstraction.

imtizāj, admixture.

imām, leader.

indikhāl, inclusion (members distinct from one another).

infiṣāl, disjunction (in syllogism).

infiṣāl, separation or disjunction.

insāniyya, idea "man."

irṣād jismānī, physical observation.

irṣād rūḥānī, spiritual observation.

ishrāq wa mushāhada, illumination and vision.

ishrāq, illumination.

ishrāqāt 'ulwiyya, heavenly illuminations.

ism, name.

isti'dād al-nuṭq, capacity to reason.

istighrāq, inclusion (members non-distinct from the whole).

istiqrā', induction.

Isāghūjī, *Isagoge*.

ittiḥād, union.

ittiṣāl, connection.

iḍāfa ishrāqiyya, illuminationist relation.

iḍāfa, relation.

'illa fā'iliyya, agent cause.

'ilm al-anwār, science of lights.

'ilm al-bārī, knowledge of God.

'ilm al-manṭiq, science of logic.

'ilm bi-anfusinā, knowledge of oneself.

'ilm ishrāqī ḥuḍūrī, knowledge based on illumination and presence.

'ilm ishrāqī, illuminationist knowledge.

'ilm thālith, metaphysics.

'ilm ḥuḍūrī shuhūdī, science based on presence and vision.

'ilm ḥuḍūrī, knowledge by presence.

'ilm ṣaḥīḥ, true science.

'ilm ṣūrī, formal knowledge.

'ilm, or *ma'rifa*, knowledge.

'inād, disjunction.

'ījāb, affirmation.

ījād = *ta' līf* + *iktisāb*, coming into being.

Jadal, *Topics*.

jam' ta'līfī, combination by composition.

jam' tarkībī, combination by synthesis.

jam', combination.

jamī' al-ṣifāt, collectivity of attributes.

jamī', totality.

jawhar ghāsiq, dark substance.

jawhar shā'ir bi-dhātihi, substance conscious of its own essence.

jawhariyya, substantiality.

jawāhir, substances.

jazā', apodosis.

jins ba'id, summum genus.

jins, genus.

jismiyyat al-shu'ā', corporeality of rays.

kamā huwa, as-it-is.
khalawāt, retreats.
khalsa, ecstasy.
Khiṭāba, Rhetoric.
khārijiyyāt, externals.
kull wāḥid wāḥid, each and every.
kull, all.(quantifier)
kull, the whole.
kulliyāt, universals.

lāūlawiyya, relation of one thing to many things.
ladhdha, pleasure.
lafẓ ʻāmm, class name.
lafẓ shākhiṣ, proper name.
lafẓ, utterance.
lawniyya, idea "color."
lawāzim, concomitants.
lawḥ ḥiss al-mushtarak, tablet of the sensus communus.
laḥẓa, moment.
lisān al-ishrāq, language of illumination.
luzūm, implication.

mādda, matter.
mādiyya, material.
māhiyya, quiddity.
maʻnā shākhiṣ, particular meaning.
maʻlūm, known.
maʻna ʻāmm, general meaning. or universal (illuminationist term).
maʻnā, meaning.
maʻrifa mutayaqqana, certain knowledge.
ma'khūdhāt, received (premises).
mafhūm, concept.
majhūl, unknown.
majmūʻ al-ʻulūm. knowledge as a whole.
majāziyya, metaphorical.
manī, I-ness.
maqbūlāt, acceptable premises.
maqāla, treatise.
maqām al-tajrīd, state of abstraction.
maqām, station.
Maqūlāt, Categories.
mas'alat al'ilm, question of knowledge.
mashhūrāt, generally accepted premises.
mawhūm, non-real.
mawḍūʻ, subject.
maḥabba, love.
maḥmūl, predicate.
maḥsūs, sensible.
maḥsūsāt, sense data.
maṭālib, questions.
maẓnūnāt, supposedly true, the alleged (premises).
mithāl min nūr Allah, idea of the light of God.
mithāl, idea.
muʻtabar, valid.
mubṣar, object.
mufāraqāt, separate substances.

Mughālaṭāt, Sophistical Refutations.

muhmala ba'ḍiyya, universal definite proposition.

mujarrabāt, empirical (premises).

mujarradāt mufāraqa, separate entities.

mukhayyalāt, imagined (premises).

muktasab, acquired.

mukāshafāt, revelations.

mumkin, possible.

mumtani', impossible.

munāzalāt, moments of revelation.

muqaddam, antecedent.

muqaddama, premise.

muqaddamāt yaqīniyya, certain premises.

muqawwimāt, constituent elements.

murakkab, composite.

musammā, named.

mushshabbahāt, premises that only appear true.

mushāhada ishrāqiyya, illuminationist vision.

mushāhada wa mukāshafa, personal revelation and vision.

mushāhada, seeing or vision.

mushāhada-ishrāq, vision-illumination.

mushāhadāt, seen (premises).

mushāhadāt, visions.

mustanīr, illuminated object.

mutafāwit, separate.

mutasāwiq, co-extensive.

mutawātirāt, repetitive (premises).

muḥīṭa, universal indefinite.

mūjiba ḍarūriyya, necessary affirmative.

nafs nāṭiqa, rational soul.

nafs al-ẓuhūr wa al-nūriyya, light-as-such.

naẓar manṭiqī, logical deduction.

naẓarī, speculative.

nufūs mujarrada, abstract souls.

Nūr al-anwār, Light of Lights.

nūr aqrab, Closest Light.

nūr awwal, First Light.

nūr bāriq ladhīdh, flashing pleasurable light.

nūr fī ḥaqīqa nafsihi, light in itself.

nūr ilāhī, Divine light.

nūr khāliq, creative light.

nūr maḥḍ, pure light.

nūr mudabbir, managing light.

nūr mujarrad, abstract light.

nūr āriḍ, accidental light.

nūr, light.

nūriyya, luminosity.

qahr, control.

qawl mu'allaf, composed formula.

qawl shāriḥ, expository proposition.

qawl, formula.

qawāʿid, theorems.

qawāʿid al-mashshāʾīn, Peripatetic principles of philosophy.

qayyim ʿalaʾl-ishrāq, proficient in illumination.

qaḍiyya muwajjaha, modal proposition.

qaḍiyya ḥamliyya, predicative proposition.

qaḍiyya, proposition.

qisma, division, or dichotomy.

qiyās iqtirānī, hypothetical syllogism.

qiyās istithnāʾī, disjunctive syllogism.

qiyās khulf, *reduction ad impossible* (in syllogism).

qiyās ḍamīr, *enthymeme*.

Qiyās, *Prior Analytics*.

qiyās, syllogism.

quṭb, pole.

qāʿida ishrāqiyya, illuminationist theorem.

rasm nāqiṣ, incomplete description.

rasm tāmm, complete description.

rasm, description.

ravān bakhsh, *dator spiritus*.

riʾāsa, leadership.

riyāḍāt, ascetic practices.

rumūz, secrets.

ruṭūba jalīdiyya, vitreous humour.

rābiṭ, connective.

rābiṭa, material relation.

salb, negation.

saṭḥiyya, idea surface.

shadda, intensity.

shakl al-thālith, third figure (of syllogism).

shakl awwal, first figure (of syllogism).

shakl thānī, second figure (of syllogism).

sharṭ, protasis.

sharṭiyya munfaṣila, disjunctive conditional (proposition).

sharṭiyya muttaṣila, connective conditional (proposition).

sharṭiyyāt, conditionals (propositions).

shawq, desire.

shayʾ ghāʾib, absent thing.

shayʾ kamā huwa, thing as-it-is.

shayʾ wāḥid basīṭ, simple unitary thing.

shayʾ, thing.

shayʾiyya, thingness.

Shiʿr, *Poetics*.

shumūl, inclusion (members distinct from the whole but not from one another).

shākiṣa, specific thing.

shāriʿūn, lawgivers.

siyāsa, earthly rule.

sullam mukhallaʿa, unrestricted premise.

sūr, quantification sign.

ṣifāt, attributes.

ṣināʿa naẓariyya, speculative art.

ṣināʿa qānūniyya, axiomatic art.

ṣināʿī, artificial.

ṣuwar khayāliyya, imaginary forms.

ṣūra dhihniyya, mental form.

ṣūra, form.

ṣūrat al-shay', form of the thing.

ṣūriyya, formal.

taʿrīf bi al-tamthīl, definition by analogy.

taʿrīf musammā bi-ajzā' mafhūm tāmm, conceptual definition.

taʿrīf, making known.

ta'līf al-ḥadd, composition of definition.

ta'līf wujūdī, real composition.

tabdīl al-lafẓ, lexical definition.

tadbīr ilāhī, Divine management.

tafrīq, subtraction.

takrār, frequency.

tamthīl, analogy.

tanāquḍ, contradiction.

tanāquḍ, negation.

taqaddum, priority.

taqrīrāt, given (premises).

tarkīb dhihnī, mental synthesis.

tarkīb khabarī, enunciative composition.

tarkīb majmūʿī, synthetic combination.

tarkīb wujūdī, real synthesis.

tarkīb, synthesis.

taḥlīl, analysis.

taṣawwur, conception.

taṣdīq, assent.

tu'ī, thou-ness.

ṭabīʿī, natural.

ṭālī, consequent.

ṭarīq al-ʿulūm. methodology of science.

ṭarīq al-mashshā'īn, Peripatetic method.

ū'ī, he/she/it-ness.

ʿulūm ḥaqīqiyya, real sciences.

wahmiyyāt, fancied (premises).

wujūd ʿaynī, real being.

wujūd dhihnī, ideal being.

wujūd, existence.

wāhib al-ṣuwar, dator formarum.

wāhib al-ʿilm, dator scientiæ.

wājib, necessary.

yaqīn, certainty.

ẓāhir, evident.

ẓuhūr, apparentness or manifestation. *Evidenz* (illuminationist term).

Glossary of Terms
English Arabic

absent thing, *shay' ghā'ib*.

abstract light, *nūr mujarrad*.

abstract souls, *nufūs mujarrada*.

acceptable premises, *maqbūlāt*.

accidental light, *nūr āriḍ*.

accidental, *'araḍī*.

acquired, *ghayr fiṭrī*.

acquired, *muktasab*. (Peripatetic term)

Active Intellect, *'aql fa''āl*.

affection, *athar*.

affirmation, *'ījāb*.

agent cause, *'illa fā'iliyya*.

air, *hawā'*.

all, *kull*.

always (the modal), *dā'iman*.

analogy, *tamthīl*.

analysis, *taḥlīl*.

antecedent, *muqaddam*.

apocalyptic lights, *anwār sāniḥa*.

apodosis, *jazā'*.

apparentness, *ẓuhūr*.

archetype, *arbāb al-ṣanam*.

artificial, *ṣinā'ī*.

as-it-is, *kamā huwa*.

ascetic practices, *riyāḍāt*.

assent, *taṣdīq*.

assertoric demonstration, *burhān 'anna*.

attributes, *ṣifāt*.

axiomatic art, *ṣinā'a qānūniyya*.

bodies, *ajsām*.

Brethren of Abstraction, *Ikhwān al-tajrīd*.

capacity to reason, *isti'dād al-nuṭq*.

Categories, *Maqūlāt*.

certain knowledge, *ma'rifa mutayaqqana*.

certain premises, *muqaddamāt yaqīniyya*.

certainty, *yaqīn*.

change of phrase, *tabdīl al-lafẓ*.

chaos, *harj*.

class name, *lafẓ 'āmm*

closest light, *nūr aqrab*.

closest, *aqrab*.

co-extensive, *mutasāwiq*.

cogitation, *fikr, tafakkur*.

collectivity of attributes, *jamī' al-ṣifāt*.

combination by composition, *jam' ta'līfī*.

combination by synthesis, *jam' tarkībī*.

combination, *jam'*.

coming into being, *ījād* = *ta'līf* + *iktisāb*.

complete description, *rasm tāmm*.

composed formula, *qawl mu'allaf*.

composite, *murakkab*.

composition of definition, *ta'līf al-ḥadd*.

concept, *mafhūm*.

conception, *taṣawwur*.

conceptual definition, *ta'rīf musammā bi-ajzā' mafhūm al-tāmm*.

concomitant accidents, *'awāriḍ lāzima*.

concomitant signification, *dalālat taṭafful*.

concomitants, *lawāzim*.

conditionals (propositions), *sharṭiyyāt*.

confirmation, *'ayd*.

connection, *ittiṣāl*.

connective conditional (proposition), *sharṭiyya muttaṣila*.

connective, *rābiṭ*.

consequent, *ṭālī*.

constituent elements, *muqawwimāt*.

contradiction, *tanāquḍ*.

control, *qahr*.

controlling lights, *anwār qāhira*.

conversion (of syllogism), *'aks*.

corporeal reality, *ḥaqīqa jirmiyya*.

corporeality of rays, *jismiyyat al-shu'ā'*.

creative light, *nūr khāliq*.

dark form, *hay'a ẓulmāniyya*.

dark substance, *jawhar ghāsiq*.

dator formarum, *wāhib al-ṣuwar*.

dator scientiæ, *wāhib al-'ilm*.

dator spiritus, *ravān bakhsh*.

definition by analogy, *ta'rīf bi al-tamthīl*.

demonstration, *burhān*.

description, *rasm*.

desire, *shawq*.

differentia, *faṣl*.

discursive philosophy, *ḥikma baḥthiyya*.

disjunction, *infiṣāl*.

disjunction (in syllogism), *'inād*.

disjunctive conditional (proposition), *sharṭiyya munfaṣila*.

disjunctive syllogism, *qiyās istithnā'ī*.

Divine light, *bāriq ilāhī*, *nūr ilāhī*.

Divine management, *tadbīr ilāhī*.

Divine philosopher, *ḥakīm muta'llih*, *ḥakīm ilāhī*.

Divine philosophy, *ḥikma muta'alliha*.

division, or dichotomy, *qisma*.

duration-less instant, *ān*.

each and every, *kull wāḥid wāḥid*.

earthly rule, *siyāsa*.

ecstasy, *khalsa*.

emanation, *fayḍ*.

empirical premises, *mujarrabāt*.

enthymeme, qiyās ḍamīr.

enunciative composition, *tarkīb khabarī*.

equivocal sense, *bi al-tashkīk*.

essence, *dhāt*.

essential, *dhātī*.

essentialist definition, *ḥadd*..

essentials, *dhātiyyāt*.

evident, *ẓāhir*.

Evidenz, ẓuhūr.

existence, *wujūd*.

expository proposition, *qawl shāriḥ*.

external vision (sight), *ibṣār*.

externals, *khārijiyyāt*.

eye, *baṣar*.

fancied premises, *wahmiyyāt*.

final cause, *'illa ghā'iyya*.

First Light, *al-nūr al-awwal*.

first figure (of syllogism), *al-shakl al-awwal*.

flashing pleasurable light, *nūr bāriq ladhīdh*.

form of the thing, *ṣūrat al-shay'*.

form, *ṣūra*.

formal knowledge, *'ilm ṣūrī*.

formal, *ṣūriyya*.

formula, *qawl*.

frequency, *takrār*.

general essential, *dhātī al-'āmm*.

general meaning, or universal, *al-ma'na al-'āmm*.

generally accepted premises, *mashhūrāt*.

genus, *jins*.

given premises, *taqrīrāt*.

habitual intellect, *'aql bi' l-malaka*.

he/she/it-ness, *ū'ī*.

heavenly illuminations, *ishrāqāt 'ulwiyya*.

heavenly rules, *ḍawābiṭ 'arshiyya*.

hidden, *ghayr ẓāhira*.

holy intellect, *'aql qudsī*.

homonymous names, *asmā' mushtaraka*.

hypothetical syllogism, *qiyās iqtirānī*.

I-ness, *manī*.

idea "color," *lawniyya*.

idea "man," *insāniyya*.

idea "surface", *saṭḥiyya*.

idea of the light of God, *mithāl min nūr Allah*.

idea, *mithāl*.

ideal, or mental, being, *wujūd dhihnī*.

illuminated, *mustanīr*.

illumination and vision, *ishrāq wa mushāhada*.

illumination, *ishrāq*.

illuminationist knowledge, *'ilm ishrāqī*.

illuminationist relation, *iḍāfa ishrāqiyya*.

illuminationist theorem, *qā'ida ishrāqiyya*.

illuminationist vision, *mushāhada ishrāqiyya*.

illuminationist wisdom, *ḥikma ishrāqiyya*.

imaginary forms, *ṣuwar khayāliyya*.

imagined premises, *mukhayyalāt*.

implication, *luzūm*.

implicit signification, *dalālat al-ḥīṭa*.

impossible (the mode), *mumtani'*.

inclusion (members distinct from one another), *indikhāl*.

inclusion (members distinct from the whole but not from one another), *shumūl*.

inclusion (members non-distinct from the whole), *istighrāq*.

incomplete description, *rasm nāqiṣ*.

incomplete essentialist definition, *ḥadd nāqiṣ*.

independent differentia, *faṣl mustaqil*.

induction, *istiqrā'*.

innate, *fiṭrī*.

insight, *firāsa*.

instantaneously, *daf'atan*.

intellectual perception, *idrāk 'aqlī*.

intensity, *shadda*.

intermediary, *barzakh*.

intuitive philosophy, *ḥikma dhawqiyya*.

intuitive premises, *ḥadsiyyāt*.

ipseity, *dhāt*.

Isagoge, *Madkhal*.

judgement, *ḥukm*.

judgements of intuition, *aḥkām al-ḥads*.

knowledge as a whole, *majmū' al-'ilūm*.

knowledge based on illumination and presence, *'ilm ishrāqī ḥuḍūrī*.

knowledge by presence, *'ilm ḥuḍūrī*.

knowledge of God, *'ilm al-bārī*

knowledge of oneself, *'ilm bi-anfusinā*.

knowledge, *'ilm*, or *ma'rifa*.

known, *ma'lūm*.

language of illumination, *lisān al-ishrāq*.

lawgivers, *shāri'ūn*.

leader, *imām*.

leadership, *ri'āsa*.

lexical definition, *tabdīl al-lafẓ*.

Light of Lights, *Nūr al-anwār*.
light in itself, *nūr fī ḥaqīqa nafsihi*.
light of God, *bāriq ilāhī*.
light, *nūr*.
light-as-such, *nafs ẓuhūr wa al-nūriyya*.
light-ray, *ḍaw'*.
logical deduction, *naẓar manṭiqī*.
love, *maḥabba*.
luminosity, *nūriyya*.
luminous object, *mustanīr*.

making known, *ta'rīf*.
managing light, *nūr mudabbir*.
manifestation, *ẓuhūr*.
masters of vision, *aṣḥāb mushāhada*.
material relation, *rābiṭa*.
material, *mādiyya*.
mathematicians, *aṣḥāb al-ta'ālīm*.
matter, *barzakh* (iluminationist term).
matter, *mādda*.
meaning, *ma'nā*.
mental concept, *amr i'tibārī*.
mental form, *ṣūra dhihniyya*.
mental synthesis, *tarkīb dhihnī*.
messengers, *ahl al-sifāra*.
metaphorical, *majāziyya*.
metaphysics, *'ilm thālith*.
methodology of science, *ṭarīq al-'ulūm*.
middle term, *ḥadd awsaṭ*.
mixture, *imtizāj*.
mixture, *imtizāj*.
modal proposition, *qaḍiyya muwajjaha*.
moment, *laḥẓa*.
moments of revelation, *munāzalāt*.
more evident, *aẓhar*.
most apparent, *aẓhar*.

name, *ism*.
named, *musammā*.
natural, *ṭabī'ī*.
necessary (the mode), *ḍarūra*.
necessary affirmative (proposition), *mūjiba ḍarūriyya*.
necessary, *wājib*.
negation, *salb*.
negation, *tanāquḍ*.
nominal substitutions, *tabdīl al-lafẓ*.
non-apparent, *ghayr ẓāhir*.
non-being, *'adamī*.
non-composite, *basīṭ*.
non-real, *mawhūm*.
non-simple, *ghayr basīṭa*.

object (the seen), *mubṣar*.
objectified ipseity, *huwa*.
On Interpretation, *fī al-'Ibāra*.
opaque, *ḥājiz*.

particular essential, *dhātī khāṣṣ*.

particular meaning, *ma'nā shākhiṣ*.

perception of one's own self-consciousness, *idrāk al-anā'iyya*.

perception of what a thing is in itself, *idrāk mā huwa huwa*.

perception, *idrāk*.

Peripatetic method, *ṭarīq al-Mashshā'īn*.

Peripatetic principles of philosophy, *qawā'id Mashshā'īn*.

personal revelation and vision, *mushāhada wa mukāshafa*.

philosophia generalis, *ḥikma 'āmma*.

physical observation, *irṣād jismānī*.

pleasure, *ladhdha*.

Poetics, *Shi'r*.

pole, *quṭb*.

poor, *faqīr*.

possible (the mode), *mumkin*.

Posterior Analytics, *Burhān*.

poverty, *faqr*.

predicate, *maḥmūl*.

predicative proposition, *qaḍiyya ḥamliyya*.

premise, *muqaddama*.

premises that only appear true, *mushshabbahāt*.

presence of the thing, *ḥuḍūr al-shay'*.

presence, *ḥuḍūr*.

primacy of essence, *aṣālat al-māhiyya*.

primacy of existence, *aṣālat al-wujūd*.

primary premises, *awwaliyyāt*.

Prior Analytics, *Qiyās*.

priority, *taqaddum*.

proficient in illumination, *qayyim 'ala' l-ishrāq*.

proof, *ḥujja*.

proofs, *ḥujjaj*.

proper name, *lafẓ shākhiṣ*.

proposition, *qaḍiyya*.

protasis, *sharṭ*.

pure light, *nūr maḥḍ*.

quantification sign, *al-sūr*.

question of knowledge, *mas'alat al'ilm*.

questions, *maṭālib*.

quiddity, *māhiyya*.

rational soul, *nafs nāṭiqa*.

real being, *wujūd 'aynī*.

real composition, *ta'līf wujūdī*.

real definitions, *ḥudūd ḥaqīqiyya*.

real sciences, *'ulūm ḥaqīqiyya*.

real synthesis, *tarkīb wujūdī*.

real thing, *'aynī*.

reality out there, *fi' l-a'yān*.

realizing or obtaining, *ḥuṣul*.

received premises, *ma'khūdhāt*.

reduction ad impossible (in syllogism), *qiyās khulf*.

relation of one thing to many things, *lāūlawiyya*.

relation, *iḍāfa*.

repetitive premises, *mutawātirāt*.

retreats, *khalawāt*.

revelations, *mukāshafāt*.

Rhetoric, *Khiṭāba*.

rich, *ghanī*.

richness, *ghinā'*.

rules of the tablet, *ḍawābiṭ lawḥiyya*.

rules, *ḍawābiṭ*.

science based on presence, and vision, *'ilm ḥuḍūrī shuhūdī*.

science of lights, *'ilm al-anwār*.

science of logic, *'ilm al-manṭiq*.

second figure (of syllogism), *shakl thānī*.

secrets, *rumūz*.

sections, *fuṣūl*.

seeing or vision, *mushāhada*.

seeing subject, *bāṣir*.

seen premises, *mushāhadāt*.

self-consciousness, *anā'iyya*.

self-emanating, *fayyaḍ bi-al-dhāt*.

self-evident, *badīhī*.

sense data, *maḥsūsāt*.

sense-perception, *idrāk ḥissī*.

sensible, *maḥsūs*.

separate accidents, *'awāriḍ mufāraqa*.

separate entities, *mujarradāt mufāraqa*.

separate substances, *mufāraqāt*.

separate, *mutafāwit*.

separation or disjunction, *infiṣāl*.

shape, *hay'a*.

sight, *ibṣār*.

signification by concomitance, *dalālat al-iltizām*.

signification by correspondence, *dalālat al-muṭābaqa*.

signification by implication, *dalālat al-taḍammum*.

signification by intention, *dalālat al-qaṣd*.

signification, *dalāla*.

simple mental counterparts, *basā'iṭ dhihniyya*.

simple real things, *basā'iṭ ḥaqīqiyya*.

simple unitary thing, *shay' wāḥid basīṭ*.

singular, *basīṭ*.

sometimes (the modal), *ba'ḍ al-awqāt*.

Sophistical Refutations, *Mughālaṭāt*.

specific essential, *dhātī khāṣṣ*.

specific thing, *shākiṣa*.

speculative art, *ṣinā'a naẓariyya*.

speculative, *naẓarī*.

spiritual observation, *irṣād rūḥānī*.

state of abstraction, *maqām al-tajrīd*.

state, *ḥāl*.

station, *maqām*.

subject, *mawḍū'*.

substance conscious of its own essence, *jawhar shā'ir bi-dhātihi*.

substances, *jawāhir*.

substantial reality, *ḥaqā'iq jawhariyya*.

substantiality, *jawhariyya*.

subtraction, *tafrīq*.

summum genus, jins ba'id.

supposedly true, or the alleged, premises, *maẓnūnāt*.

syllogism, *qiyās*.

synonymous names, *asmā' mutarādifa*.

synthesis, *tarkīb*.

synthetic combination, *tarkīb majmū'ī*.

tablet of the *sensus communus, lawḥ ḥiss al-mushtarak*.

technical terms is in science, *asmā' iṣṭilāḥiyya fi' l-'ilm*.

term, *ḥadd*.

the "I," *'ana*.

the whole, *al-kull*.

theorems, *qawā' id*.

thing, *shay'*.

thing as-it-is, *shay' kamā huwa*

thingness, *shay' iyya*.

things, *ashyā'*.

third figure (of syllogism), *shakl al-thālith*.

thou, *anta*.

thou-ness, *tu'ī*.

thought, *fikr*.

tool, *āla* =ὄργανον.

Topics, *Jadal*.

totality (the organic whole), *ijtimā'*.

totality, *jamī'*.

treatise, *maqāla*.

true science, *'ilm ṣaḥīḥ*.

truths, *ḥaqā' iq*.

union, *ittiḥād*.

units, *āḥād*.

universal definite (proposition), *muhmala ba'ḍiyya*.

universal indefinite (proposition), *muḥīṭa*.

universal meaning, *ma'nā 'āmm*.

universal reality, *ḥaqīqa kulliya*.

universal, *ma'nā 'āmm*.

universals, *kulliyāt*.

univocally, *bi-m'nā wāḥid*.

unknown differentiæ, *fuṣūl majhūla*.

unknown, *majhūl*.

unrestricted premise, *sullam mukhalla'a*.

unseen, *ghayb*.

utterance, *lafẓ*.

valid, *mu'tabar*.

vision-illumination, *mushāhada-ishrāq*.

visions, *mushāhadāt*.

vitreous humour, *ruṭūba jalīdiyya*.

well-known premises, *mashhūrāt*.

whole, *ijtimā'*.

why demonstration, *burhān lima*.

you are you (thou-ness), *anta anta*.

Bibliography

Abelson, Raziel. "Definition." *Encyclopedia of Philosophy.* vol. 2, pp. 314-324. Edited by Paul Edwards. New York: Macmillan, 1967.

Afnan, Soheil. *A Philosophical Lexicon in Persian and Arabic.* Beirut: Daar El-Machreq, 1969.

Alfarabi. *Ārā' Ahl al-Madīna al-Faīḍla* [The opinions of the Inhabitants of the Virtuous City]. Edited by M. al-Kurdī. Cairo, 1948.

________. *al-Alfāẓ al-Musta'mala fī' l-Manṭiq* [Utterences Employed in Logic]. Edited by Muhsin S. Mahdi. Beirut: Dar El-Machreq, 1968.

________. *al-Jam' Bayn Ra'yay al-Ḥakīmayn: Aflāṭūn al-Ilāhī wa Arisṭūṭālīs* [Harmonization of the Opinions of the Two Philosophers: the Divine Plato and Aristotle]. Edited by A.N. Nader. Beirut: Dar El-Machreq, 1968.

________. *Kitāb al-Ḥurūf* [The Book of Letters]. Edited by Muhsin S. Mahdi. Beirut: Daar El-Machreq, 1972.

Aristotle. *Metaphysics.* Translated with commentaries and glossary by Hippocrates G. Apostle. Bloomington and London: Indiana University Press, 1966.

________. *Physics.* Translated with commentaries and glossary by Hippocrates G. Apostle. Bloomington and London: Indiana University Press, 1969.

________. *The Works of Aristotle Translated into English.* vol. 1. Edditedby W.D. Ross. Oxford: Clarendon Press, 1966.

Ashtiyānī, Sayyid Jalāl al-Dīn. *Hastī* [Being]. Mashhad: Khurāsān Prress, 1379 A.H.

Avicenna. *Kitāb al-Ishārāt wa al-Tanbīhāt* [The Book of Directives and Remarks]. Edited by Mahmoud Shahābī. Tehran: Tehran University Press, 1339 A.H. solar.

________. *Livres des Définitions.* Edited and translatedby A.-M. Goichon. Cairo: Publications de l'Institut Français d'Archeologie Orientale du Caire, 1963.

________. *Livre des directives et remarques* Translated by A.-M. Goichon. Paris: J. Vrin, 1951.

________. *Mabda' wa Ma'ād* [Origin and Resurrection]. Translated into Persian by Mahmoud Shahābī. Tehran: Tehran Uiversity Press, 1332 A.H. solar.

________. *Manṭiq al-Mashriqiyyīn* [Logic of the Easterners]. Cairo, 1910.

________. *al-Najāt* [The Deliverance]. Edited by M. al-Kurdī. Cairo, 1948.

________. *al-Shifā' :al-Burhān* [The Healing: Demonstration]. Edited by A.R. Badawi. Cairo, 1954.

________. *al-Shifā' :fi' l-Ibāra* [The Healing:On Interpretation]. Edited by M. al-Khuīayrī. Cairo,1970.

________. *al-Shifā' :al-Jadal* [The Healing:The Dialectic]. Edited by A.F. El Ehwani. Cairo, 1965.

________. *al-Shifā' :al-Ilāhiyyāt* [The Healing:Metaphysics]. Edited by G.C. Anawati and S. Zāyid. Cairo, 1960.

________. *al-Shifā' :al-Madkhal* [The Healing:Isagoge]. Edited by Ibrahim Madkour. Cairo, 1952.

________. *al-Shifā' :al-Maqūlāt* [The Healing:Categories]. Eddited by G.C. Anawati, et al. Cairo,1959.

________. *al-Shifā' :al-Qiyās* [The Healing:Syllogism]. Edited by S. Zāyid. Cairo, 1964.

al-Baghdādī, Abu'l-Barakāt. *al-Mu'tabar* [The Evidential]. Haydarabad, Deccan, 1357 A.H.

Beck, Lewis W. "Kant's Theory of Definition." *The Philosophical Review*, vol. 65, 2 (374) (April, 1956), pp. 179-191.

Corbin, Henry. *Archange empourpré, Quinze traités et récits mystiques traduits du persan et de l'arabe*, présentés et annotés par Henry Corbin Paris: Fayard, 1976.

________. *En Islam iranien.* Four Volumes. Paris: Gallimard1971.

________. *Le Livre de la Sagesse Orientale, Kitāb Ḥikmat al-Ishrāq.* Traduction et notes par Henry Corbin, établies et introduit par Christian Jambet. Paris: Verdier, 1986.

________. *Les Motifs zoroastriens dans la philosophie de Sohravardī* Tehran, 1946.

________. *L'Homme de Lumière dans le soufisme iranien* Paris: Sisteron, 1971.

________. *Suhrawardī d'Alep, fondateur do la doctrine illuminative.* Paris, 1939.

Cornford, Francis M. *Plato's Cosmology*. New York: Arts Press, 1957.

Fakhry, Majid. *A History of Islamic Philsophy*. New York: Columbia University Press, 1970.

Flūṭirkhus. *al-Ārā' al-Ṭabī'iyya*. Published in *Arisṭū fī al-nafs,* ed. A. Badawi , Beirut, 1954, pp. 95-188.

al-Ghazālī, Abū Ḥāmid Muḥammad. *Miḥak al-Naẓar* [Critical Test of Speculation]. Edited by al-Na'sānī. Beirut, 1966.

________. *Mi'yār al-'Ilm* [Standard for Knowledge]. Edited by Solayman Dunya. Cairo, 1961.

Gilson, Étienne. *Being and some Philosophers*. Toronto: Pontifical nstitute of Mediæval Studies, 1949.

Goichon, A.-M. *Lexique de la longue philosophique d'Ibn Sīnā*. Paris: Desclée de Brouwer, 1938.

________. *Lexique de la longue philosophique d'Ibn Sīnā: Supplément.* Paris: Desclée de Brouwer, 1939.

Guthrie, W.K.C. *A History of Greek Philosophy*. Cambridge: Cambridge University Press, 1969.

Haeri, Mehdi. *Hiram-i Hastī* [the Pyramid of Being]. Tehran, 1980.

Hamlyn, D.W. *Sensation and Perception.* London: Routledge & Kegan Paul, 1961.

Harawī, Muḥammad-Sharīf. *Anwāriyya: An 11th century A.H. Persian translation and commentary on Suhrawardī's Ḥikmat al-Ishrāq.* Edited with introduction and notes by Hossein Ziai. Tehran: Amir Kabir, 1980, second edition 1984.

Hirst, R.J. "Perception." *Encyclopedia of Philosophy*. Edited by Paul Edwards. vol. 6, pp. 79-87. New York: Macmilan, 1967.

Hörten, Max. *Die Philosophie der Erleuchtung nach Suhaawardī.* Halle, 1912.

Ḥunayn ibn Isḥāq. "Fi'l-ḍaw' wa ḥaqīqatihi." *al-Machreq (*1899), pp. 1105-1113.

Ibn Abī Uṣaybi'a. *Ṭabaqāt al-Aṭibbā'*. Edited by A Müller. Köningsberg i Pr., 1884.

Ibn Kammūna, Sa'd b. Manṣūr. *Sharḥ al-Talwīḥāt*. Printed in *Manṭiq al-Talwīḥāt* [Logic of the Intimations]. Edited by A.A. Fayyāz. Tehran: Tehran University Press, 1334 solar.

________. *Tanqīḥ al-Abḥāth li' l-Milal al-Thalāth*. Edited by Moshe Perlman. Berkeley and Los Angeles: University of California Press,1971.

Iqbal, Muhammad. *The Development of Metaphysics in Persia*. London: Luzac, 1908.

Ivry, Alfred. *al-Kindī's Metaphysics*. Albany: State University of New York Press, 1974.

Izutsu, Toshihiko. "The Problem of Quiddity and Natural Universal in Islamic Metaphysics." *Études Philosophique*. Edited by Osman Amine. Cairo: Gebo, 1974.

Jadaane, Fehmi. *L'Influence du stoicisme sur la pensée musulmane*. Beirut: Dar El-Machreq, 1968.

Kal, Victor. *On Intuition and Discursive Reasoning in Aristotle*. Leiden: E.J. Brill, 1988.

Kant, Immanuel. *Logic*. Translated by R. Hartman and W. Schwartz. New York: Library of Liberal Arts., 1974.

Kneale, William and Martha. *The Development of Logic*. Oxford: Oxford University Press, 1968.

Massignon, Louis. *Receuil de textes inédits*. Paris: Paul Geuthner, 1929.

Mates, Benson. *Stoic Logic*. Berkeley: University of California Press, 1973.

Matthews, Gwyneth. *Plato's Epistemology and Related Logical Problems*. London: Faber and Faber, 1972.

Merlan, Philip. *From Platonism to Neoplatonism*. 3rd ed., rev. The Hague: Martinus Nijhoff, 1968.

________. *Monopsychism Mysticism Metaconsciousness*. The Hague: Martinus Nijhoff, 1963.

Mishkāt al-Dīnī, A.M. *Taḥqīq dar Ḥaqīqat-i 'Ilm* [Examining the Reality of Knowledge]. Tehran: Tehran University Press, 1344 A.H. solar.

Nasr, Seyyed Hossein. *An Introduction to Islamic Cosmological Doctrines*. London, 1978

________. *Three Muslim Sages* . Cambridge: Harvard University Press, 1964.

Perlman, Moshe. *Sa'd b. Manṣūr Ibn Kammūna's Examination of the Inquiries into the Three Faiths: A Thirteenth-Century Essay in Comparative Religion*. Berkeley and Los Angeles: University of California Press, 1967.

Peters, F.E. *Aristotle and the Arabs*. New York: New York University Press, 1968.

Pines, Solomon. *Nouvelles études sur Awḥad al-Zamān Abu'l-Barakāt al-Baghdādī*. Paris: Librarie Durlaches, 1953.

________. "Studies in Abu'l-Barakāt al-Baghdādī's Poetics and Metaphysics." In Scripta Hierosolymitana, Volume VI, *Studies in Philosophy*. Edited by S.H. Bergman. Jerusalem: The Magnes Press of The Hebrew University (1960), pp. 120-198.

Pistorius. *Plotinus and Neoplatonism*. Cambridge: Bower and Bower, 1952.

Plato. *The Collected Dialogues*. Edited by Edith Hamilton and Huntington Cairns. Princeton: Princeton Uiversity Press, 1969.

Plotinus. *The Enneads*. Translated by Stephen Mackenna. New York: Pantheon Books, 1969.

al-Qifṭī. *Tārīkh al-Ḥukamā'* [History of the Philosophers]. 11th c. Persian trans. Edited by Bahman Dārā'ī. Tehran: Tehran University Press, 1347 A.H. solar.

Rahman, F. *Avicenna's De Anima*. London: Oxford University Press, 1959.

________. Avicenna's Psychology. London: Oxford University Press, 1952.

________. *Prophecy in Islam*. London: George Allen & Unwin Ltd., 1958.

Rist, J.M. *Plotinus: The Road to Reality*. Cambridge: Cambridge University Press, 1967.

Ritter, Helmut. "Philologika IX: Die vier Suhrawardī." *Der Islam*. vol. 24 (1937), pp. 270-286 and vol. 25 (1938), pp. 35-86.

Robinson, Richard. *Definition*. Oxford: Oxford University Press, 1972.

________. Plato's Earlier Dialectic. Oxford: Clarendon Press, 1970.

Russel, Bertrand. *Introduction to Mathematical Philosophy*. London: George Allen & Unwin, 1924.

Sagal, Paul T. "Implicit Definition." *The Monist*, vol. 57, no. 3, (July, 1973) pp. 443-450.

Sajjādī, Seyyed Ja'far. *Shihāb al-Dīn Suhrawardī*. Tehran: Intishārāt-i Falsafa, 1984.

al-Sāwī, 'Umar ibn Sahlān. *Tabṣira va du Risāla-yi dīgar dar Manṭiq* [The Beacon on Two Other Logical Treatises]. Edited by M.T. Danesh Pajouh. Tehran: Tehran University Press, 1958.

Sayre, M. *Plato's Analytic Method*. Chicago: University of Chicago Press, 1969.

Shahābī, Mahmoud. *Būd va Numūd* [Being and Appearance]. Tehran: Tehran University Press, 1335 A.H. solar.

Shahrazūrī, Shams al-Dīn Muḥammad. *Nuzhat al-Arwāḥ*. MS. Istanbul: Yeni Cami, 1908.

________. *Nuzhat al-Arwāḥ wa Rawḍat al-Afrāḥ fī Tārīkh al-Ḥukamā' wa'l-Falāsifa*. Edited by Seyed Khurshid Ahmed. Hayderabad: Osmania Oriental Publications Bureau, 1976.

________. *Nuzhat al-Arwāḥ wa Rawḍat al-Afrāh*. A 16 th century Persian translation by Maqṣūd 'Ali Tabrīzī, edited with an introduction on histories of Islamic philosophy, by M.T. Danesh-Pajouh and M. S. Mawlā'ī. Tehran, 1986.

Sharīf, M.M. *A History of Muslim Philosophy*. Wiesbaden: Otto Harrassowitz, 1963.

Shīrāzī, Quṭb al-Dīn. *Sharḥ Ḥikmat al-Ishrāq* [Commentary on the Philosophy of Illumination]. Tehran, 1313 A.H.

Shīrāzī, Ṣadr al-Dīn, "Mulla Ṣadrā." *Ta'līqāt: Sharḥ Ḥikmat al-Ishrāq*. Tehran, 1313 A.H.

Smith, N.K. *A Commentary to Kant's Critique of Pure Reason*. London: Macmillan, 1923.

Stigen, Anfinn. *The Structure of Aristotle's Thought*. Oslo: Universitetsforlaget, 1966.

Suhrawardī, Shihāb al-Dīn Yaḥyā. *Kalimat al-Taṣawwuf* [Maxim on Sufism]. MS. Tehran: Majlis, Majmū'a 3071.

________. *Kitāb al-Lamaḥāt* [The Flashes of Light]. Edited by Emile Maalouf. Beirut: Dar an-Nahar, 1969.

________. *Manṭiq al-Talwīḥāt* [Logic of the Intimations]. Edited by A.A. Fayyāī. Tehran: Tehran University Press, 1334 solar.

________. *al-Mashāri' wa' l-Muṭāraḥāt* [The Paths and Havens]. MS Leiden: Or. 365.

________. *Oeuvres philosophiques et mystiques: Opera Metaphysica et Mystica II*. Edited with an Introduction by Henry Corbin. Theran: Insatitut Franco-Iranien, 1954.

________. *Opera Metaphysica et Mystica I*. Edited with an Introduction and Notes by Henry Corbin. Istanbul: Maarif Matbaasi, 1945.

________. *Opera Metaphysica et Mystica III* Edited by Seyyed Hossein Nasr. Tehran: Insatitut Franco-Iranien, 1970.

________. *al-Talwīhāt* [The Intimations]. MS. Berlin 5062.

Tūnī, Muḥammad Hossein. *Ilāhiyyāt*.Tehran: Tehran University Press, 1333 A.H.

Index

a priori, 44, 101
Abū Yazīd al-Bastāmī, 21
accidents, 85, 132, 180; the concomitant, 62; the separate 62
acquired, 43, 45, 64, 137
Active Intellect, 21, 143, 144-146, 153; as *dator formarum,* 153; as *dator scientiæ*, 153, 174; as *dator spiritus,* 153; union with, 21
Agathodæmon, 176
Aleppo, 15, 16, 17, 18, 33, 34
Alfarabi, 11, 27, 87, 159, 160
Alkindi, 11
all, 103; as collection, 87, 90; relation between one and the whole, 96; as total, or whole, 115
all, the universal quantifier, 69
allegorical tales, 18
allegory, 28, 145
analogy, 53, 72
analysis, 183, 184
Apposites, 9, 23, 24, 29, 30, 31
Arabic and Persian philosophy and logic, 77
Arabic language, 68
archetype, 153
Aristotelian formal method, 84, 88
Aristotelian philosophy, 39, 86, 88, 96, 97, 100, 103. *See also* Peripatetic philosophy.
Aristotelian quick wit, 155. *See also* intuition.
Aristotle, 21-23, 37, 38, 64, 67, 78, 80, 81, 83, 87-89, 91-97, 101, 105, 122, 124, 125, 129, 145, 146, 147, 159, 160, 176, 182; Suhrawardī's dream-vision of, 21, 145
artificial, 184
ascetic and mystical practices, 25, 35, 146
Asclepius, 176
assent, 42, 44, 45, 46, 47, 60, 80, 99, 136, 137, 138, 139, 140, 141. *See also* conception.
astronomy, 178
Atomists, 180
atoms, 180
Avicenna, 27, 41, 42, 46, 51, 56, 57, 69, 98, 100, 101, 102, 104, 105, 108, 109, 111, 112, 113, 148, 169
Avicennan doctrine, 148
Avicennan ontology, 169
Avicennan philosophy,7, 11, 19, 45, 111. *See also* Peripatetic philosophy.
axiomatic art, 47. *See also* logic.
Ayer, Alfred J., 127
Ayyūbid Ṣalāḥ al-Dīn, 17, 33

Baghdad, 16
Baghdādī, Abu'l-Barakāt al-, 2, 6, 17, 19, 113, 116, 183
being, 2, 27, 58, 149, 163; equivocal sense of 169, 170; univocal sense of 131, 132, 167, 169, 170; of one who is instantaneously created, 147; as entity cognizant of its essence, 150; homonymous being,168; characterized by nobility, 171; non-being, 56; as ontic entity, 131; ontological view, 87; outside the mind, 108; perfection of, 164, 171; characterized by poverty and richness,165, 69; primary being,170; as prior, 86, 179; as simple entity, 134; theory of, 121,

131, 166; the ideal, or mental, being 57
body, 132, 144, 157, 170; admixture in, 56; animal bodies, 152; human bodies, 153
Book of Definitions, 100, 105
brethren of abstraction, 29, 147, 157
Brouwer, E.I.J., 126
Buzurjmihr, 175

Carra de Vaux, 7
categories as part of the subject matter of physics and metaphysics, 51
Categories, 50, 73
cause, the agent, 104, 112; the final,104; the four causes, 104; relation between definition and the four causes, 103
celestial motion, 156
certitude, 54, 121, 129, 130, 137, 138, 154; psychological foundations of, 138
chaos, 44
circular arguments, 113
cogitation, 43, 175
cognition, 61, 102, 111, 114; illuminationist theory of, 121
combination, 103, 183; by composition, 183; by synthesis 183, 184
companions, 32
concept, 56, 82; the derived, abstracted, 167; the derived, mental, 170
conception, 42, 44, 46, 47, 60, 80, 136-141; conception that includes assent, 136; conception-assent, 130. *See also* assent.
consciousness, 127, 143, 149, 15; as principle of illuminationist knowledge, 151; as cosmic, 151; as human, 51; human levels of, 155; intermediary principle of, 149
Corbin, Henry, 7, 8, 14, 25, 58, 139
corporeal, 61, 65, 151, 153; as reality, 180; the thing, 61; corporeality, 152 corporeality of rays, 158; non-corporeal, 130, 153
cosmic level, 156
cosmic lights, 151. *See also* light.
cosmic order, 149
cosmology, 4

data, as empirical, 54, 72; as given, 44; as non-sensible, 61; as sense-data, 35, 44, 61, 178
Dawwānī, Jalāl al-Dīn 3, 13
De Anima, 147
definition, 4, 42, 45, 50, 52, 54, 64, 65, 66, 74, 75, 77, 78, 81, 82-89, 91, 92, 94, 95, 97-100, 104, 106, 108, 110, 112, 115, 116, 122, 133, 179, 181, 183; Aristotelian view of the Socratic, 88; as subject of propositions, 112; by extension, 127; by intention, 127; by analogy, 57, 112; by genus and differentiæ, 95; in demonstration, 83; in use, 127; into two complementary parts, 98; as the premise in demonstration, 83; of man, 66; of number, 126; of soul, 57; as the first step in science, 83; the explicit,127 five types of, 79, 82, 104; the definiendum, 97; analytic and synthetic,126; Aristotelian formula for, 87, 88, 90, 96; Aristotelian real definition, 88, 98; can it be demonstrated? 103; the complete essentialist, 179, 03,104, 107, 114; the composite, 104; the conceptualist, 77, 79, 81, 82. 110; critique of, 102, the general, 88, the implicit, 83 the lexical, 117, 127, 179; methodology of, 85; the ostensive, 82, 83, 101, 112; the persuasive, 89; recognitional sense of, 90, 110; Russell's view of,

127; the Aristotelian, 94, 96, 98, 127; theory of 102, 111; two approaches to, nominal and real, 95, 97, 101; unity of, 101, 102, 103, 110; the valid, 25; relation to demonstration, 103, 113
demiurgus, 162
Democritus, 92, 93
demonstration, 20, 45, 54, 57, 71, 79, 81, 106, 124, 130, 155; as knowledge, 114 ; and definition, 55; as result of definition, 103; matter of, 71; conclusion of, 104; method of, 87, 119; the Aristotelian, 35, 83; the assertoric, 72; the why and the assertoric, 55
description, 52, 64, 74, 100, 102, 112, 117, 180 descriptive definition, 82, 80, 116; the complete, 79, 102; the incomplete, 79. *See also* definition.
desire, 156
dialectic, 54
dialectical means, 89
dialectical method, 84
dialectical method of the dialogue, 94
dichotomy, 87, 90, 113
difference, 165
differentia, 66, 95, 100, 120, 168, 108, 181; differentiæ 96, 97, 100, 111, 120, 159, 184; the independent, 108; the unknown, 131
Directives and Remarks, 11, 111
discursive (as method in philosophy), 10, 22, 24, 30, 125; discursive analysis, 26, 35; discursive, analytic and ordinary mode of expression, 28; discursive knowledge, 129; discursive methodology, 3; discursive Peripatetic philosophy, 27; discursive philosopher, 176; discursive philosophical problems, 21 discursive philosophy, 14, 21, 22, 25, 30, 37, 129, 130, 176, 177; discursive principles, 14; discursive scientific knowledge, 36; discursive thought, 11
Divine assistance, 136
Divine inspiration, 136
Divine light, 25, 34, 35, 58, 177
Divine management, 177
Divine philosopher, 37, 176
Divine philosophy, 37
Divine spirit, 44, 139
division, 53, 87, 90, 113, 124, 183, 184
durationless instant, 141, 159, 161
durationless, discrete moment, 165

Eastern philosophers, 109, 113
Eastern theorem of light and darkness, 175
ecstasy, 146
elemental realm,163
elemental world, 165
emanation, 152, 161, 162, 163; exclusion of creation in,162; Plotinian doctrine of, 162; the idea of control in, 153
Empedocles, 175
Enneads, 163
enthymeme, 53
enumeration, 100, 103, 114, 121; as discrete one-by-one, 114
Enunciative Composition (division in illuminationist logic), 52, 57
epistemology, 2, 13, 21, 27, 34, 58, 65; epistemological foundation of definition, 85; epistemological priority, 129; epistemological process 77; epistemological question, 64; the four epistemological divisions 43
Eros, 162
essence, 5, 87, 89, 95, 96, 106, 107, 108, 119, 131, 135, 139, 142, 147, 148, 150, 151, 157, 167, 169, 170, 180; of man, 110, 118, 127; of things, 138, 141; essences and attributes, 126; non-

corporeality of the subject's own,148; unity of, 95, 99, 107, 114
essential, 63, 85, 181; essential attributes, 118, 123, 133, 134, 159 essential causes, 103; essential constituents, 86; essential nature, 87, 95, 96; essential element, 168; the particular, 66, 96; the specific,119, 181; the general, 119
essentialist definition, 77, 78, 80-82, 100-106, 108, 111, 113, 114, 117-119, 121, 123, 127, 138, 154, 155, 180-182; the incomplete, 79. *See also* definition.
essentials, 66, 101, 118, 120, 121, 180, 181; of the thing, 106; complete sum of,100; totality of, 121
Eternity, 162
Euclid 160
evident subject,13. *See also* subject.
evident thing, 86. *See also* thing.
Evidential (the book), 2, 17, 19, 183
Evidenz, 150, 154, 159
existence, 167, 168, 170; in the univocal sense, 168. *See also* being, quiddity, essence.
existent entity, 168. *See also* thing.
experience, 27, 29, 32, 34, 35, 36, 89, 125, 126, 129; of illumination 24, 28; as personal, 21, 25, 34
experiential knowledge, 10, 21, 26, 28
experiential sciences, 21
external reality, 126
external senses, 158
external vision, 158, 160
external world, 108

Fakhr al-Dīn al-Mārdīnī, 16
Farshāwashtar, 175
finite number of essential attributes, 67
finite, 162, 163
finite, the partly, 162
finitude, 164
First Teacher, 20. *See* Aristotle.
Flashes of Light (the book),11, 30, 175
form, 27, 46, 88, 89, 90, 92, 112, 150, 180; of the thing 42, 60; of the object, 144, dark form, 170
formal, 74, 104; formal and material logic, 74, 98; formal construction, 90; formal definition, 125, 126; formal knowledge, 142; formal logic, 48, 49, 69, 71, 75, 123; formal method, 45, 89; formal problems of logic, 45, 75; formal rules, 47, 65, 94, 98; formal validity, 129, 136; formal validity of science 137
Forms, 84, 89, 93, 124, 125, 129
formula, 80, 82, 100, 102, 105, 110, 114; of definition, 66, 79, 83, 113; of proximate genus plus differentiæ 182
forty-day retreat, 35
Galen, 82
genus, 66, 95, 96, 97, 111, 119, 168, 181, 184; *genus longinquum,* 106; the proximate 100; *summum genus,* 101, 107; genera, 100, 108, 111, 120, 159, 184;
God, 4, 27, 143, 175, 176
God's vicegerent, 176
Greek philosophy, 164
Greek Wisdom, 9
Greeks, 91, 164
Guthrie, A.K., 89
Ḥallāj, Manṣūr, 21
Harmonization of the Opinions of Plato and Aristotle (the book), 87, 159
Hayākil al-Nūr (the book),13
Healing (the book), 11, 41, 44, 45, 51, 52, 57, 101, 113
Heavenly Sun, 156
Hermes, 37, 175, 176
History of Philosophy, 36; Iranian branch of, 37

Holy Spirit, 153
holy intellect, 155
Hörten, Max 7
human-ness, 180
humours, 184
Husserl, Edmund, 154
Hūrakhsh, the cosmic sun,156

Ibn Kammūna, Sa'd b. Manṣūr, 1, 2, 55
idea, 44, 61, 106, 140, 142, 151; of color, 108, 132; of man, 118, 119, 66, 107; of animal 107
ideal, 131
idealism, 85
Ideas, 84, 93, 162
illumination, 13, 27, 35, 44, 48, 88, 94, 126, 150, 156, 161, 163; and vision 111, 165; language of, 26, 27, 28; moment of, 157, 159
illuminationist method in philosophy, 12, 23, 30
illuminationist logical and epistemological principles, 42
illuminationist visionary experience, 146
illuminationist ontology, 133, 166, 169
illuminationist epistemology, 4, 29, 43, 64, 65, 67, 71, 129, 130-32, 144, 146, 151, 154
illuminationist knowledge, 34, 35, 139, 141, 142, 143, 149
illuminationist logic, 52, 58, 98, 115
illuminationist philosophy, 13, 22, 24, 27, 28, 30
illuminationist principles, 22, 24, 29, 61, 110
illuminationist realism, 132
illuminationist relation, 134, 135, 141, 142, 150, 154
illuminationist theory,97, 110, 127
illuminationist theory of definition, 85, 88, 112
imagery of light and darkness 27
imagination, as creative acts of the illuminated subject, 161; faculty of 157, 161
impossible (the mode), 69, 169
inclusion, 68, 86
induction, 53, 72, 83, 103, 121, 159
inductive argument, 88
inference, 44, 155; rules of 70; valid inferences, 68
infinite, 162, 163, 164; link with the finite, 164; the partly,162
infinitesimal, 164; as the moment of illumination-vision, 164. *See also* durationless.
infinity, 164; infinite order infinity, 163; finite order infinity,163
initiates, 32
innate, 42, 43, 45, 64, 117, 137, 168; innate idea, 64, 113, 118, 124; as the grounds for knowledge, 64; innate knowledge, 44, 117; innate visions and intuitions, 137; innately known, 66, 113
insight, 53. *See also* intuition.
inspiration, 35, 44, 45; as personal, 1, 113
intellect, 27, 112, 131, 154; the habitual, 155
intelligibility, 124
intelligibles, 155
intermediary, 170
intuition, 21, 34, 35, 45, 72, 88, 89, 114, 118, 125, 130, 141, 155, 173, 175; certainties of, 17; creative act of, 14, 22; position of,34; intuitive premises, 72; intuitive, 44, 54, 125; intuitive ability, 37; intuitive grasp of the whole, 28, 29,130; intuitive judgements, 155; intuitive knowledge, 135, 136, 138; intuitive mode of cognition, 150; intuitive philosophy, 14, 22, 30, 37; primary intuition, 2, 21, 27, 119, 126

intuitionist, 14
ipseity, 27, 66, 85, 97, 146, 147, 149; "I", 146-149, 152, 170; I-ness, 13; he (as objective reality), 148; he/she/it-ness, 13; thou, 148; thou-ness, 13
Iran, 15
Iranian philosophy and wisdom, the ancient, 9
Iranian speculative mysticism, 1
Iranian thought, the ancient, 8
Iranian wisdom, 9, 36
Isagoge, 42, 43, 45, 50, 51, 56, 64, 74, 99
Isfahan, 16
Isfahbad al-Nāsūt, 152, 53, 154. *See also* Active Intellect.

Jewish mysticism, 3
judgement, 42
Jāmāsf, 175

Kant, 126
Kitāb al-Alwāḥ al-'Imādī, 13
Kitāb al-Jadīd fi'l-Ḥikma, 1
Kneale, William, 92
knowable, deductively, intuitively, or innately, 86
Knowing self, 138. *See also* self.
knowing being, 117
knowing subject, 2, 13, 119, 134, 141, 140, 159
knowledge, 2, 4, 14, 21, 34, 43, 44, 61, 93, 95, 99, 113, 138; as a whole 47; based on illumination and presence, 141, 142, 150; based on intuition, 129, 142; by experience, 10, 21, 22, 26, 28, 130, 142; by presence, 137, 139, 142 of compound things, 134; of essence, 129, 141; of God, 142; of incorporeal separate entities, 142; of multiplicity, 97; of oneself, 142; of simple things, 134; the obtained, 98; Aristotelian notion of pre-existent, 117; the certain, 66; distinguished from belief, 91; foundation of, 61, 124; question of, 146; theory of, 4, 64; two-fold division of, 64; basis for, 113; universal knowledge, 134; unrestricted knowledge, 157
known, 66, 181

Laches, 88, 90
language, allegorical 13; allegorical and symbolic 1, 10; technical, 14; use of metaphor in, 28, 147, 32, 63, 125, 175; of the early philosophers,175; oral teachings and, 18, 28, 89; position in the reconstruction of metaphysics, 27; special 27; and the symbolic mode of expression, 27; the technical, 12, 22, 27, 38; use of in philosophy, 26, 27
law of mean terms, 162
lawgivers, 176
leadership on earth, 177
light, 117, 125, 156, 157, 159, 161, 163, 169; in itself, 169, 170; is its own definition, 125; degrees of intensity of, 27; of God, 35, 173; gradation of, 169; intensity of, 152, 165, 169, 171; luminosity of, 157; characterized as absolutely poor, 169; characterized as absolutely rich, 169; abstract light, 149, 150, 152, 153, 156, 159, 161, 165, 166; accidental light, 63, 170; apocalyptic light, 35, 129, 157, 166, 177; archetypal light, 166; Closest Light, 164, 166; creative light, 157; First Light, 163, 164, 165, 166; flashing pleasurable light, 157; glittering light, 146; noncorporeal light, 161; principal, abstract lights, 165; pure light, 151, 170; self-subsisting light, 149, 170; controlling

light, 152, 156, 166; light-as-such, 151; Isfahbad lights, 153, 156, 157; managing lights, 152, 156, 166
Light of Lights, 4, 58, 156, 157, 161-166
Logic of the Easterners (the book), 101, 109, 112
logic, 9, 11, 12, 24, 41-49, 51, 56, 58; as part of philosophy, or not? 47; as a speculative art, 47; of the Peripatetics, 41; illuminationist subjects of, 49; non-Aristotelian, 2; problems of, 50, 51, 55, 65; rules of, 48, 74; structure of, 74; its subject is non-real, 47; as tool, 44, 45, 47, 48
logical deduction, 46
logical investigation, 44
love, 153, 165

magus, the infidel, 175
Majd al-Dīn al-Jīlī, 16, 17
Malik Ẓāhir Shāh, 17, 19, 33
man, 110; as substance conscious of its own essence, 144; man's reality 133
manifest, the, 5, 133. *See also* thing.
manifestation, 154; of essence, 143
many in formula, 96
Marāgha, 16
Massignon, Louis, 7
Master of the Philosophy of Illumination, 7
Masters of Vision, 157
material logic, 52, 54, 79, 123
material, 74, 104, 112
materialist view, 65
mathematical rules, 47, 116, 183, used in constructing definitions, 183
mathematical terminology, 116
mathematicians, 160
mathematics, 9, 47, 93, 108
matter, 27, 46, 152, 165, 166, 180
meaning, 46, 59-61, 106, 117; the general, 55, 63; the particular, 62; the universal, 61, 184
Meno, 124
mental, the,131, 183: as concept, 108, 112, 132, 168; mental form, 108; mental synthesis, 184; mental composition, 184.
messengers, 176
metaphore, 128, 147, 75
metaphorical language, 32, 63, 125. *See also* language
metaphysica generalis, 132, 168
metaphysics, 9, 11, 12, 20, 24, 55, 58, 73, 85, 88, 95, 96, 103, 158, 159
method of hypothesis, 90
mind, 42, 60, 134
modality, 70; the iterated, 99
mode necessary, 69
mode possible, 69, 169
modus ponens, 68, 70
modus tollens, 68, 70
monads, 4, 170
Muhammad Iqbāl, 8
Mullā Ṣadrā, *see* Ṣadr al-Dīn al-Shīrāzī.
multiplicity, 111; of constituents 107; of attributes 114
mystical experience, 9, 27, 30, 79, 113, 130
mystical vision 1, 130
Mārdīn, 16
Mārdīnī, Fakhr al-Dīn, 16, 17

name, 63, 110, 180; class name, 62; homonymous names, 63; proper name, 62; synonymous name, 63; as the word man, 118
name-giver, 180
Nasr, S.H., 7, 8, 58
natural philosophers, the ancient, 180
Necessary Existent, 169
necessary, 69, 169

negation, 49, 50, 68, 69, 70, 71, 75
Neoplatonist, 86
Neoplatonists, 162
nominal and real definitions, 101
nominal definition, 117, 95, 112
nominal substitutions, 65
nominal, 117
nominalism, 85
nominalist, 77, 81, 83
non-essential attributes, 118, 132
Nous, 162, 163

object, 5, 120, 134, 141, 142, 143, 149, 150, 154, 156, 161; object as-it-is, 154; is seen, 133, 134, 139, 161; itself is illuminated, 156; apparentness of, 151, 154, 159; immediate, a-temporal grasp of, 150; as knowable, 2; the luminous, 160; reality of, 141; the apparent, 133, 151, 183
objective ipseity, 148, 149
Observations (the book), *17*
On Interpretation, 51, 52, 67, 74
one in form, 96
one in formula, 96
one in number, 96
One, 163; One beyond Being, 164
Organon, 45, 50, 51, 52, 53, 65, 73, 74, 98
Orientalist philological tradition, 4
Orientalists, 7

pahlavī, or *fahlavānī,* or *kiyānī,* philosophers, 37
Parts of Animals, 88
perception, 61, 118, 120, 135, 140, 141, 144, 149, 154; of one's own self-consciousness 150; intellectual perception, 141
Peripatetic (philosophy), 4, 18, 22, 25, 26, 27, 44, 46, 48, 60, 62, 65, 73, 74, 78, 100, 102, 104, 106, 107, 113, 118, 127, 168; definition of man as rational animal, 57; doctrine, 31; formal rules of definition, 50; formula of definition, 66, 83, 99, 112, 121, 123, 129, 119, 181; formula of definition, objections to, 66; logic, 41, 50, 51, 74, 98; method, 11, 20, 21, 23, 25, 29, 30, 175, 177; philosophy, 1, 11, 12, 14, 27, 31, 37, 81; philosophy, distinguished from Eastern philosophy 109; principles of philosophy, 12, 109; teachings, 11; theory of being,131; thoeoy of knowledge, 130, 131, 142
Peripatetics, 17, 20, 25, 46, 49, 50, 55, 65, 67, 69, 73, 78, 80, 83, 85, 98, 101, 103, 107, 109, 110, 119, 120, 122, 124, 131-136, 138, 139, 143, 147, 150, 151, 175, 118, 180-182; approach in philosophy 26; the later, 104
Persian and Arabic allegorical tales, 13
Persian Khusrawāni sages, 109
Persian philosophers, 175
petitio principii, 114
philosophia generalis, 109
philosophia specialis, 109
philosophy of illumination, passim
philosophy, Græco-Egyptian branch, 37, foundation of, 29, method of, principles of, 85; terminology of, 82. *See also* Peripatetic philosophy.
physical entities, 93
physical observation, 130
physical order, 149
physics, 9, 11, 12, 24, 55, 58, 144, 158; problems of, 73
Plato, 21, 37, 81, 83, 84, 87-93, 96, 124, 160, 162-165, 175, 176
Platonic philosophy, 1,19, 86, 88, 97, 103, 110, 124; Platonic approach, 97; Platonic dialectic, 88; Platonic

dialogues, 92; Platonic method, 88, 90, 96; Platonic method of definition, 94, 113, 116; Platonic position in philosophy, 84; Platonic theory of Forms, 92; Platonic view of Ideas 117
pleasure, 146
Plotinian One, 162, 163, 164
Plotinus, 162, 163, 164; concept of Nous, 163
poetry, 54
Posterior Analytics, 35, 51, 52, 55, 64, 65, 67, 72, 74, 83, 88, 92, 94, 98, 99, 103, 113, 123, 129
power, 157
predicate, 67, 69, 70, 135; common predicate, 168
predicative proposition, 67-69, 135, 142
predicative being,168
predicative knowledge, 135, 149, 150
premise, 70, 94, the accepted 54, of demonstrations 94, whose validity is certain 71; classes of, 54; the fancied, 54; the given, 54; the observed 54, 71; the received, 54; the repetitive, 54; the self-evident, 86, 137, 168; the supposedly true, 54; the unrestricted, 78; the intuitive, 72 ; the generally accepted, 72; the imagined, 54, 72; the primary, 54, 71, 130; the self-evident, 130
presence, 32, 150, 154; of the object, 141, 143; of the thing, 149
presuppositions, 56
primacy of essence, ontological position of, 167
primacy of existence, ontological position of, 167
primary and secondary intelligibles, 27
primary axiom, 14, 86
primary being, 168
primary knowledge, 137
primary truths, 95
principle of illuminationist vision,149
principle of things, 93
principle realities, 100
principles and rules of philosophy, 25, 30, 41; non-Aristotelian, 50
principles of Eastern philosophy,109
principles of knowledge, 93
principles of logic, 45
principles of proof, 74
Prior Analytics, 51, 53, 54, 67, 74
priority, epistemological, 86, 124
priority, ontological, 169, 171
proficient in illumination (the person), 25, 28, 29
proof, 44-46, 49, 52, 53, 57, 67, 71, 78, 79, 81, 175
proposition 45, 54, 57, 67, 68, 70, 80; affirmation in 68, 70; the always necessary affirmative, 69, 75; antecedent in, 68; apodosis in, 68, argument of, 80; the compound, 68; the connective conditional, 67; consequent in, 68; contradiction in, 53, 70; conversion of, 53, 70; the existential, 135; the expository, 44-46, 52, 56, 78-81, 99, 104; the iterated modal, 50, 70; the modal, 53, 57, 69; modalities in, 53, 56, 165; the non-predicative, 141; reduction of, 69; the universal indefinite, 68; the universal, 69; protasis in, 67; the conditional, 46, 68, 71
Pythagoras, 175
Pythagoreans, 92

quality, abstracted, 108
quantification sign, 68
quantification, 50, 70
quantity, absolute, 180
questions, 55, 72, 85, 112
quiddity, 56, 62, 63, 167, 168. *See also* essence.

Quires on Philosophy, 109
Qur'ānic exegesis, 13

rational animal, 66, 85, 107, 110, 118, 127, 180
rational soul, 112, 149
rational substance, 101
rational, 107, 112
rays, 158
real being, 57, 89
real composition, 184
real definition, 65, 81, 82, 88, 95, 117, 118, 180. *See also* definition.
real essence, 112. *See also* essence, being, quiddity.
real knowledge, 118. *See also* knowledg.
real sciences, 35, 54, 71, 132
real synthesis, 184
real thing, 63, 108, 134. *See also* thing, light.
real, 183
realism, 85. *See also* philosophy of illumination.
realist 81
reality, 9, 61, 62, 117, 152, 155; of a thing, 63, 121; of man 118, 180; outside the mind, 63; fundamental basis of, 125
realizing, 141. *See also* intuition, perception.
really out there, 47
reason, 17
reasoning, capacity for, 118, 112, 180
reflection, personal, 17, 26
relation, 61, 134, 138, 141, 149
Republic, 88
retreats, 173
revelation, 1, 35, 45, 173
Rhetoric, 51, 54
Rist, J.M. 163, 164
Risāla fī I'tiqād al-Ḥukamā', 31
Ritter, Helmut, 7
Russell, Bertrand,127

Ṣadr al-Dīn al-Shīrāzī, 3, 167, 170
sagesse orientale, 1
Saladin, see Ayyūbid Ṣalāḥ al-Dīn
sameness, 165; and difference 112
science, 43, 47, 80, 95, 96, 106, 137; based on presence and vision,146; first step in , 65; methodology of, 14, 44; rules of, 20; of lights, 169, 175; science of logic, 44; sciences 25, 119;
scientific knowledge, 83
scientific method,72, 83
secondary intelligibles, 47
seeing, 135
seer, 159
self, 143, 144, 146; the knowing, 138; and consciousness 117
self-as-self, 146
self-conscious, 13, 85, 152, 157, 159
self-consciousness, 4, 13, 97, 114, 117, 124, 126, 138, 144, 146-157, 163, 166, 169; as a cosmic principle, 149, 153; as a psychological principle, 149
self-emanating, 157. *See also* Light of Lights.
self-emanation, 162
self-knowledge, 4, 22, 66, 119, 145-151, 153, 156. *See also* innate.
self-manifestation, 154
self-realization, 143
self-subsistent, 170. *See also* thing, monad.
semantic problems, 59, 61, 74
semantic theory, 52, 65
semantics, 26, 52, 63, 74, 99
semiotics, 98, 106, 115, 123
sense-perception , 20, 134, 141, 147, 155, 159, 183
sensible nature, 93. *See also* thing.
sensus communis, 157
separate entities, 63, 143

separate parts, 108
separation, 143
Shahrazūrī, 2, 16, 139
shape, 165, 166, 169, 170
Sharī'a, 33
Shaykh al-Ishrāq, 7
Shīrāzī, Quṭb al-Dīn 3, 30, 32, 60, 62, 139, 140, 141, 142
sight, 137, 149, 156, 159, 161; objects of 158. *See also* vision.
signification, 59, 106; by complete correspondence, 106; of concomitance, 60; of correspondence, 60; of implication, 60; of intention, 60; by concomitance, 60, 106; the implicit, 60, 106, 107; the incomplete, 100, 107; by indication,106; types of, 106
Sikanjibīn, 184
Socrates, 88, 89, 92, 93
Socratic attempt to define ethical terms, 91
Socratic fallacy, 90
Socratic method of definition, 89
Sophistical Refutations, 49, 51, 55, 73, 74
soul, 27, 119, 146, 150, 181; soul's knowledge; 22 soul's knowledge of itself, 14; abstract souls, 157. *See also* self, ipseity.
spheres, 165
Spies, Otto, 7
spiritual observation, 130
statement, 45, 80
Stoic theory of categories, 51
subject, 5, 67, 69, 70, 118, 120, 126, 132, 138, 141-143, 149, 150, 154, 160, 161; correspondence between the subject and the object, 138; the perceiving, 135; self of, 27
substance, 87, 95, 96, 101, 131, 134; the dark, 170; the separate, 131
substantial reality, 112
substantiality, 131
subtraction, 184
ṣūfī states, 147
ṣūfī *ṭarīqa,* 35
Suhraward, village of, 15
Suhrawardī, passim.
Sun Rays (the book), 13
supposition, theory of, 50
surface, 108
syllogism, 54, 67, 70, 73; conversion of 49; the dialectical, 159; disjunction in, 143, 156; the disjunctive, 68, 70; fallacies in, 68; figures of, 46, 47; first figure of, 71, 99; forms of, 54; the hypothetical, 68, 70; matter of, 53, 54; middle term of, 70, 155; *reduction ad impossible* in,71; reduction of second and the third figures to the first, 50; second and the third figures of, 75, second figure of, 71; sophistical errors in, 55; third figure of, 71
symbol man, 127
symbol, 28, 175
symbolic language, 26, 28
symbolic mode 30, 126
symbolic, 36, 125; and metaphorical expression, 27, 29, 124
symbolism, 32
Symposium, 91
synthesis, 87, 90, 100, 101, 103, 124, 183, 184
synthetic combination,144
Syria, 16, 17

temporal extension, 44, 141, 159
temporal modalities, 68, 69, 70; in propositions, 70, 99
temporal process, 141
terminology, non-standard, 23
The Development of Metaphysics in Persia (the book), 8
the named, 57

the whole, 152. *See also* all.
theosophy, 1, 176, 177
Theætetus, 88, 90, 91
thing, 59, 96, 179, in itself, 61, 65, 150; and its attributes 111; as it exists externally 107; as-it-is 62, 108, 133, 137, 143, 149; the defined,179, 181; in an unrestricted sense, 168; man as, 110, 118; as the named. 180; as the seen, 108, 131, 159; to be defined, 65; essential attributes of, 99; thing's reality. 131; the absent 61, 140; aggregate all of,179, 181; organic whole of,179, 181; all the attributes of, 110, 111, 113; attributes of, 66, 124, 132, 181; the closest, 19; the composite 46, 62; the composite real, 101; the existing, 96; externals of, 118, 180; idea of in the mind, 107; concomitants of, 60, 63, 85, 132, 180; constituent elements of, 100, 108, 121; the luminous, 161; the more apparent, 116, 117, 179; the more evident, 65; the more known, 117; the more prior, 65; the most apparent, 117, 132; the most apparent and most prior, 117; the most intelligible, 125; the most known, 117; the most prior, 66, 86, 113, 117, 125; the non compound, 133; non-apparent attributes of, 121; the non-real, 47; the non-sensible, 61; the non-simple, 62; properties of, 132; as real, 63, 108, 134; reality of, 179; as sensed, 120, 181, 133; the sensible 61, 180; sensible parts of, 180; the simple, 62, 85, 133, 107; the specific, 63; sum of the constituents of, 107; that-ness of, 149; the apparent, 117, 121; totality of, 66, 67, 69, 78, 122, 124; quiddity of, 6; what-it-is, 62; what-ness of, 168;
thingness, 168
thinking, 47
thought, 43 *See also* cogitation.
time, *see* durationless
time-space, 21
Timæus, 163
Topics, 51, 52, 65, 88, 98, 100, 103, 105, 116, 123
totality of existence, 2
translatability of symbols, 127
true science, 35, 44, 178
truths of a symbolic nature, 21

'Umar ibn Sahlān al-Sāwī,17, 52
union, 143
unit(s), 65, 115, 119, 179, 183
unitary formula, 96, 114, 123
unity, 97, 111, 143; of the subject and object, 143; of the thing defined 97
universal principles, 96
universal reality, 66, 120, 181
universal, 56, 63, 63, 96
universals, 150
unknown 66, 181. *See also* known.
utterance, 46, 59, 60, 61, 62, 105, 106, 107, 117, the compound, 106; the simple, 101, 136; the single, 46 101

virtue, 110
vision, 35, 45, 133, 135, 137, 141, 149, 156, 158-161, 165, 175; the internal, 158; moment of, 156; theory of, 158
vision-illumination, 124, 155, 156, 161
visionary data, 36
visionary experience, 36, 157
vitreous humour, 158

whole of reality, 130
whole, 2, 65, 134. *See also* all.
wisdom, 2, 22, 33

Ẓahīr al-Fārsī, 17

Index of Greek Terms

ἀγχίνοια, 53n, 72n, 135n, 155, 155n
ἀξίωμα, 42n, 67n

δαιμόνιον, 22n
διαγραφή, 82n

ἐπιστήμη, 129n

ἰδέα ποιότητος, 62n

κοινὴ ποιότης, 62n

λεκτόν, 59n, 60n, 62n; αὐτοτελές, 62n; ἐλλιπές, 62n
λόγος, 80n, 91n, 95n
λόγος ἀποφαντικός, 42n, 67n
μονάδες, 116n
μοναδιστί, 116n

νοῦς ποιητικός, 116n, 154n
νόησις, 42n

οὐσία, 87, 95n
ὀνόματα, 62n
ὃλον, 115n
ὁρισμός, 88, 80n
ὃρος, 88

πειθώ, and ἀνάγκη, 135n
περι φαντασίς, 42n
περιγραφή, 82n
προσηγορίαι, 62n
τὰ πρῶτα, 71n
προφορικὸς λόγος, 80n

σημαῖων, 60n
σύγκρισις, 115n
σύνολος, 115n
σύστημα, 115n
συύθεσις, 115n
σόφια , 2

τυγχάνον, 60n

ὑπογραφή, 82

φαντασία λογική, 42n
φωνή, 60n

Brown Judaic Studies

140001	*Approaches to Ancient Judaism I*	William S. Green
140002	*The Traditions of Eleazar Ben Azariah*	Tzvee Zahavy
140003	*Persons and Institutions in Early Rabbinic Judaism*	William S. Green
140004	*Claude Goldsmid Montefiore on the Ancient Rabbis*	Joshua B. Stein
140005	*The Ecumenical Perspective and the Modernization of Jewish Religion*	S. Daniel Breslauer
140006	*The Sabbath-Law of Rabbi Meir*	Robert Goldenberg
140007	*Rabbi Tarfon*	Joel Gereboff
140008	*Rabban Gamaliel II*	Shamai Kanter
140009	*Approaches to Ancient Judaism II*	William S. Green
140010	*Method and Meaning in Ancient Judaism*	Jacob Neusner
140011	*Approaches to Ancient Judaism III*	William S. Green
140012	*Turning Point: Zionism and Reform Judaism*	Howard R. Greenstein
140013	*Buber on God and the Perfect Man*	Pamela Vermes
140014	*Scholastic Rabbinism*	Anthony J. Saldarini
140015	*Method and Meaning in Ancient Judaism II*	Jacob Neusner
140016	*Method and Meaning in Ancient Judaism III*	Jacob Neusner
140017	*Post Mishnaic Judaism in Transition*	Baruch M. Bokser
140018	*A History of the Mishnaic Law of Agriculture: Tractate Maaser Sheni*	Peter J. Haas
140019	*Mishnah's Theology of Tithing*	Martin S. Jaffee
140020	*The Priestly Gift in Mishnah: A Study of Tractate Terumot*	Alan. J. Peck
140021	*History of Judaism: The Next Ten Years*	Baruch M. Bokser
140022	*Ancient Synagogues*	Joseph Gutmann
140023	*Warrant for Genocide*	Norman Cohn
140024	*The Creation of the World According to Gersonides*	Jacob J. Staub
140025	*Two Treatises of Philo of Alexandria: A Commentary on De Gigantibus and Quod Deus Sit Immutabilis*	David Winston/John Dillon
140026	*A History of the Mishnaic Law of Agriculture: Kilayim*	Irving Mandelbaum
140027	*Approaches to Ancient Judaism IV*	William S. Green
140028	*Judaism in the American Humanities*	Jacob Neusner
140029	*Handbook of Synagogue Architecture*	Marilyn Chiat
140030	*The Book of Mirrors*	Daniel C. Matt
140031	*Ideas in Fiction: The Works of Hayim Hazaz*	Warren Bargad
140032	*Approaches to Ancient Judaism V*	William S. Green
140033	*Sectarian Law in the Dead Sea Scrolls: Courts, Testimony and the Penal Code*	Lawrence H. Schiffman
140034	*A History of the United Jewish Appeal: 1939-1982*	Marc L. Raphael
140035	*The Academic Study of Judaism*	Jacob Neusner
140036	*Woman Leaders in the Ancient Synagogue*	Bernadette Brooten
140037	*Formative Judaism: Religious, Historical, and Literary Studies*	Jacob Neusner
140038	*Ben Sira's View of Women: A Literary Analysis*	Warren C. Trenchard
140039	*Barukh Kurzweil and Modern Hebrew Literature*	James S. Diamond

140040	*Israeli Childhood Stories of the Sixties: Yizhar, Aloni,Shahar, Kahana-Carmon*	Gideon Telpaz
140041	*Formative Judaism II: Religious, Historical, and Literary Studies*	Jacob Neusner
140042	*Judaism in the American Humanities II: Jewish Learning and the New Humanities*	Jacob Neusner
140043	*Support for the Poor in the Mishnaic Law of Agriculture: Tractate Peah*	Roger Brooks
140044	*The Sanctity of the Seventh Year: A Study of Mishnah Tractate Shebiit*	Louis E. Newman
140045	*Character and Context: Studies in the Fiction of Abramovitsh, Brenner, and Agnon*	Jeffrey Fleck
140046	*Formative Judaism III: Religious, Historical, and Literary Studies*	Jacob Neusner
140047	*Pharaoh's Counsellors: Job, Jethro, and Balaam in Rabbinic and Patristic Tradition*	Judith Baskin
140048	*The Scrolls and Christian Origins: Studies in the Jewish Background of the New Testament*	Matthew Black
140049	*Approaches to Modern Judaism I*	Marc Lee Raphael
140050	*Mysterious Encounters at Mamre and Jabbok*	William T. Miller
140051	*The Mishnah Before 70*	Jacob Neusner
140052	*Sparda by the Bitter Sea: Imperial Interaction in Western Anatolia*	Jack Martin Balcer
140053	*Hermann Cohen: The Challenge of a Religion of Reason*	William Kluback
140054	*Approaches to Judaism in Medieval Times I*	David R. Blumenthal
140055	*In the Margins of the Yerushalmi: Glosses on the English Translation*	Jacob Neusner
140056	*Approaches to Modern Judaism II*	Marc Lee Raphael
140057	*Approaches to Judaism in Medieval Times II*	David R. Blumenthal
140058	*Midrash as Literature: The Primacy of Documentary Discourse*	JacobNeusner
140059	*The Commerce of the Sacred: Mediation of the Divine Among Jews in the Graeco-Roman Diaspora*	Jack N. Lightstone
140060	*Major Trends in Formative Judaism I: Society and Symbol in Political Crisis*	Jacob Neusner
140061	*Major Trends in Formative Judaism II: Texts, Contents, and Contexts*	Jacob Neusner
140062	*A History of the Jews in Babylonia I: The Parthian Period*	Jacob Neusner
140063	*The Talmud of Babylonia: An American Translation. XXXII: Tractate Arakhin*	Jacob Neusner
140064	*Ancient Judaism: Debates and Disputes*	Jacob Neusner
140065	*Prayers Alleged to Be Jewish: An Examination of the Constitutiones Apostolorum*	David Fiensy
140066	*The Legal Methodology of Hai Gaon*	Tsvi Groner
140067	*From Mishnah to Scripture: The Problem of the Unattributed Saying*	Jacob Neusner
140068	*Halakhah in a Theological Dimension*	David Novak

140069	*From Philo to Origen: Middle Platonism in Transition*	Robert M. Berchman
140070	*In Search of Talmudic Biography: The Problem of the Attributed Saying*	Jacob Neusner
140071	*The Death of the Old and the Birth of the New: The Framework of the Book of Numbers and the Pentateuch*	Dennis T. Olson
140072	*The Talmud of Babylonia: An American Translation. XVII: Tractate Sotah*	Jacob Neusner
140073	*Understanding Seeking Faith: Essays on the Case of Judaism. Volume Two: Literature, Religion and the Social Study of Judiasm*	JacobNeusner
140074	*The Talmud of Babylonia: An American Translation. VI: Tractate Sukkah*	Jacob Neusner
140075	*Fear Not Warrior: A Study of 'al tira' Pericopes in the Hebrew Scriptures*	Edgar W. Conrad
140076	*Formative Judaism IV: Religious, Historical, and Literary Studies*	Jacob Neusner
140077	*Biblical Patterns in Modern Literature*	David H. Hirsch/ Nehama Aschkenasy
140078	*The Talmud of Babylonia: An American Translation I: Tractate Berakhot*	Jacob Neusner
140079	*Mishnah's Division of Agriculture: A History and Theology of Seder Zeraim*	Alan J. Avery-Peck
140080	*From Tradition to Imitation: The Plan and Program of Pesiqta Rabbati and Pesiqta deRab Kahana*	Jacob Neusner
140081	*The Talmud of Babylonia: An American Translation. XXIIIA: Tractate Sanhedrin, Chapters 1-3*	Jacob Neusner
140082	*Jewish Presence in T. S. Eliot and Franz Kafka*	Melvin Wilk
140083	*School, Court, Public Administration: Judaism and its Institutions in Talmudic Babylonia*	Jacob Neusner
140084	*The Talmud of Babylonia: An American Translation. XXIIIB: Tractate Sanhedrin, Chapters 4-8*	Jacob Neusner
140085	*The Bavli and Its Sources: The Question of Tradition in the Case of Tractate Sukkah*	Jacob Neusner
140086	*From Description to Conviction: Essays on the History and Theology of Judaism*	Jacob Neusner
140087	*The Talmud of Babylonia: An American Translation. XXIIIC: Tractate Sanhedrin, Chapters 9-11*	Jacob Neusner
140088	*Mishnaic Law of Blessings and Prayers: Tractate Berakhot*	Tzvee Zahavy
140089	*The Peripatetic Saying: The Problem of the Thrice-Told Tale in Talmudic Literature*	Jacob Neusner
140090	*The Talmud of Babylonia: An American Translation. XXVI: Tractate Horayot*	Martin S. Jaffee
140091	*Formative Judaism V: Religious, Historical, and Literary Studies*	Jacob Neusner
140092	*Essays on Biblical Method and Translation*	Edward Greenstein
140093	*The Integrity of Leviticus Rabbah*	Jacob Neusner
140094	*Behind the Essenes: History and Ideology of the Dead Sea Scrolls*	Philip R. Davies

140095	*Approaches to Judaism in Medieval Times, Volume III*	David R. Blumenthal
140096	*The Memorized Torah: The Mnemonic System of the Mishnah*	Jacob Neusner
140097	*Knowledge and Illumination*	Hossein Ziai
140098	*Sifre to Deuteronomy: An Analytical Translation. Volume One: Pisqaot One through One Hundred Forty-Three. Debarim, Waethanan, Eqeb*	Jacob Neusner
140099	*Major Trends in Formative Judaism III: The Three Stages in the Formation of Judaism*	Jacob Neusner
140101	*Sifre to Deuteronomy: An Analytical Translation. Volume Two: Pisqaot One Hundred Forty-Four through Three Hundred Fifty-Seven. Shofetim, Ki Tese, Ki Tabo, Nesabim, Ha'azinu, Zot Habberakhah*	Jacob Neusner
140102	*Sifra: The Rabbinic Commentary on Leviticus*	Jacob Neusner/ Roger Brooks
140103	*The Human Will in Judaism*	Howard Eilberg-Schwartz
140104	*Genesis Rabbah: Volume 1. Genesis 1:1 to 8:14*	Jacob Neusner
140105	*Genesis Rabbah: Volume 2. Genesis 8:15 to 28:9*	Jacob Neusner
140106	*Genesis Rabbah: Volume 3. Genesis 28:10 to 50:26*	Jacob Neusner
140107	*First Principles of Systemic Analysis*	Jacob Neusner
140108	*Genesis and Judaism*	Jacob Neusner
140109	*The Talmud of Babylonia: An American Translation. XXXV: Tractates Meilah and Tamid*	Peter J. Haas
140110	*Studies in Islamic and Judaic Traditions*	William Brinner/Stephen Ricks
140111	*Comparative Midrash: The Plan and Program of Genesis Rabbah and Leviticus Rabbah*	Jacob Neusner
140112	*The Tosefta: Its Structure and its Sources*	Jacob Neusner
140113	*Reading and Believing*	Jacob Neusner
140114	*The Fathers According to Rabbi Nathan*	Jacob Neusner
140115	*Etymology in Early Jewish Interpretation: The Hebrew Names in Philo*	Lester L. Grabbe
140116	*Understanding Seeking Faith: Essays on the Case of Judaism. Volume One: Debates on Method, Reports of Results*	Jacob Neusner
140117	*The Talmud of Babylonia. An American Translation. VII: Tractate Besah*	Alan J. Avery-Peck
140118	*Sifre to Numbers: An American Translation and Explanation, Volume One: Sifre to Numbers 1-58*	Jacob Neusner
140119	*Sifre to Numbers: An American Translation and Explanation, Volume Two: Sifre to Numbers 59-115*	Jacob Neusner
140120	*Cohen and Troeltsch: Ethical Monotheistic Religion and Theory of Culture*	Wendell S. Dietrich
140121	*Goodenough on the History of Religion and on Judaism*	Jacob Neusner/ Ernest Frerichs
140122	*Pesiqta deRab Kahana I: Pisqaot One through Fourteen*	Jacob Neusner
140123	*Pesiqta deRab Kahana II: Pisqaot Fifteen through Twenty-Eight and Introduction to Pesiqta deRab Kahana*	Jacob Neusner
140124	*Sifre to Deuteronomy: Introduction*	Jacob Neusner

140126	*A Conceptual Commentary on Midrash Leviticus Rabbah: Value Concepts in Jewish Thought*	Max Kadushin
140127	*The Other Judaisms of Late Antiquity*	Alan F. Segal
140128	*Josephus as a Historical Source in Patristic Literature through Eusebius*	Michael Hardwick
140129	*Judaism: The Evidence of the Mishnah*	Jacob Neusner
140131	*Philo, John and Paul: New Perspectives on Judaism and Early Christianity*	Peder Borgen
140132	*Babylonian Witchcraft Literature*	Tzvi Abusch
140133	*The Making of the Mind of Judaism: The Formative Age*	Jacob Neusner
140135	*Why No Gospels in Talmudic Judaism?*	Jacob Neusner
140136	*Torah: From Scroll to Symbol Part III: Doctrine*	Jacob Neusner
140137	*The Systemic Analysis of Judaism*	Jacob Neusner
140138	*Sifra: An Analytical Translation Vol. 1*	Jacob Neusner
140139	*Sifra: An Analytical Translation Vol. 2*	Jacob Neusner
140140	*Sifra: An Analytical Translation Vol. 3*	Jacob Neusner
140141	*Midrash in Context: Exegesis in Formative Judaism*	Jacob Neusner
140143	*Oxen, Women or Citizens? Slaves in the System of Mishnah*	Paul V. Flesher
140144	*The Book of the Pomegranate*	Elliot R. Wolfson
140145	*Wrong Ways and Right Ways in the Study of Formative Judaism*	Jacob Neusner
140146	*Sifra in Perspective: The Documentary Comparison of the Midrashim of Ancient Judaism*	Jacob Neusner
140148	*Mekhilta According to Rabbi Ishmael: An Analytical Translation Volume I*	Jacob Neusner
140149	*The Doctrine of the Divine Name: An Introduction to Classical Kabbalistic Theology*	Stephen G. Wald
140150	*Water into Wine and the Beheading of John the Baptist*	Roger Aus
140151	*The Formation of the Jewish Intellect*	Jacob Neusner
140152	*Mekhilta According to Rabbi Ishmael: An Introduction to Judaism's First Scriptural Encyclopaedia*	Jacob Neusner
140153	*Understanding Seeking Faith. Volume Three*	Jacob Neusner
140154	*Mekhilta According to Rabbi Ishmael: An Analytical Translation Volume Two*	Jacob Neusner
140155	*Goyim: Gentiles and Israelites in Mishnah-Tosefta*	Gary P. Porton
140156	*A Religion of Pots and Pans?*	Jacob Neusner
140157	*Claude Montefiore and Christianity*	Maurice Gerald Bowler
140158	*The Philosopical Mishnah Volume III*	Jacob Neusner
140159	*From Ancient Israel to Modern Judaism Volume 1: Intellect in Quest of Understanding*	Neusner/Frerichs/Sarna
140160	*The Social Study of Judaism Volume I*	Jacob Neusner
140161	*Philo's Jewish Identity*	Alan Mendelson
140162	*The Social Study of Judaism Volume II*	Jacob Neusner
140163	*The Philosophical Mishnah Volume I : The Initial Probe*	Jacob Neusner
140164	*The Philosophical Mishnah Volume II : The Tractates Agenda: From Abodah Zarah Through Moed Qatan*	Jacob Neusner

140166	*Women's Earliest Records*	Barbara S. Lesko
140167	*The Legacy of Hermann Cohen*	William Kluback
140168	*Method and Meaning in Ancient Judaism*	Jacob Neusner
140169	*The Role of the Messenger and Message in the Ancient Near East*	John T. Greene
140171	*Abraham Heschel's Idea of Revelation*	Lawerence Perlman
140172	*The Philosophical Mishnah Volume IV: The Repertoire*	Jacob Neusner
140173	*From Ancient Israel to Modern Judaism Volume 2: Intellect in Quest of Understanding*	Neusner/Frerichs/Sarna
140174	*From Ancient Israel to Modern Judaism Volume 3: Intellect in Quest of Understanding*	Neusner/Frerichs/Sarna
140175	*From Ancient Israel to Modern Judaism Volume 4: Intellect in Quest of Understanding*	Neusner/Frerichs/Sarna
140176	*Translating the Classics of Judaism: In Theory and In Practice*	Jacob Neusner
140177	*Profiles of a Rabbi: Synoptic Opportunities in Reading About Jesus*	Bruce Chilton
140178	*Studies in Islamic and Judaic Traditions II*	William Brinner/Stephen Ricks
140179	*Medium and Message in Judaism: First Series*	Jacob Neusner
140180	*Making the Classics of Judaism: The Three Stages of Literary Formation*	Jacob Neusner
140181	*The Law of Jealousy: Anthropology of Sotah*	Adriana Destro
140182	*Esther Rabbah I: An Analytical Translation*	Jacob Neusner
140183	*Ruth Rabbah: An Analytical Translation*	Jacob Neusner
140184	*Formative Judaism: Religious, Historical and Literary Studies*	Jacob Neusner
140185	*The Studia Philonica Annual*	David T. Runia
140186	*The Setting of the Sermon on the Mount*	W.D. Davies
140187	*The Midrash Compilations of the Sixth and Seventh Centuries Volume One*	Jacob Neusner
140188	*The Midrash Compilations of the Sixth and Seventh Centuries Volume Two*	Jacob Neusner
140189	*The Midrash Compilations of the Sixth and Seventh Centuries Volume Three*	Jacob Neusner
140190	*The Midrash Compilations of the Sixth and Seventh Centuries Volume Four*	Jacob Neusner
140191	*The Religious World of Contemporary Judaism: Observations and Convictions*	Jacob Neusner
140192	*Approaches to Ancient Judaism: Volume VI*	Jacob Neusner/ Ernest S. Frerichs
140193	*Lamentations Rabbah: An Analytical Translation*	Jacob Neusner
140194	*Early Christian Texts on Jews and Judaism*	Robert S. MacLennan
140195	*Lectures on Judaism*	Jacob Neusner
140196	*Torah and the Chronicler's History Work*	Judson R. Shaver
140197	*Song of Songs Rabbah: An Analytical Translation Volume One*	Jacob Neusner
140198	*Song of Songs Rabbah: An Analytical Translation Volume Two*	Jacob Neusner
140199	*From Literature to Theology in Formative Judaism*	Jacob Neusner

140201	*The Canonical History of Ideas*	Jacob Neusner
140202	*Maimonides on Perfection*	Menachem Kellner
140203	*The Martyr's Conviction*	Eugene Weiner/Anita Weiner

Brown Studies on Jews and Their Societies

145001	*American Jewish Fertility*	Calvin Goldscheider
145003	*The American Jewish Community*	Calvin Goldscheider
145004	*The Naturalized Jews of the Grand Duchy of Posen in 1834 and 1835*	Edward David Luft
145005	*Suburban Communities: The Jewishness of American Reform Jews*	Gerald L. Showstack
145007	*Ethnic Survival in America*	David Schoem

Brown Studies in Religion

147001	*Religious Writings and Religious Systems Volume 1*	Jacob Neusner, et al
147002	*Religious Writings and Religious Systems Volume 2*	Jacob Neusner, et al
147003	*Religion and the Social Sciences*	Robert Segal